WISDOM
LITERATURE
JOB, PROVERBS, RUTH, CANTICLES, ECCLESIASTES, and ESTHER

Roland E. Murphy, O. Carm.

The Forms of the Old Testament Literature
VOLUME XIII
Rolf Knierim and Gene M. Tucker, editors

WILLIAM B. EERDMANS PUBLISHING COMPANY
GRAND RAPIDS, MICHIGAN

Copyright © 1981 by Wm. B. Eerdmans Publishing Co.
255 Jefferson Ave. S.E., Grand Rapids, MI 49503

Reprinted, June 1983

Library of Congress Cataloging in Publication Data

Murphy, Roland Edmund, 1917-
 The wisdom literature.

 (The Forms of the Old Testament literature; v. 13)
 1. Wisdom literature—Criticism, Form. 2. Bible.
O.T. Job—Criticism, Form. 3. Bible. O.T. Ruth—
Criticism, Form. 4. Bible. O.T. Esther—Criticism,
Form. I. Title. II. Series: Forms of the Old Testament
literature; v. 13.
BS1455.M87   223'.066   81-3191
ISBN 0-8028-1877-3   AACR2

Contents

ABBREVIATIONS AND SYMBOLS

JCS	Journal of Cuneiform Studies
JEOL	Jaarbericht . . . ex oriente lux
JQR	Jewish Quarterly Review
KAT	Kommentar zum Alten Testament
LD	Lectio divina
LUÅ	Lunds universitets årsskrift
LXX	Septuagint
MT	Masoretic Text
NAB	New American Bible
NEB	New English Bible
OBO	Orbis Biblicus et Orientalis
OTL	Old Testament Library
RB	Revue biblique
RGG	Religion in Geschichte und Gegenwart
RTP	Revue de théologie et de philosophie
RSV	Revised Standard Version
SANT	Studien zum Alten und Neuen Testament
SB	Sources bibliques
SBLASP	Society of Biblical Literature Abstracts and Seminar Papers
SBLDS	Society of Biblical Literature Dissertation Series
SBM	Stuttgarter biblische Monographien
SBS	Stuttgarter Bibelstudien
SBT	Studies in Biblical Theology
Scr	Scripture
STU	Schweizerische Theologische Umschau
TBü	Theologische Bücherei
ThSt	Theologische Studiën
ThSt (B)	Theologische Studien, ed. K. Barth (and M. Geiger)
TUMSR	Trinity University Monograph Series in Religion
TZ	Theologische Zeitschrift
VF	Verkündigung und Forschung
VS	Verbum salutis
VT	Vetus Testamentum
VTSup	Vetus Testamentum, Supplements
WMANT	Wissenschaftliche Monographien zum Alten und Neuen Testament
ZAW	Zeitschrift für die alttestamentliche Wissenschaft
→	The arrow indicates a cross reference to another section of the commentary

EDITORS' FOREWORD

THIS BOOK is the first in a series of twenty-four volumes planned for publication throughout the nineteen-eighties. The series eventually will present a form-critical analysis of every book and each unit of the Old Testament (Hebrew Bible) according to a standard outline and methodology. The aims of the work are fundamentally exegetical, attempting to understand the biblical literature from the viewpoint of a particular set of questions. Each volume in the series will also give an account of the history of the form-critical discussion of the material in question, attempt to bring consistency to the terminology for the genres and formulas of the biblical literature, and expose the exegetical procedure in such a way as to enable students and pastors to engage in their own analysis and interpretation. It is hoped, therefore, that the audience will be a broad one, including not only biblical scholars but also students, pastors, priests, and rabbis who are engaged in biblical interpretation.

There is a difference between the planned order of appearance of the individual volumes and their position in the series. While the series follows basically the sequence of the books of the Hebrew Bible, the individual volumes will appear in accordance with the projected working schedules of the individual contributors. The number of twenty-four volumes has been chosen for merely practical reasons which make it necessary to combine several biblical books in one volume at times, and at times to have two authors contribute to the same volume. The present volume is an exception to the arrangement according to the sequence of the Hebrew canon in that it omits Lamentations. The commentary on Lamentations will be published with that on the book of Psalms.

The initiation of this series is the result of deliberations and plans which began some fifteen years ago. At that time the current editors perceived the need for a comprehensive reference work which would enable scholars and students of the Hebrew scriptures to gain from the insights that form-critical work had accumulated throughout seven decades, and at the same time to participate more effectively in such work themselves. An international and interconfessional team of scholars was assembled, and has been expanded in recent years.

Several possible approaches and formats for publication presented themselves. The work could not be a handbook of the form-critical method with some examples of its application. Nor would it be satisfactory to present an encyclopedia of the genres identified in the Old Testament literature. The reference work would have to demonstrate the method on all of the texts, and identify genres only through the actual interpretation of the texts themselves. Hence, the work had to be a commentary following the sequence of the books in the Hebrew Bible (the

Kittel edition of the *Biblia Hebraica* then and the *Biblia Hebraica Stuttgartensia* now).

The main purpose of this project is to lead the student to the Old Testament texts themselves, and not just to form-critical studies of the texts. It should be stressed that the commentary is confined to the form-critical interpretation of the texts. Consequently, the reader should not expect here a full-fledged exegetical commentary which deals with the broad range of issues concerning the meaning of the text. In order to keep the focus as clearly as possible on a particular set of questions, matters of text, translation, philology, verse-by-verse explanation, etc. are raised only when they appear directly relevant to the form-critical analysis and interpretation.

The adoption of a commentary format and specific methodological deliberations imply a conclusion which has become crucial for all the work of form criticism. If the results of form criticism are to be verifiable and generally intelligible, then the determination of typical forms and genres, their settings and functions, has to take place through the analysis of the forms in and of the texts themselves. This leads to two consequences for the volumes in this series. First, each interpretation of a text begins with the presentation of the *structure* of that text in outline form. The ensuing discussion of this structure attempts to distinguish the typical from the individual or unique elements, and to proceed on this basis to the determination of the *genre*, its *setting*, and its *intention*. Traditio-historical factors are discussed throughout this process where relevant; e.g., is there evidence of a written or oral stage of the material earlier than the actual text before the reader?

Second, in contrast to most traditional form-critical work, the interpretation of the texts accepts the fundamental premise that we possess all texts basically at their latest written stages, technically speaking, at the levels of the final redactions. Any access to the texts, therefore, must confront and analyze that latest edition first, i.e., a specific version of that edition as represented in a particular text tradition. Consequently, the commentary proceeds from the analysis of the larger literary corpora created by the redactions back to any prior discernible stages in their literary history. Larger units are examined first, and then their subsections. Therefore, in most instances the first unit examined in terms of structure, genre, setting, and intention is the entire biblical book in question; next the commentary treats the individual larger and then smaller units.

The original plan of the project was to record critically all the relevant results of previous form-critical studies concerning the texts in question. While this remains one of the goals of the series, it had to be expanded to allow for more of the research of the individual contributors. This approach has proved to be important not only with regard to the ongoing insights of the contributors, but also in view of the significant developments which have taken place in the field in recent years. The team of scholars responsible for the series is committed to following a basic design throughout the commentary, but differences of emphasis and even to some extent of approach will be recognized as more volumes appear. Each author will ultimately be responsible for his own contribution.

The use of the commentary is by and large self-explanatory, but a few comments may prove helpful to the reader. This work is designed to be used alongside a Hebrew text or a translation of the Bible. The format of the interpretation of the texts, large or small, is the same throughout, except in cases—as partly in this volume—where the biblical material itself suggests a different form of presentation. Individual books and major literary corpora are introduced by a general bibliography referring to wider information on the subjects discussed, and to works relevant for the subunits of that literary body. Whenever available, a special form-critical bibliography for a specific unit under discussion will conclude the discussion of that unit. In the outline of the structure of units, the system of sigla attempts to indicate the relationship and interdependence of the parts within that structure. The traditional chapter and verse divisions of the Hebrew text are supplied in the right-hand margin of the outlines. Where there is a difference between the Hebrew and English versification the latter is also supplied in parentheses according to the *Revised Standard Version*.

In addition to the commentary on the biblical books, this volume includes an introduction to the major genres found in the Old Testament wisdom literature and a glossary of the genres discussed in the commentary. Most of the definitions in the glossary were prepared by Professor Murphy, but some have arisen from the work of other members of the project on other parts of the Old Testament. Each subsequent volume will include such a glossary. Eventually, upon the completion of the commentary series, all of the glossaries will be revised in the light of the analysis of each book of the Old Testament and published as Volume XXIV of the series. The individual volumes will not contain special indices but the indices for the entire series will be published as Volume XXIII.

The editors wish to acknowledge with appreciation the contribution of numerous persons and institutions to the work of the project. All of the contributors have received significant financial, secretarial, and student assistance from their respective institutions. In particular, the editors have received extensive support from their Universities. Without such concrete expressions of encouragement the work scarcely could have gone on. At Claremont, the Institute for Antiquity and Christianity has from its own inception provided office facilities, a supportive staff, and the atmosphere which stimulates not only individual but also team research. Emory University and the Candler School of Theology have likewise provided tangible support and encouragement.

To be singled out for their work on this project are many research assistants and associates from the Old Testament Graduate Departments of Claremont and Emory. From Claremont they were Kent Richards, John Connally, Gene Roop, Anthony Campbell, Charles Mabee, Michael Floyd, Frederick Tiffany, Judy Orr, Rodney Hutton, K. C. Hanson, and—for the last three years—Eleanor Johnston. From Emory they were Lynne Deming, Stephen Reid, Andrew Dearman, and Gail Preston.

ROLF KNIERIM
GENE M. TUCKER

Preface

It will be clear to the careful reader that only three (Proverbs, Job, Ecclesiastes) of the six books treated here are technically "wisdom literature." The others are included to assure a convenient distribution of the biblical material in these volumes. The choice is a happy one, however. The Song of Songs is unmistakably a collection of love poems. But recent scholarship (J.-P. Audet, E. Würthwein, B. Childs) has been open to ascribing the preservation and transmission of these poems to the sages of Israel. As a whole, the Song emphasizes values which are primary in wisdom thought (cf. Proverbs 1–9). Esther is hardly to be classified as a wisdom story, as will be seen from the treatment below. The very fact that the case could be argued well and seriously by S. Talmon, however, is a sign that it is conveniently placed in this volume. Finally, the genre of Ruth is not among the forms associated with Israelite wisdom. But the idyllic nature of the story puts it within the purview of the sages' goals.

The writer has attempted to glean the best from the relevant form-critical studies of the past. The general reader of the Bible will be the judge of how sharply this tool cuts into the material and lays it out for exposition. The scholar will be the judge among the differing points of view, and may sense the need of more "rhetorical criticism," which is a growing concern in biblical studies. Also, much remains to be done in the area of proverbial sayings, as the recent dissertations of Carole Fontaine and Brian Kovacs remind us. The writer wishes to express his gratitude to his colleagues in the form-critical project, from whom he learned much about form criticism. He is also grateful for a sabbatical from Duke University during which most of this work was accomplished.

Roland E. Murphy, O. Carm.
Duke University

Bibliography

W. Baumgartner, "The Wisdom Literature," in *The Old Testament and Modern Study* (ed. H. H. Rowley; London, 1951); 210-37; S. H. Blank, "Wisdom," *IDB*; J. Crenshaw, ed., *Studies in Ancient Israelite Wisdom* (New York, 1976); idem, "Wisdom," in *Old Testament Form Criticism* (ed. J. H. Hayes; TUMSR 2; San Antonio, 1974); 225-64; H. Duesberg and I. Fransen, *Les scribes inspirés* (rev. ed.; Maredsous, 1966); O. Eissfeldt, *Der Maschal im Alten Testament* (BZAW 24; Giessen, 1913); J. Fichtner, *Die altorientalische Weisheit in ihrer israelitisch-judischen Ausprägung* (BZAW 62; Giessen, 1933); C. R. Fontaine, "The Use of the Traditional Saying in the Old Testament" (Diss., Duke University, 1979); E. Gerstenberger, *Wesen und Herkunft des "apodiktischen" Rechts* (WMANT 20; Neukirchen-Vluyn, 1965); idem, "Zur alttestamentlichen Weisheit," *VF* 14 (1969) 28-44; H. Gese, *Lehre und Wirklichkeit in der alten Weisheit* (Tübingen, 1958); H.-J. Hermisson, *Studien zur israelitischen Spruchweisheit* (WMANT 28; Neukirchen-Vluyn, 1968); W. A. Irwin, "The Wisdom Literature," *IB*; C. B. Kayatz, *Einführung in die alttestamentliche Weisheit* (BibS [N] 55; Neukirchen, 1969); idem, *Studien zu Proverbien 1–9* (WMANT 22; Neukirchen-Vluyn, 1966); W. McKane, *Prophets and Wise Men* (SBT 1/44; London, 1965); idem, *Proverbs, A New Approach* (OTL; Philadelphia, 1970); J. L. McKenzie, "Reflections on Wisdom," *JBL* 86 (1967) 1-9; R. E. Murphy, "Form Criticism and Wisdom Literature," *CBQ* 31 (1969) 475-83; idem, "The Interpretation of Old Testament Wisdom Literature," *Int* 23 (1969) 289-301; H. D. Preuss, "Erwägungen zum theologischen Ort alttestamentlicher Weisheitsliteratur," *EvT* 30 (1970) 393-417; G. von Rad, *Wisdom In Israel* (tr. James D. Martin; Nashville, 1972); O. S. Rankin, *Israel's Wisdom Literature* (Edinburgh, 1936); W. Richter, *Recht und Ethos* (SANT 15; Munich, 1966); H. H. Schmid, "Hauptprobleme der altorientalischen und alttestamentlichen Weisheitsliteratur," *STU* 35 (1965) 68-74; idem, *Wesen und Geschichte der Weisheit* (BZAW 101; Berlin, 1966); R. B. Y. Scott, "The Study of the Wisdom Literature," *Int* 24 (1970) 20-45; idem, *The Way of Wisdom in the Old Testament* (New York, 1971); P. Skehan, *Studies in Israelite Poetry and Wisdom* (CBQMS 1; Washington, 1971); O. Skladny, *Die ältesten Spruchsammlungen in Israel* (Göttingen, 1962); C. Westermann, "Weisheit im Sprichwort," in *Schalom* (*Fest.* A. Jepsen; AzT 1/46; Stuttgart, 1971) 73-85; R. N. Whybray, *The Intellectual Tradition in the Old Testament* (BZAW 135; Berlin, 1974); W. Zimmerli, "Zur Struktur der alttestamentlichen Weisheit," *ZAW* 51 (1933) 177-204.

For translation of pertinent texts, see: E. Gordon, *Sumerian Proverbs* (Philadelphia, 1959); J. Khanjian, "Wisdom," in *Ras Shamra Parallels* II (ed. L. Fisher; AnOr 50; Rome, 1975) 373-400; W. Lambert, *Babylonian Wisdom Literature* (Oxford, 1960); J. Pritchard, ed., *ANET* (Princeton, 1968); D. E. Smith, "Wisdom Genres in RS 22.439," in *Ras Shamra Parallels* II (ed. L. Fisher; AnOr 50; Rome, 1975) 215-47. For general orientation, see: M. Noth and D. W. Thomas, eds., *Wisdom in Israel and the Ancient Near East* (VTSup 3; *Fest.* H. H. Rowley; Leiden, 1955); J. Leclant et al., *Les sagesses du Proche-Orient ancien* (Paris, 1963).

"WISDOM LITERATURE" is not a form-critical term; it is merely a term of convenience, derived apparently from ecclesiastical usage, to designate the books of Proverbs, Job, and Ecclesiastes, and among the Apocrypha, Ben Sira and the Wisdom of Solomon. It has been adopted also by Egyptologists and cuneiform specialists to designate a variety of extrabiblical literature that is similar to the biblical works. The term can be justified as a characterization of the literature because it is concerned for the most part with *ḥokmâ* ("wisdom"). Certain genres and themes are common to these works and so give a semblance of unity to them and a validity to the common classification.

Recent research, however, has been claiming a broad range of wisdom literature within the historical and prophetical writings (see the bibliography in Whybray, 1-2). G. von Rad started this trend with his study of the Joseph narrative, which he described as "a didactic wisdom-story" (cf. "The Joseph Narrative and Ancient Wisdom," in Crenshaw, *Studies*, 439-47; esp. p. 447). Von Rad's thesis with regard to the Joseph narrative is discussed by Crenshaw (cf. "Method in Determining Wisdom Influence Upon 'Historical' Literature," in *Studies*, 481-94). The critique offered by Crenshaw is justified, especially in light of his conclusion that such attempts to discover wisdom influence upon historical literature must be made only with great caution.

Nevertheless, the role of wisdom in the OT is better evaluated in the light of wisdom thinking, or what von Rad has called the sapiential "understanding of reality" (*Wisdom in Israel*, passim). It is not a question of direct influence of the sages or of wisdom literature, but of an approach to reality that was shared by all Israelites in varying degrees. Admittedly certain genres, such as the sayings and admonitions, were cultivated by the teachers. The teachers were, so to speak, the experts who catalogued the lessons and insights of experience as the basis of human conduct. But the sapiential understanding of reality was shared by all Israelites; it was not a mode of thinking that belonged to only one class. The mentality was far broader than the literary remains that have come down to us as "wisdom literature." Thus it should come as no surprise that Isaiah, or any other prophet, should use a parable. But Isaiah is not to be classified among the sages, nor is his writing part of "wisdom." False problems are raised by a rigid plotting of genres and the extent of the wisdom vocabulary. The author of the book of Job moved outside of strict wisdom genres when he used a legend concerning Job the partiarch as the framework for his sapiential discussion of a wisdom problem. In a similar way, a broader basis for judging "wisdom psalms" can be reached by going beyond the arguments of form criticism. If we understand wisdom as reflecting a certain approach to reality, we can find it represented in Genesis 1–3. Isaiah makes frequent use of parable (e.g., 28:23-29), and prophetic themes seem to be used in Proverbs 1–9 (e.g., 1:28; cf. Isa 65:2, 12; 66:4). But the judgments of form criticism are not to be confused with an understanding of reality.

This introduction will treat the following topics: basic wisdom genres; the setting of wisdom literature; and the significance of extrabiblical literature of the ancient Near East for wisdom genres.

I. Basic Wisdom Genres

We will describe only the more prominent genres; the reader is referred to the introductions of individual books for specific genres, such as the INSTRUCTION in Proverbs, the DISPUTATION and SUMMARY-APPRAISAL FORMULA in Job, or the REFLECTION in Ecclesiastes.

1. THE SAYING

The SAYING is a sentence normally expressed in the indicative mood, and usually based on experience. Three types deserve discussion here: the PROVERB, the experiential SAYING, and the didactic SAYING.

The PROVERB draws a conclusion from experience and formulates it in a pithy, succinct way; for such a conclusion to become truly proverbial, it must gain currency among a people. Here one can point to several authentic·proverbs in the Bible (cf. O. Eissfeldt, 45ff.). "Out of the wicked comes forth wickedness" is called a "proverb" (*māšāl*) of the ancients (1 Sam 24:14). The question in Jer 23:28 has the ring of a saying that has gained some currency: "What has straw in common with wheat?" The same is true of the advice (here, obviously, not in the indicative mood) in 1 Kgs 20:11, "Let not him that girds on his armor boast as he that puts it off." These are examples of the popular proverb (*Volkssprichwort*), strictly speaking. They are pungent sayings growing out of concrete situations, and striking enough to be taken into the patrimony of the people. It is possible that transmission among the people also contributed to the final formation of the saying, but we have no way to check on such a process for the biblical proverb. It would appear that very few popular proverbs have been preserved in the wisdom literature; at least, it is extremely difficult to make a case for certain sayings as having been popular proverbs before they were collected for the book of Proverbs.

An experiential (or observational) SAYING merely presents some aspect of reality. It tells it "the way it is," and leaves the practical conclusion(s) for the hearer/reader to draw. Several of the sayings in Proverbs are merely experiential, such as the paradox in 11:24, "One man pretends to be rich, yet has nothing; another pretends to be poor, yet has great wealth." Again, although some wisdom sentences warn against bribery, there is the following observation: "A man's gift makes room for him and brings him before great men" (Prov 18:16). It belongs to the very nature of the saying to allow for ambiguities and antinomies. Thus, "He who restrains his words has knowledge, and he who has a cool spirit is a man of understanding," but "even a fool who keeps silent is considered wise; when he closes his lips he is deemed intelligent" (Prov 17:27-28). Such sayings, therefore, remain open for further verification, even for limitation. They are essentially tied to the experience from which they derive, and to the tradition (handed down among those who found them meaningful) that gave them status and importance. It is the context of the collections in Proverbs that lends a didactic orientation to experiential sayings that originally were sheer observations.

The didactic (or learned) SAYING goes beyond a mere statement about reality; it characterizes a certain act or attitude in such a way as to influence human conduct. Some value is being inculcated, and this can be done in several ways. In Prov 14:31, one's relation to God is defined in terms of treatment of the poor; no doubt is left about the course of action to be pursued:

> *He who oppresses the poor blasphemes his Maker,*
> *but he who is kind to the needy glorifies him*
> (Prov 14:31; cf. 19:17; 22:22-23).

Such direction is obvious in sayings that speak of wisdom, justice, etc.:

> *The fear of the Lord is training for wisdom,*
> *and humility goes before honors* (Prov 15:33).
> *The memory of the just will be blessed,*
> *But the name of the wicked will rot* (Prov 10:7).

C. Westermann points out that such generalizations are formed according to a very general theme: the conduct and the (corresponding) fate of the wise/foolish and the just/wicked. He remarks (p. 85) that "if one reads all these sayings one after another, it becomes convincingly clear that they all say essentially the same thing and so are a development of one theme." They do not arise from and speak to specific situations, as do, for example, the comparisons (Prov 10:26, "As vinegar to the teeth, and smoke to the eyes, is the sluggard to those who use him as a messenger"). The concern about the just and the wicked is not peculiar to the book of Proverbs; it is found throughout the Hebrew Bible. It would appear that such a broad theme was a part of the Israelite ethos and was not merely a preoccupation of the wisdom tradition, although it was emphasized there. Such themes contrast vividly with other concerns typical of wisdom: work and its fruits, silence and speech, diligence and laziness, etc.

The didactic SAYING is often characterized as an "artistic saying" (*Kunstspruch*), i.e., a saying that is carefully and deliberately formed with an eye to literary polish and finesse. Such literary finish was always a concern of the sage who held it up as a goal:

> *There is joy for a man in his utterance;*
> *a word in season, how good it is*
> (Prov 15:23; cf. 25:11; 26:25).

It is written of Qohelet that he sought to find "pleasing sayings, and to write down true sayings with precision" (Eccl 12:10). In the discussion about the setting of the sayings it will become apparent that it is not possible to restrict such literary achievement to the "school" alone; even the common, relatively uneducated people had their own power of expression, as the sayings in Samuel and Kings demonstrate.

2. COMMANDS AND PROHIBITIONS

The sage instructed not only by offering the lessons enshrined in sayings. He also imposed his will by a COMMAND (imperative or jussive mood) or by a PROHIBITION. These commands and prohibitions abound in the genre of INSTRUCTION (→ Introduction to Proverbs). But they also appear in isolated form in Proverbs and Ecclesiastes. At times the command will be in parallelism with the prohibition, and both are saying the same thing:

> Hear instruction and be wise,
> and do not neglect it (Prov 8:33).

The command (or the prohibition) can make explicit a point that is only implicitly or indirectly urged in a saying, as can be seen by comparing the following:

> Entrust your works to the Lord,
> and your plans will succeed (Prov 16:3).
> He who plans a thing will be successful;
> happy is he who trusts in the Lord (Prov 16:20).

Similarly, one can compare Prov 23:22 with 10:1 and 22:22 with 14:31.

Is there any particular import to this interchangeability of command/ prohibition with a wisdom saying? It suggests that when the issue is teaching or inculcating a value, the genre itself is an indifferent factor. The intensity of the charge may vary, calling for either a prohibition or merely a saying that goes counter to something undesirable. The setting remains the same: a didactic situation. But the variation in the genre is due to the psychological factors involved in attempting to convince another. Both genres belong to the educational task. An experiential saying challenges the one who hears it, and who is in a sense a kind of partner to the one who utters or writes it; but it is not compelling in the way that a didactic saying, a command, or a prohibition is. Hence the two genres, saying and command/prohibition, do not necessarily correspond to two different settings (contra Westermann, 76-78).

In the wisdom tradition the commands and prohibitions are usually provided with motive clauses (some implicit, others introduced by kî ["because"] or pen ["lest"], etc.). A very wide range of motives is adduced, from practical considerations of danger (Prov 22:24-25), to the action of the Lord (Prov 22:22-23). They indicate a certain amount of reflection; the teacher is engaged in persuading and convincing and he pitches his motivation to the various levels that he considers apposite. But there is no particular significance to be attached to the fact that motive clauses may be omitted or introduced only implicitly.

II. THE SETTING OF WISDOM LITERATURE

The setting of wisdom literature is a difficult problem because of the dearth of information about its origins and the channels by which it was handed down. In the most general way, the situation can be described as didactic; information is being passed on by someone in authority, and someone is being instructed about human conduct or about life in general. When one examines the sociological institutions where such advice would have been preserved and imparted, several alternatives (not necessarily exclusive) appear.

The first possibility is the home, where parental instruction would have been imparted to the children and would have been oral. There are several hints of this within Proverbs, as 10:1 indicates: "A wise man makes his father glad, but a foolish son is a grief to his mother" (cf. 15:20; 29:13). The role of the father can be taken for granted, but the part played by the mother is not to be minimized (Prov 6:20, "the teaching of your mother"; cf. Prov 31:26, 28). The frequent address, "my son," is not merely stylistic and indicative of a teacher-pupil relationship in scholastic instruction. It reaches back into the family, where a responsible relationship between parents and children (Prov 17:21, 25; 28:7; 29:3) would have first been emphasized. Along with teaching went discipline, as testified by the sayings concerning physical punishment (Prov 13:24; 19:18; 22:15; 23:13-14; 29:15).

Unquestionably the family was one locus of instruction, particularly instruction of youth. Presumably this was on an oral level, and for centuries before a book like Proverbs, for instance, was written. Examples of this can be seen in the instruction that Tobit gives to Tobias (Tob 4:5-21; cf. 12:6-10), or the traditions of Jonadab that were preserved among the Rechabites (Jeremiah 35). Such teachings range from simple wisdom sayings to exhortations and commands about conduct. The ideals held forth in familial instructions were normally formed by the larger society of which the family was part. The standards of the family could not fly in the face of the community, as the sense of collective unity in Israel abundantly shows. Hence the formative role of the tribal ethos as a source of instruction has been emphasized by such recent scholars as E. Gerstenberger (*Wesen und Herkunft*). Here the commands and prohibitions would have set forth certain ideals of character and conduct in no uncertain fashion. The indicative (in contrast to the imperative) style of the saying served the same purpose, but in a more subtle way. In portraying reality "as it is," the wisdom saying invited the learner to feel the impact of experience and authority, and thus to give assent to the saying. As indicated above, it would be too rigid to conclude as Westermann does (p. 76) that these two forms (volitive and indicative) postulate *different* settings. Both are common to a didactic situation and merely represent different modes of achieving the same purpose. For this reason one may question the line of development presented by Westermann (p. 77) that there is a movement from indicative sayings (in the older collections, Proverbs 10ff.) to the volitives (commands and prohibitions in the later instructions, Proverbs 1-9). It is true, however, in the perspective of the *book* of Proverbs, that the collections of sayings in Proverbs 10ff. have become a body of traditional learning that is now to be taught; such is the import of Proverbs 1-9, especially 1:1-7, which was written as an introduction to the collections.

The second possible setting is the school, where a teacher-student relationship would be found. Although, unfortunately, we have no direct evidence of schools in Israel, H. Hermisson (pp. 97-136; for a contrary view, see Whybray) has argued forcefully for the existence of such institutions. First, it is reasonable to presume that the cultivation of reading and writing would have been indispensable for the political working of the state. Certainly the court officials, the priests and temple personnel, etc., would have found a school necessary for carrying out their tasks. Simple family instruction would not have sufficed; an institution where a larger number of "students" could be accommodated would have emerged. It is natural to think that the earliest historical writing (such as J, E, or the "book of the law" of 2 Kgs 22:8) would have flourished in such a milieu, and recently scholars have been pointing out wisdom influence in such preexilic writings as the Joseph story (Genesis 37–50) and the succession narrative (2 Samuel 9–1 Kings 2). Already by the time of Jeremiah (Jeremiah 36) there were secretaries like Baruch.

Second, there is the argument from analogy with the schools established in both Mesopotamia and Egypt. Israel would not have lagged behind them, especially when one considers the great influence of the Egyptian court upon that of Jerusalem. Several of the administrative offices established in the period of David and Solomon were borrowed from the Egyptian bureaucracy: the secretary, the herald, the house minister, and probably the scribal school (cf. T. Mettinger, *Solomonic State Officials* [ConB OT 5; Lund, 1971]). It is almost inconceivable that Israel would not have adopted the equivalent of the Egyptian court school in order to carry out the responsibilities of the new monarchy. Another indication of such a school in Israel is the acquaintance with the Egyptian wisdom literature (especially Amenemope and Prov 22:17–24:22). This literature was transmitted in the Egyptian schools, whose primary purpose was to serve the state, and this suggests that there must have been a court school in Jerusalem where also the traditional wisdom was cultivated. Wisdom literature, from Proverbs to the Wisdom of Solomon, has royal associations, and it was not without some reason that the name of Solomon (even if he was not an "author") was connected with it. Finally, the mention of the "men of Hezekiah," the Judaean king, in Prov 25:1, as well as the many sayings about the "king" in the collections of Proverbs 10ff., confirm the probable existence of a royal circle where the sayings would have been cultivated. The spectrum of life represented in Proverbs—from farm to court—cannot determine the setting of the authors. But the high literary quality of the sayings points to origins, or at least cultivation, among a scribal class that had some expertise with words and ideas.

Thus far we have been discussing a setting in the preexilic period when there was a monarchy. What of the postexilic period? This question is all the more pressing in view of the fact that the wisdom books, *in their present form* (Proverbs, as edited with chs. 1–9, and 31:10-31; Job in all probability; and certainly Ecclesiastes) are postexilic. Here one can only surmise that the scribal (lay) class was the vehicle by which Israelite wisdom was preserved and transmitted. Concretely one can point to a sage like Qohelet, of whom it is said (Eccl 12:9) that he "taught the people knowledge and weighed, scrutinized, and arranged many proverbs." Since Ben Sira speaks of *bêt midrašî* ("my school," 51:23), presumably he was at the head of a school in which the wisdom traditions were transmitted. Hence we may conclude that wisdom schools existed, certainly in the postexilic period. Here the wisdom movement, as it came more and more under the influence of the Torah (cf. Sirach 24), was continued among the Jews.

By way of summary, several levels are to be recognized in the setting of wisdom literature. The general situation is didactic, and this may be in the context of family or tribe, the court school, or the postexilic scribal school.

But one must also consider the setting that a book creates for a given wisdom genre. Thus, the adoption of a legal genre within the book of Job gives it a new setting. The preoccupation is not that of "justice at the gates," but of theological argument for justice before God. The statement of purpose about the proverbs in Prov 1:1-6 does more than indicate the advantages of wisdom. It serves to introduce a book that is essentially a collection of instructions and sayings, which, despite their original setting, now appear in a new light by virtue of their collection into a book. The book has become the setting of material that was once communicated in oral instruction, whether in the family or in school. If the book is highly structured, as P. W. Skehan (pp. 27-45) argues for Proverbs, having its "seven pillars" (Prov 9:1) and constituting a "house" on the model of the temple, then each part has a particular setting within the book. Similarly, the question style of the Yahweh speeches in Job 39–41 takes on a new setting when the speeches are spoken by the Lord in the denouement of the action within the book. Or again, the use of particular wisdom sayings in Ecclesiastes is to be determined by the new setting in which they are found within the book itself.

III. WISDOM GENRES IN ANCIENT NEAR EASTERN LITERATURE

The literatures that are pertinent here are Mesopotamian (Sumerian, Akkadian), Egyptian, Canaanite, and Greek. W. Lambert (p. 1) observes that "wisdom is strictly a misnomer as applied to Babylonian literature." Perhaps this judgment could be extended to all the other literatures as well, since it is really the OT classification that has been pressed into service to describe the comparable phenomenon in the other literatures. Nonetheless, some significant parallels do exist, and their study throws light on the OT wisdom genres. One may recall that Israel herself compared her wisdom, in the person of Solomon, to "the wisdom of all the people of the East, and all the wisdom of Egypt" (1 Kgs 4:29-34 [MT 5:9-14]). Only a survey is presented here; for details, see the discussion of the individual wisdom books.

1. MESOPOTAMIA

Sumerian wisdom, which has come to be translated and understood only in recent times, contains far more genres than those found in Israel. Prof. E. Gordon has listed several such genres ("A New Look at the Wisdom of Sumer and Akkad," *BO* 17 [1960] 122-52): proverbs, fables and parables, folktales, miniature "essays," riddles, tensons (wisdom disputations), satirical dialogues, precepts, etc. Obviously this list is more inclusive than the collection preserved for us in the Bible. A view of the Sumerian proverbs literature can be obtained from Gordon's *Sumerian Proverbs* and from Lambert.

The preservation of these sayings, and indeed of all ancient Mesopotamian literature, is due to the fact that they were written on clay tablets. The immortality of these tablets, however, was secured by the strenuous activity of the Sumerian and Babylonian scribes. In the *edubba* ("tablethouse"), or school, the ancient works (epics, omen literature, prayers, etc., as well as the wisdom corpus) were copied diligently by the scribes, who were themselves organized in a kind of guild system and deeply imbued with the idea of tradition. The schools were associated with temple and palace, and served the purposes of these institutions. The scribes have been characterized as a "poor aristocracy," but their learning was formidable. It is likely that their widest contact with the people came from their transmission of popular sayings.

In the course of time the sayings came to be preserved in bilingual texts (Sumerian and Akkadian), of which several are found in Lambert (pp. 225-74). Lambert also points out that Babylonian proverbs apparently were not cultivated in the traditional literature of the Babylonians and Assyrians—perhaps because the scribes were satisfied with the bilingual collections and took a dim view of the sayings that were passed around among the uneducated (pp. 275-76).

In addition to sayings, there was also the "instruction," such as the *Counsels of Wisdom* (perhaps 14th-13th centuries B.C.; cf. Lambert, 101-5; *ANET*, 595-96). These "counsels" are moral exhortations, presumably of a high courtier to his son, and the typical phrase, "my son," is used. They resemble Proverbs and also the Egyptian *Sebayit*, and the familiar sapiential topics are treated: avoidance of bad companions, improper speech, kindness to the needy, women, conduct at court, friends, etc. There are frequent commands and prohibitions.

One of the significant parallels to Proverbs is the wisdom contained in the *Story of Ahiqar* (*ANET*, 427-30). Although the earliest text transmitted to us is in Aramaic, it goes back to an Akkadian original. In it are two speeches that contain the usual wisdom maxims: guarding one's tongue, conduct before the king, respect for secrets, etc. Again, the genre is that of instruction. The figure of Ahiqar himself has been incorporated into the book of Tobit (Tob 1:22; 2:10; 11:17; 14:10), and both Ahiqar and Tobit impart wisdom teaching.

The Babylonian similarities to Job and Qohelet are to be found in theme rather than in genre (Lambert, 21-89; *ANET*, 596-604). Hence the *Ludlul* poem, "I will praise the Lord of Wisdom," and the *Dialogue about Human Misery* (or *Babylonian Theodicy*), and the *Dialogue of Pessimism* constitute their own genres. The genre of the *Ludlul* poem is really thanksgiving, although H. Gese (p. 63) calls it a "paradigm of answered lament" and correlates it with Job. The *Babylonian Theodicy* seems to have greater similarity to Job; it is at least a dialogue between a sufferer and his friend. A Sumerian parallel to Job, "Man and his God" (*ANET*, 589-91), can perhaps be justifiably called similar to Job in theme, but certainly not in literary genre.

2. EGYPT

Egyptian literature has provided the most striking parallels to OT wisdom literature, particularly in the *Sebayit* or instruction, and in the onomastica, or name lists.

The instruction follows a fixed pattern: "the instruction that X made for his son/student, Y." Often a prose introduction indicates the circumstances under which it was written, and also the purpose; then the wisdom sentences follow.

The bases of the instruction are experience and tradition. The central concept is *ma'at*, translated as "justice," "order," etc. This is the divinely established harmony between nature and society, an order that must be preserved or restored, and hence the goal of human activity. About a dozen instructions, known after the names of the authors (Ptah-hotep, Merikare, Amenemope, etc.) have been preserved for us; the texts are available in *ANET*, 405-24, and summaries are given in McKane (*Proverbs*, 51-150) and Schmid (*Wesen*, 8-84).

The instructions are clearly aimed at the training of young men for court life (cf. the introduction to Amenemope, *ANET*, 421), and the ideals propounded in the teaching have marked similarity to those of Proverbs: diligence, honesty, reliability, self-control, etc. The setting seems to be obvious: the court school.

Another important genre is the onomasticon, or name list, which is an encyclopedic catalogue of various objects, used for the training of scribes. The lists are found in both Mesopotamia and Egypt. The onomasticon of Amenemope contains the names of hundreds of persons and things; the concern is with what Ptah has created: heaven, earth, mountains, waters, etc. Such a list seems to underlie passages like Job 38:12-41; Sir 43:1-25; Dan 3:59-83 (cf. G. von Rad, "*Job* XXXVIII and Ancient Egyptian Wisdom," in *The Problem of the Hexateuch and Other Essays* [New York, 1966] 281-91).

Finally, there are several Egyptian works that have been compared to Job and Qohelet. The comparison is less in the area of genre, however, than in common preoccupations about the central problems of life. Comparisons have been made with the "Harper's Songs" (*ANET*, 467), and the *Dispute over Suicide* (or, *The Man Who Was Tired of Life*, *ANET*, 405-7). The *Satirical Letter* of Hori (*ANET*, 476-78) exemplifies the tone of questioning that the Lord directs against Job (38:4ff.).

3. CANAANITE

Canaanite influence (esp. that of Ugarit) has been strikingly exemplified in OT poetry, especially the poetry of the Psalms. Parallelism, the repetition of favorite word pairs, motifs, and stylistic characteristics—all these have been important for the interpretation of Hebrew poetry. But as far as the genres of wisdom literature are concerned, there is very little to point to. The phase of "Edomitic wisdom" has more or less passed, since the wisdom was actually that of the OT (esp. parts of Job), and archaeology has not unearthed any Edomitic wisdom texts. W. F. Albright pointed out an archaic Hebrew proverb in an Amarna Letter ("An Archaic Hebrew Proverb in an Amarna Letter from Central Palestine," *BASOR* 89 [1943] 29-32) that is reminiscent of the ant proverbs in Prov 6:6; 30:28: "if ants are smitten, they do not accept [the smiting] quietly, but they bite the hand of the man who smites them." Presumably many more such sayings existed, but they have not been preserved. Another wisdom genre, or better, wisdom formula, can be exemplified: the numerical saying, an example of which is found in the Ugaritic Baal epic (II AB, iii, 17-20; *ANET*, 132). This form is found in Ps 62:12-13 and Amos 1-2, but especially in the wisdom literature: Prov 6:16-19; 30:7-31; Job 5:19-22; 13:20-22; 33:14-15; cf. Eccl 4:12; 11:2. Interestingly, the numerical saying is not found in Mesopotamia and Egypt, although numbers exerted an attraction for both cultures (cf. G. Sauer, *Die Sprüche Agurs*

[BWANT 81; Stuttgart, 1963]). The one exception is the wisdom of Ahiqar, which provides one example (*ANET*, 428). Thus far, the studies of the Ugaritic wisdom of Shube'awelum (RS 22.439) have yielded only modest results. One finds wisdom sayings, admonitions, and exhortations; the work seems to be in the genre of the Akkadian *Counsels of Wisdom*. See the studies of D. E. Smith ("Wisdom Genres in RS 22.439") and J. Khanjian ("Wisdom") in *Ras Shamra Parallels* II (ed. L. Fisher; AnOr 50; Rome, 1975) 215-47 and 373-400.

4. GREEK

The influence of Greek culture and literature upon Jewish wisdom is raised for Ecclesiastes, Sirach, and the Wisdom of Solomon (the last probably written in the 1st century B.C. in Egypt). If one grants that Palestinian Judaism was already exposed to Hellenism from the 4th century on, there is a matrix, influenced by Greece, in which these books arose. Debate about the Greek influence upon Ecclesiastes has gone on for about a century, but no firm conclusions can be drawn. Where similarities exist, these largely concern content, not genre. At the most it seems reasonable to suppose that Qohelet was influenced by the *Zeitgeist* of his day (ca. 350 B.C.). Certain features in Ecclesiastes have been compared to the Greek "diatribe," but it cannot be said that this is the genre of Ecclesiastes (→ Ecclesiastes).

Bibliography

P. Dhorme, *A Commentary on the Book of Job* (London, 1967); Michael B. Dick, "The Legal Metaphor in Job 31," *CBQ* 41 (1979) 37-50; G. Fohrer, *Das Buch Hiob* (KAT 16, 2nd ed.; Gütersloh, 1963); H. Gese, *Lehre und Wirklichkeit in der alten Weisheit* (Tübingen, 1958); R. Gordis, *The Book of God and Man* (Chicago, 1965); N. Habel, "Appeal to Ancient Tradition as a Literary Form," in SBLASP I (ed. Geo. MacRae; Missoula, 1973) 34-50; G. Hölscher, *Das Buch Hiob* (HAT 17, 2nd ed.; Tübingen, 1952); F. Horst, *Hiob* (*BKAT* XVI/1; Neukirchen-Vluyn, 1968); H. P. Müller, *Hiob und seine Freunde* (ThSt [B] 103; Zurich, 1970); M. Pope, *Job* (AB 15; 3rd ed.; New York, 1973); G. von Rad, "*Job* xxxviii and Ancient Egyptian Wisdom," in *The Problem of the Hexateuch and Other Essays* (New York, 1966) 281-91; H. Richter, *Studien zu Hiob* (Theologische Arbeiten XI; Berlin, 1959); P. W. Skehan, *Studies in Israelite Poetry and Wisdom* (CBQMS 1; Washington, 1971); F. Stier, *Das Buch Hiob* (Munich, 1954); A. Weiser, *Das Buch Hiob* (ATD 13; ·2nd ed.; Göttingen, 1956); C. Westermann, *Der Aufbau des Buches Hiob* (BHT 23; Tübingen, 1956); J. W. Whedbee, "The Comedy of Job," in *Semeia 7: Studies in the Book of Job* (ed. R. Polzin and D. Robertson; Missoula, 1977) 1-39.

CHAPTER 1

THE BOOK AS A WHOLE

Structure

The above structure is broadly accepted by scholars, but not all would agree with the separation of Job's soliloquy (it is *not* addressed to the friends) in ch. 3 from the cycle of speeches. The question is: does Job speak up, and the friends then answer? Or do the friends speak first, while Job replies? Westermann, Richter, and Dhorme separate ch. 3, but Fohrer and Pope include it in the cycle. It seems better to recognize two soliloquies by Job (chs. 3, 29–31), which deserve to be set off. There is reason to suspect that later additions, especially chs. 28 and 32–37, were made to the book. The prologue and epilogue form the narrative framework of the dialogue between Job and the friends and of the divine theophany. This story of Job is, in the opinion of scholars, a very old tradition (cf. the mention of Job with Noah and the Ugaritic Dan[i]el in Ezek 14:12-23). It is generally recognized that the text has been scrambled in chs. 24–27, where no speech is attributed to Zophar, and Job appears to say things inconsistent with his own position; but the many solutions offered for this defect are a sign that there is as yet no solution to the problem. It is customary to divide the speeches of Job and the friends into three cycles (3/4–14; 15–21; 22–27), but since the third cycle is defective, not much is to be gained by this.

The coherence of the speeches within the dialogue (chs. 4–27) is very loose in that there is no logical progression in thought and argument. Yet the structure of the book as a whole is well articulated when the function of the dialogue is seen. It aims to controvert the traditional theory of retribution. The description of Job as a God-fearing man in the prologue has provided the author with the situation he needs: a holy man is suffering without cause, and this fact underlies the whole debate. Indeed, one may say that the intention of the book (see below) dominates the articulation of the structure, even if the poem on wisdom and the speeches of Elihu are judged as relatively marginal.

Genre

According to M. Pope, "there is no single classification appropriate to the literary form of the Book of Job. It shares something of the characteristics of all the literary forms that have been ascribed to it, but it is impossible to classify it exclusively as didactic, dramatic, epic, or anything else. The book viewed as a unit is *sui generis* and no single term or combination of terms is adequate to describe it" (p. XXXI). Similarly, H. Ringgren judged the genre as unique (*einzigartig*, *TZ* 24 [1968] 469). The soundness of these judgments is underlined by the unsuccessful, if valuable, attempts of scholars to capture the overall genre of the book.

Pursuing an idea of A. Bentzen (*Introduction*, I, 182), C. Westermann has argued that the literary genre of Job is a dramatization of a lament. Job laments; he does not argue. The three friends argue. Such is the pattern of the dialogue or dispute in chs. 4–27 that is sandwiched in between the laments in chs. 3 and 29–31. The DIALOGUE is properly a *Trostrede* or consolation—that is what friends are for, and what Job expects (e.g., 16:2; 21:34), but the dialogue becomes a dispute bearing the theological arguments of the friends as a reply to Job's complaints. Chs. 38–42 contain another dispute, this between the Lord and Job. All this is placed in the framework of the prose narrative (prologue and epilogue; chs. 1–2 and 42:7-17), which in effect gives the dialogue the nature of a happening. The usual three figures in a complaint—self, God, enemies—are to be found in the book: Job, God, and the three friends. Ch. 28 becomes an intermezzo in the pause between the first and second act of the drama, a speech that closes out the dialogue with the friends and warns them that wisdom is not the easily available commodity which they make it out to be.

Westermann is quite correct in underscoring the role of the complaint in Job (which he terms "lament," but cf. these two genres in the Glossary), and his observations are helpful; exegetes are now more sensitive to the complaint motifs than in the past. But the "dramatization of a lament" is not a literary genre, and it does not adequately characterize the entire work. The phrase has the virtue of emphasis, but that is its only strength.

No less one-sided is the interpretation of Heinz Richter. He characterizes the genre of Job as that of a judicial process: "The all-pervasive basis of the drama of Job are the genres taken from law" (p. 131). He follows the lead of L. Köhler (*Hebrew Man* [Nashville, 1956]), who used Job as a source of information for Israelite legal forms. Richter counts 444 verses as belonging to the judicial genres, as opposed to 346 given over to wisdom genres, and it is the former that are truly constitutive (and not merely ornamental) for the book. Thus, chs. 4–14 are an attempt at a preliminary settlement, and chs. 15–31 contain the formal legal settlement between Job and the friends and also his prayer for a divine settlement (*Gottesurteil*), which is provided in the secular lawsuit (38:1–42:6) of the Yahweh speeches. For these various legal processes Richter points to the rather sparse data that are scattered throughout the rest of the Bible.

The theories of Westermann and Richter exemplify one pitfall of form criticism. The most exact and careful analysis of forms and motifs must be carried out with a sense for the broad perspective. The mere occurrence of certain genres is not enough to determine the literary genre of the work. How are the genres used? Often there is a contrast between the use of a genre and its ordinary function, and one has to stand away from the work in order to appreciate this. Nevertheless, it is important to recognize that several genre elements do exist within Job. Thus, the importance of the legal genres and motifs is that they make the reader aware of the strong claims made by Job. As F. Stier reminds us: "Job imposes judicial responsibility upon God. We deprive the book of the monstrous element to which it witnesses, namely that a man engages in a judicial process against God, were we to see in its judicial setting merely literary dress" (p. 217).

The general designation for Job by H. Gese is that it is a "paradigm of the answered lament" (*Klageerhörungsparadigma*). He patterns his understanding of the literary form upon Mesopotamian models, especially the *Ludlul bel nemeqi* ("I will praise the Lord of Wisdom," *ANET*, 434-37), and the Sumerian "Man and his God." In all three texts the main figure is one who is suffering, apparently without cause. All relate a complaint by the sufferer, who is eventually restored by the divinity. This type is characterized by two features: a complaint (which Gese terms "lament," but cf. Glossary), and a trusting appeal to God when in distress (so at least, the *Ludlul* poem). Thus the sequence is: distress, complaint, divine response, and restoration. Gese claims that the author of Job took over this type, only to change it. The mechanical theory of retribution is replaced by a theology of God's transcendence. The relation of Job to the Mesopotamian model is not very compelling, however, and Gese's view overrates the role of the epilogue.

Form-critical analysis of Job must take another path than that usually pursued. Not many clear and simple genres retain their separate identity within a speech, and thus enable the expositor to point to them at various levels in a history of development of tradition. Perhaps the use of proverbs and wisdom sayings are exceptions. But even in these cases it is not helpful to separate them from their larger setting in the speech or to speculate about their possible original setting. In other words, the danger of atomizing the disputation speeches must be avoided. G. Fohrer has pointed out that the speeches are a mixture of genres and genre elements from at least three different areas: law (litigation), wisdom, and the Psalms (especially complaint and hymn). It seems best to attend to these elements within the framework of the speeches in which they appear—without dissection of minutiae which would have to be placed in theoretical and improper fashion in various presumed settings. This is particularly true of the legal subgenres; we have no real knowledge of due process in ancient Israel, and to reconstruct it from Job is working in a vicious circle. The speeches of Job and his friends can rightly be classified as DISPUTATION SPEECHES, which employ various subgenres. Job's soliloquy in chs. 29-31, while it incorporates items from wisdom and law, approaches the genre of the COMPLAINT of an individual, in which the individual describes his distress (notice the "then" and "now" motif of the DIRGE in chs. 29-30), and asserts his innocence (ch. 31). While the Lord's response in chs. 38-40 is also a DISPUTATION SPEECH aimed at Job, it too incorporates genres from law and wisdom. See the commentary by G. Fohrer (pp. 50-53).

A stout and stimulating analysis of the book of Job as belonging to the genre of COMEDY has been presented by J. W. Whedbee ("The Comedy of Job"). Such a claim had already been made by eminent literary figures such as Northrop Frye and Christopher Fry. Even if the definition of comedy may not be universally agreed upon, Whedbee's presentation is very appealing. He defines comedy in terms of two central ingredients: a vision of incongruity that involves the ironic, the ludicrous, and the ridiculous, and a basic story line in which ultimately the hero arrives at happiness and is restored to a harmonious society.

The last point is most evident in the book of Job. The prologue describes the holy Job and his prosperous life, while it also provides the reader with the basic information which is kept secret from Job and the friends. The epilogue reintegrates Job to his world, a "comic upturn."

Incongruity (or at least ambiguity) surfaces already in the prologue when God himself admits, "You have incited me against him without cause" (2:3). This is a foreshadowing of the underside of God that Job will develop at length in his speeches (chs. 7, 9, 12). But incongruity, manifested in irony and the ridiculous, appears throughout the work. In Job's opening complaint (ch. 3) the reader is confronted with the incongruity of the Job of the prologue and the Job of the dialogue. Caricature is particularly evident in the treatment of the friends. They begin with silence (2:13), to which Job later refers as their only wisdom (13:5). Eliphaz is a parody of the "wise counsellor." His description of Job's "ripe old age" (5:26; cf. 8:5-7; 11:13-19) is an ironic anticipation of the epilogue! The stereotyping of the righteous and the wicked, in which the friends indulge, turns to their own ridicule; Job is the wrong person for these bromides. Their moralizing is cut down by his harsh words (12:2-3; 13:12; 16:2-5; 26:2-4). The friends, far from being wise men, thus represent the *alazon*, the classical comic figure of the impostor or fool. But the friends are not Job's real enemy; it is God, and to God Job addresses several sallies. He parodies Psalm 8 in 7:17-18, and he turns the traditional song of praise into a song to the God of terror and destruction (9:2-10). He forces God's hand in 31:35-37, and who appears? Elihu, the interloper, another *alazon*, an "angry young man," whose prosy and bombastic style befits his platitudes. In the Yahweh speeches there is obvious irony in the questions addressed to Job (38:2-5; 40:1, 6-14; etc.). But there is a double irony here, insofar as Job has already anticipated in 9:3-4, 11-12, how God would act! The theophany provides Job with double vision: of God and also of the world from God's point of view (as von Rad has pointed out, God lets nature do the talking for him in these speeches). The two divine speeches and the two replies of Job (40:3-5 and 42:1-6) are understood by Whedbee to be a "two-stage movement" from silence to repentance; what seems to the reader to be the climax is only a prelude to the final word of the Lord. Job's reaction is genuine, but also paradoxical. He has seen God (42:5), but he also sees that he does not see; he does not see all.

Finally, the studies of P. W. Skehan (pp. 96-126), not directly concerned with genre, have pointed out several peculiarities about the speeches in Job. These studies affect the exterior form of the poems, their visible structures; it would appear that the author deliberately wrote speeches of specific length and with acrostic features. The following features are noteworthy:

(1) A normal speech length in chs. 4–14 emerges: usually twenty-two or twenty-three lines. This length seems to derive from the pattern of the ACROSTIC POEM frequently employed in the Bible (Lamentations, Psalms). The twenty-two lines are the deliberate equivalent of the strict acrostic, although the sequence of 'aleph, beth, is not preserved.

(2) In chs. 4–14, the speeches are multiples of the acrostic patterns. Thus, Eliphaz's discourse (chs. 4–5) is contained in two speeches which are ALPHABETIZING POEMS, 4:2–5:2 (twenty-two lines) and 5:3-27 (twenty-three lines, plus 5:28, an appeal to listen). Job responds to this in a double length speech (6:1–7:21) which exceeds that of Eliphaz by seven lines. The pattern is that Job's reply will always be just a little longer.

(3) Acrostic features are noteworthy in chs. 4–14. For example, Job's speech in ch. 9 is twenty-three lines long in units that break down according to sense into three-line stanzas (except for vv. 11-12). The initial letters of the lines follow a deliberate arrangement: 'aleph, 'aleph, ḥeth; he, he, he; nun, 'ayin, 'ayin; etc. The resultant picture is striking: thus, Eliphaz speaks generally in five-line units; Job answers him consistently in three-line and four-line units.

(4) "In response to the plea of Job in 29–31, the author composed the Lord's reply, 38–41, to overmatch it, not only in quality, but likewise in measurable quantity, with recognizable relationships between the two, corresponding to the relationships in quantity between the speeches of the friends and the speeches of Job in the earlier dialogue. Both Job's final plea and the Lord's reply are tripartite structures, comparable to those found in chs. 9–10 and 12–14" (Skehan, 114). Thus, the first portion of the Lord's speech (38:2-38) goes beyond the thirty-three lines of Job 29:2-30:8, the first part of Job's plea. The second is longer (some thirty-four lines in all) than the second part of Job's soliloquy (twenty-two lines in 30:9-31). Finally, the third part of the Lord's speech (40:7–41:26) yields fifty lines, well beyond the forty lines of Job in 31:1-40.

N. Habel (pp. 34-50) has called one of the wisdom genres appearing in Job the APPEAL TO ANCIENT TRADITION. Its basic structure is the appeal itself, the citation of the tradition, and its application; cf. 8:8-13; 12:7-12; 15:17-35; 20:4-29. In this connection, B. Childs has independently pointed out the SUMMARY-AP-PRAISAL FORMULA (*Isaiah and the Assyrian Crisis* [SBT 2/3; Naperville, 1967]): "Such is. . . ." See Job 8:13; 18:21; 20:29.

Setting

From the remarks on genre it is clear that the subgenres of judicial process and wisdom would have been at home in several appropriate settings: judicial court, the school, etc. However, a reconstruction of a detailed setting, such as a given element in a legal process, is exceedingly hypothetical. It seems better to recognize that within the speeches there are *imitations* of judicial processes, but the evidence will not bring us beyond that. Hence the most important setting is the book itself: how do the genres and subgenres combine in this work?

The setting of the book must be placed in the wisdom movement. Whatever one may think of the theories of its growth (by various additions), the work is a product of the sages who found the optimism of Proverbs to be an oversimplifi-cation. The doctrine of divine retribution, which Proverbs shares with the Deu-teronomic theology and the general biblical tradition, needed to be confronted with the "difficult case," and this is Job. There is no proof that it was written out of a personal experience of suffering.

Commentators generally place the work in the postexilic period (5th-3rd centuries), but several scholars place it before the exile (e.g., M. Pope). However, there are no convincing arguments for a fixed date. If the book has received additions, the final form of the work is probably postexilic (and certainly before Ben Sira, ca. 200 B.C.). But this does not eliminate the possibility of much earlier material having been used. Certainly the reference to Job in Ezek 14:14, 20 suggests that some form of the Job story was known about 600 B.C. On the whole, one can make no firm conclusions about setting in terms of the date.

Intention

Interpreters are not agreed in pinpointing the message of the book. Several points seem to emerge in the book. According to chs. 1–2, disinterested piety is not only possible, it is real. While the description of the debate between Job and the friends is tilted in Job's favor, a good part of the theology of the friends is standard wisdom doctrine (cf. Psalm 37). It is the relevancy of this to Job's case that is at issue. Ch. 28 seems to underline the lack of human wisdom to solve the case at hand. The contribution of Elihu is a moot point; but perhaps his modest effort lies in putting forth the medicinal aspect of suffering (33:16-22; 36:9-12). The intervention of the Lord does not add any really new theology; but it is enough to bring Job to yield to him, without surrendering to the views of his friends. Finally, even the traditional theory of retribution receives some (qualified) support in the epilogue, in which Job is restored.

But on the whole, the intention of the book is clearly to show the inadequacy of the traditional theory of retribution; human justice does not secure blessings from God. In the end, Job accepts the divine freedom in this matter, which remains mysterious.

CHAPTER 2
THE INDIVIDUAL UNITS

PROLOGUE, 1:1–2:13

Structure

I. A description of Job's piety and prosperity	1:1-5
II. First scene in the heavenly court	1:6-12
A. Introduction of the Satan, who functions among the sons of God	6-7
B. Satan's challenge: Job is not God-fearing "without cause"	8-11
C. Acceptance of the challenge by Yahweh	12
III. Job's first test	1:13-22
A. Announcement of four successive catastrophes	13-19
B. Description of Job's pious reaction	20-21
C. Verdict of the writer on Job's conduct	22
IV. Second scene in the heavenly court	2:1-6
A. Introduction of the Satan	1-2
B. Yahweh challenges the Satan who has incited him against Job "without cause"	3
C. Satan challenges Yahweh to inflict a personal evil	4-5
D. Acceptance of challenge by Yahweh	6
V. Job's second test	2:7-10
A. Description of Job's suffering	7-8
B. Description of Job's reaction: fidelity, despite wife's words	8-10
VI. Announcement of the visit of the three friends	11-13

The above structure, in its main outline (two heavenly court scenes and two trials endured patiently by Job), is recognized by practically all commentators. The structure has to be articulated in terms of the progress of thought: "without cause" (*ḥinnām;* 1:9; 2:3) ties together the heavenly court scenes, and Job's reaction to the tests highlights the events transpiring on earth. With the appearance of the three friends, the stage is set for the dialogue.

Genre

The prologue forms part (with 42:7-17) of the NARRATIVE FRAME of the whole book. It can be classified as an edifying STORY of a pious man who remains faithful to God in every trial (and who in the end—ch. 42—is rewarded by God).

No little artistry is to be found in this prologue. Repetition, a beloved feature in Hebrew narrative, is found in 1:6-9 and 2:1-3a. The report of the four messengers (1:13-19) is carefully constructed. The succession of catastrophes corresponds in inverted order to the listing of Job's possessions in 1:2-3. The catastrophes themselves are each made up of two factors: possessions and people are afflicted, till finally in the fourth event Job's family is wiped out; the events are outlaws, lightning, raiders, and a storm. All this is portrayed in the messengers' announcements of the bad news on the heels of the preceding messenger in set, formulaic language ("I alone have escaped to tell you," 1:15, 16, 17, 19).

Setting

This kind of story (fidelity in trial) exemplifies the brave optimism expressed in Prov 3:11-12 (cf. Genesis 22; Sir 1:1-6), and it would have been cultivated by the sages. In the book it is used to provide background to the ensuing dialogue, so that the reader knows from the outset that Job is truly one who suffers innocently.

Intention

In itself the story illustrates the principle that piety can and should be disinterested; the service of God is not to rest upon the condition of his gifts to men. The author does not belabor this point; in the total context chs. 1–2 are designed as a mise-en-scène against which the claims of Job and the three friends are to be measured.

JOB'S SOLILOQUY (COMPLAINT), 3:1-26

Text

Read 3:5-6 with *NAB*: *Kamrîrê laylâ hayyôm hahû'*, "the blackness of night (affright it! May obscurity seize) that day."

Structure

I. Introduction	1-2
II. The complaint (24 lines: 4/4/3/3/3/4/3)	3-26
A. Curse of day	3-6
B. Curse of night	7-10
C. Complaint motif: why born?	11-12, 16
D. Description of residents in Sheol: a surcease from suffering	13-15, 17-19
E. Complaint motif: why is life given?	20-23
F. Description of personal distress	24-26

On this structure see Skehan (pp. 99-100). Fohrer divides into strophes, and A. Weiser into "sections," as follows: vv. 3-10, 11-19, 20-26—a division that is also advocated by C. Westermann (pp. 31-33) and D. N. Freedman (*Bib* 49 [1968] 503-8) with detailed argument.

The poem begins clearly at v. 3. The cursing of the day (vv. 3-6) is balanced by the cursing of the night (vv. 7-10), and in v. 10 the *kî* ("because") clause justifies both curses in fact, though it is applied to the night. The complaint motif is introduced by the characteristic "why?", actually, "why not?" (vv. 11, 16). Set off from this is a description of the shades; their peace—in contrast to Job's suffering—is developed in vv. 13-15 (united by the *'im* ["if"] constructions which depend upon *yānûaḥ lî* ["I should have been at rest"] in v. 13) and in vv. 17-19 (verses that are tied together by *šām* ["there"]). The complaint motif is sounded again in v. 20, in which the *lĕ'āmēl* ("to him that is in misery") is syntactically associated with *lĕgeber* ("to a man") in v. 23. The final strophe (vv. 24-26) reflects a motif frequent in Psalms of complaint: the description of one's suffering.

Genre

Most scholars hold that this is a COMPLAINT (*Klage*), and Westermann has argued strongly for it. The usual invocation for help is lacking; instead, there is a curse (cf. Jer 20:14-18). The complaint about God is in the third person, not the second (vv. 20-23). The use of the question "why?" and the description of distress (vv. 24-26) are, however, characteristic of the complaint. The curse formula (*'ārûr*) is not used here (but cf. *qbb* and *'rr* in v. 8), as it is in Jer 20:14. Nevertheless, vv. 3-10 are clearly a CURSE. Normally the imprecation or curse is directed against people or things to ward off some harm. Here the day and the night are personified as though they played a role in the birth of Job; hence they are cursed directly. However, Job's words amount to almost a cursing of himself; he is the accursed one.

Setting

This is the COMPLAINT of a person who is suffering grievously. In the book the complaint serves as an introduction to the cycle of speeches. Job must say something drastic to set off the response of Eliphaz et al.

Intention

Like the "confessions" of Jeremiah (esp. Jer 20:14-18) this poem lays bare the depths of human suffering—so great as to make death preferable.

SPEECH OF ELIPHAZ, 4:1 – 5:27

Structure

This is an ALPHABETIZING POEM of double length: 4:2–5:2, twenty-two lines; 5:3-27, twenty-three lines plus one; cf. Skehan, 100-1.

I. Introduction	4:1
II. Part one (strophic division: 5,5,5,5 plus 2)	4:2–5:2
A. Reasons why Job should be patient (notice quasi-acrostic features introducing each line: *h-, h-, k-, k-, h-*)	2-6
1. Rhetorical question	2
2. Argument	3-6
a. Job's past actions	3-4
b. His present inconsistency	5-6
B. Argument: the innocent cannot perish like the wicked	7-11
1. Reminder of traditional wisdom theory of retribution	7-9
2. Two wisdom sayings in support of the traditional theory	10-11

C. Description of a night vision 12-16
D. Message of the night vision (notice quasi-acrostic
   features, *h-, h-, 'aleph, m-, h-*) 17-21
   1. Rhetorical question 17
   2. An a fortiori argument 18-19
   3. Conclusion 20-21
E. Conclusion 5:1-2
   1. Rhetorical question 1
   2. Wisdom saying in support of the question 2
III. Part two (strophic division: 5,5,3,5,5, plus 1) 5:3-27
A. Statement of punishment of and origin of evildoing
   (notice quasi-acrostic features (*'aleph, y-, 'aleph,*
   k-, k-) 3-7
   1. An example story about punishment of evildoing 3-5
   2. Wisdom sayings concerning man's trouble (*'āmāl*) 6-7
B. A hymnic description of the God to whom Job should
   appeal (note quasi-acrostic features, esp. *'aleph* eight
   times in v. 8; eliminate v. 9 as reduplication of 9:10) 8-13
   1. Job is advised to appeal to God 8
   2. A doxology 10-13
      a. God's providential power 10-11
      b. God's wisdom prevails over the wicked 12-13
C. Median strophe (cf. 15:17-19; 22:12-14), which
   develops the divine action (described in vv. 8-13)
   among men 14-16
D. Encouragement to accept divine reproof (notice
   'alephs in v. 17a) 17-21
   1. "Happy is the man" saying, with motive clause 17-18
   2. Graded numerical saying (6/7) concerning divine
      deliverance 19-21
E. Description of the security of the just man (note that
   lamed begins v. 22, and *tau* opens final line, v. 26) 22-26
F. Conclusion (begins with *h-*, as does 4:2): the
   summary-appraisal, and expansion into paranetic style 27

Genre

This is a DISPUTATION SPEECH. Several subgenres and motifs common to other
genres are to be found. The RHETORICAL QUESTION (4:2) and the ensuing arguments (4:3-6, 7-11) are characteristic of wisdom style. The description of the
vision (4:12-16) is reminiscent of prophetic experience, but it was gradually recognized that since wisdom is a gift of God, channels other than instruction and
tradition were also appropriate (cf. 32:6-10; Sir 24:33). The content of the vision
(man's creatureliness) is typical wisdom teaching; v. 17 has the air of a WISDOM
SAYING, although framed as a rhetorical question (Fohrer, 135). The "call" and
"answer" of 5:1 suggest the language of the court (Fohrer, 146). The subgenres
in part two are a mixture. Wisdom types prevail in 5:3-7, but vv. 8-13 constitute
a HYMN that is continued in the median strophe (vv. 14-16). Wisdom genres then
return in vv. 17-26. A SUMMARY-APPRAISAL ends the speech in v. 27.

Setting and Intention
Within the cycle of speeches, the first words of Eliphaz are deliberately moderate. The emphasis on the "human condition" is designed to bring Job to a point where he can recognize his suffering as punishment for sin.

SPEECH OF JOB, 6:1–7:21

Structure
This section is an ALPHABETIZING POEM of double length: 6:2-23, twenty-two lines and a transition (6:24-27); 6:28–7:21, twenty-three lines and a transition (6:28-30); cf. Skehan, 102. 7:20aβ-b is better read after 7:12, with *NAB*.

I. Introduction	6:1
II. Part one (strophic division: 3,3,3,4/3,3,3,4)	6:2-27
A. A complaint, which functions as an excuse for Job's "words"	2-4
B. Justification of complaint	5-7
1. Two proverbs cited	5-6
2. Conclusion	7
C. Affirmation of loyalty in the form of a death wish	8-10
D. Motifs from complaint	11-27
1. Job's suffering is so great as to be insupportable	11-14
a. Three rhetorical questions	11-12
b. Transition to reproof of three friends	13-14
2. Job's friends fail him	15-24
a. Comparison to dry wadi	15-17
b. Comparison of self to disappointed caravans	18-20
c. Reasonableness of Job's complaint	21-23
d. Job accuses his friends	24-27
III. Part two (strophic division: 3, 3, 3, 4/3, 3, 3, 4)	6:28–7:21
A. Job challenges his friends to hear him	28-30
B. A complaint, addressed to God, concerning the human condition	7:1-21
1. Description of man's lot	1-3
2. Description of Job's sufferings	4-6
3. An (implicit) appeal to God to intervene: transient character of life	7-10
4. Complaint of being a target of God	11-12
5. Description of suffering	13-15
6. Request to be left alone by God (with parody of Psalm 8)	16-18
7. Appeal for change in divine attitude, on the ground of approaching death	19-21

Genre
This is another DISPUTATION SPEECH. Elements from the COMPLAINT Psalms predominate in this speech. The friends have become the "enemies" as in the Psalms (cf. Ps 31:11), comparable to a deceitful wadi (6:15-17; cf. Jer 15:18,

where the metaphor is used of God). In 6:21-30 there are echoes of the questions and claims that would characterize a legal hearing (Fohrer). The complaint motifs return again in ch. 7. Particularly noteworthy is the framing of Job's suffering in a broad description of the human condition (7:1-6; cf. Ps 39:5-7, 12). The motif explaining why God should intervene, so frequent in complaints, is expressed in vv. 7-10. The singular imperative in 7:7 ("remember") is a sign that Job has been addressing God directly since 7:1 (throughout the speeches he addresses God at least obliquely). In vv. 11ff., the intensity of his charges against God increases, as the parody of Psalm 8 in vv. 17-18 shows.

Setting and Intention

The only real setting is that provided by the book, whatever may have been the typical settings of the various subgenres. The setting is unique in that it allows Job to alternate between the friends and God as his addressees. Against the friends Job complains of their insensitivity. Against God, he claims that he has received unjust treatment (7:11-21).

SPEECH OF BILDAD, 8:1-22

Structure

There are seven three-line stanzas (Skehan, 103; and Fohrer)

I. Introduction	1
II. Opening of litigation	2-4
A. Rhetorical question, ridiculing opponent	2
B. Bildad's thesis, in form of a rhetorical question	3
C. Proof of thesis: treatment of Job's children	4
III. Advice	5-7
A. Conditions for deliverance	5-6aα
B. Assurance of deliverance	6aβ-7
IV. Appeal to ancient tradition	8-13
A. Experience of the fathers is wisdom	8-10
B. A proverb with explanation, to illustrate the conclusion	11-12
C. Conclusion: the fate of the godless	13
V. Description of the state of the godless	14-19
VI. Description of the fate of the blameless	20-22

Genre

Again we have a DISPUTATION SPEECH. "The first strophe (vv. 2-4) is totally determined by the elements drawn from parties in litigation" (Fohrer, 186). Ridicule is followed by a counterclaim. The typical wisdom doctrine is given in the form of conditional advice: if Job seeks God. . . . The literary genre, APPEAL TO ANCIENT TRADITION, is found in vv. 8-13; the appeal is supported by a SAYING (v. 11, of Egyptian origin?) and concluded by the SUMMARY-APPRAISAL FORMULA (v. 13). The description of the wicked (vv. 14-19) and the blameless (vv. 20-22) is standard wisdom doctrine.

Setting and Intention

Bildad's speech provides the opportunity for expressing the rigid wisdom doctrine in a compact poem. He warns Job more than Eliphaz does (Fohrer, 194), especially because of Job's reproaches in chs. 6–7.

SPEECH OF JOB, 9:1– 10:22

Structure

This unit falls into three parts (so Skehan, 103-5, and approximately, Fohrer) that in length total two-and-one-half speeches: 1) Job to his friends: 9:2-24 (twenty-three lines; 3,3,3,2/3,3,3,3); 2) Job to himself: 9:25– 10:1 (eleven lines; 4,3,4); 3) Job to God: 10:1-22 (twenty-two lines; 2,5,5,5,5).

I.	Job's speech to his friends	9:1-24
	A. Introduction	1
	B. Statement of impossibility of contending legally with God (*'aleph*, *'aleph*, *ḥeth*)	2-4
	C. Doxology: hymnic description of divine creative power	5-10
	1. First part (*he*, *he*, *he*)	5-7
	2. Second part (*nun*, *'ayin*, *'ayin*)	8-10
	D. Motif of God's superiority to man (*he*, *he*)	11-12
	E. Description of hopelessness of judicial process with God	13-21
	1. First part (*'aleph*, *'aleph*, *'aleph*)	13-15
	2. Second part (*'aleph*, *'aleph*, *lamed*)	16-18
	3. Third part (*'aleph*, *'aleph*, *tau*)	19-21
	F. Accusation of God of injustice (*'aleph*, *'aleph*, *'aleph*)	22-24
II.	Job's speech addressed to himself	9:25– 10:1a
	A. Complaint motifs	25-28
	1. Human existence transistory	25-26
	2. Inevitability of Job's suffering	27-28
	B. Legal motifs	9:29–10:1a
	1. Impossibility of Job proving his innocence (*'aleph*, *'aleph*, *'aleph*)	29-31
	2. Impossibility of judicial process with God	32-35a
	3. Conclusion	9:35b– 10:1aα
III.	Job's speech to God	10:1aβ-22
	A. Introduction to complaint (*'aleph*, *'aleph*)	1aβ-2
	B. Complaint	3-22
	1. Demand for due process	3
	2. Questions about God's motives: Is God merely human, after all?	4-7
	3. Arguments to move God against God: Job the divine handiwork	8-12
	4. Accusations against God: he hounds Job	13-17

5. Complaint motifs · 18-22
   a. Why (*lāmmâ*) was he not stillborn? · · · · · · · · · 18-19
   b. Request for respite in view of prospect of
      Sheol · 20-22

"Job is always given a few lines more than the friend after whom he speaks. Hence his double-length answer to Eliphaz . . . outstrips the speech of Eliphaz by six lines. To answer either Bildad (21 lines) or Zophar (20 lines), however, Job needs only a single-length speech. But his two-and-a-half length speech in chs. 9–10 is, first, one length of discourse to Bildad and the other friends; then a half-length soliloquy; and then a full-length address to God. Similarly, in chs. 12–14 . . ." (Skehan, 98).

Genre

The DISPUTATION SPEECH is again the genre. This speech has genre elements taken from the legal world and from Psalms (HYMN and COMPLAINT). The legal terminology occurs in 9:3 ("contend," "answer"), 14-16, 19-21, 24, 28-30, 32-35; 10:2, 6, 14-15, 17. This is in sharp contrast to chs. 6–7, where the terminology was drawn from nature and daily human experience. The use of legal patterns grows out of Job's emphatic denial of the possibility of contending legally with God (9:3, which is Job's answer to Bildad in 8:3). One cannot point here to any firm legal genres or subgenres (*pace* H. Richter), for we simply do not know enough about them. Yet it is clear that Israelite judicial process has influenced this speech, and Job is using and imitating judicial forms. The legal ordeal seems to underlie 9:30, and 9:29-31 imitates an AVOWAL OF INNOCENCE.

The doxologies in 9:5-10 are clearly imitations of the HYMN (in Hebrew, participial style), and hymnic motifs appear in vv. 11-12. Job's complaint about the hopelessness of any judicial process with God follows (vv. 13-24).

Job's soliloquy (9:25–10:1) speaks of God in the third person. Basically, it is a COMPLAINT about his situation (motifs of transitoriness of life, injustice experienced) that takes up again the theme of the impossibility of receiving justice from God.

Job's address to God (10:1-22) is primarily a COMPLAINT, but there are reflections of judicial process in it (v. 2; Fohrer, 202, characterizes vv. 4-7 as "trial inquiries"). Several LAMENT motifs appear in vv. 3-12; the questions are designed to move God to intervene in his favor. Fohrer sees originally hymnic elements in vv. 8-12, and in vv. 13-17, although an accusation is presented. Again, legal language appears (v. 14, acquittal; v. 17, witnesses), but the whole ends on a note of lament ("why", *lāmmâ*, v. 18).

Setting and Intention

"The gap between the parties in dialogue has deepened" (Fohrer, 220). Although the setting remains that of a disputation between Job and the friends, Job is using the occasion to accuse God of being unjust. The speeches will reflect a growing hostility.

SPEECH OF ZOPHAR, 11:1-20

Structure

I. Introduction	1
II. Opening of litigation	2-6
A. Rhetorical questions in due process style	2-3
B. Quotation of opponent's claim	4
C. A wish for God to teach Job	5-6
	(text uncertain in v. 6)
III. Hymnic description of God's superiority	7-12
IV. Conditional advice offered to Job, with a description of the results of heeding the advice	13-20

The speech has twenty lines in stanzas of 6,6,6,2 lines; cf. Skehan, 105.

Genre

The DISPUTATION SPEECH is used, and legal and wisdom motifs are particularly noteworthy. Zophar opens his speech in the style typical of litigation (cf. 8:2-4). Hymnic influence on vv. 7-12 is clear, but the whole is shaped in a didactic way by the rhetorical questions that are framed so as to heap ridicule on Job and move him from his convictions. The advice (vv. 13ff.) is couched along the lines of wisdom teaching and culminates in the contrast of the just (v. 14) with the wicked in the final verse (v. 20).

Setting and Intention

The dispute situation still prevails. With the speech of the third friend, it appears that the author has distributed among them the most that can be said from their point of view. The contribution of Zophar to the debate is modest, but makes its point within the limited perspective of traditional wisdom.

SPEECH OF JOB, 12:1 – 14:22

These are, in fact, three speeches of alphabetic length: 12:2-25; 13:6-27; 14:1-22 (plus 13:28?), with 13:1-5 functioning as a transition. This is the longest speech in the dialogue (i.e., before ch. 29); cf. Skehan, 105-8.

I. Part one	12:1-25
A. Introduction	1
B. Initiation of litigation	2-6
1. Ridicule of opponent	2
2. Job's claim to wisdom	3
3. Proof that opponents are wrong	4-6
C. Proof of Job's claim to wisdom	7-12
1. Even animals know the hand of God	7-10
2. Two wisdom sayings	11-12
D. Hymnic description of God's wisdom and power	13-25
II. Transition	13:1-5
A. Job's claim to wisdom (cf. 12:2-3)	1-2
B. Job's desire to confront the Lord (notice recurrent *aleph*s)	3

Genre, Setting, Intention

The "speech" is really three, by size, as indicated in the structure. The subgenres are drawn from legal practice, wisdom, and the Psalms (HYMN, COMPLAINT). Upon the litigation process (in which Job lays claim to wisdom) in 12:2-6 follows an argument in wisdom style. This sets the stage for a hymnic celebration of God's wisdom and power (vv. 13-25). It bears repeating that there is a connection between wisdom and the hymn genre, between teaching wisdom (*Naturweisheit*, or nature-wisdom) and celebrating it (so von Rad, *Wisdom in Israel*, 189).

The transitional character of 13:1-5 is marked by its "academic" character: sages dispute with one another, and Job announces his intention of pleading his case before God.

In the second "speech" Job begins with a whiplashing in legal terminology (13:6-12). He makes the friends out to be (lying) defenders of God, seeking to influence the judge (Hölscher, 35). In vv. 17-18 Job again draws on legal procedure; he makes the formal claim that he is in the right (v. 18; notice the AVOWAL OF INNOCENCE already in v. 15). He follows this with a plea to God for fair treatment (vv. 20-22), and challenges him for a bill of particulars (v. 23) with accusations of divine overkill (vv. 23-27; many read 13:28 before 14:3 [Dhorme, *NEB*] or after 14:3 [Skehan, *NAB*]).

The third "speech" is primarily a COMPLAINT and it continues the address to God begun already in 13:20. As in 7:1ff., Job frames his situation in a broad description of the human condition (14:1-3) and makes a plea for divine clemency (vv. 4-6). The following argument (vv. 7-9, 10-12) is a contrast between the tree and mankind that bears upon the future of both; this seems to belong to wisdom tradition (Fohrer, 242). Job then makes an impassioned plea for something unreal; God's recognition of him after a sojourn in Sheol (vv. 13-17); then God would recognize Job in a loving way (this is a kind of motif to make God intervene now before it is too late). The final words of the complaint (vv. 18-22) show that such a wish is truly impossible.

SPEECH OF ELIPHAZ, 15:1-35

Structure

I. Introduction	1
II. Reprimand	2-16
A. Ridicule of opponent by rhetorical questions	2-3
B. Accusation	4-6
C. Ridicule of opponent	7-11
1. Rhetorical questions	7-9
2. Claim that old age denotes wisdom on the side of the friends	10
3. Rhetorical question	11
D. Accusation of Job as sinful	12-16
1. Rhetorical questions	12-14
2. A fortiori argument against Job	15-16
III. A warning lesson from the wisdom tradition	17-35
A. Introduction: appeal to ancient tradition	17-19
B. A description of the disastrous fate of the wicked	20-34
C. A wisdom saying about the wicked	35

Again, Eliphaz speaks in five-line stanzas (vv. 2-6, 7-11, 12-16, 20-24, 25-29, 30-34), with an intermediate stanza of three lines (vv. 17-19). The last verse is a WISDOM SAYING (note infinitives absolute) that describes the wicked themselves rather than their fate; cf. Skehan, 108.

Genre, Setting, Intention

The genre is the DISPUTATION SPEECH, and the subgenres are derived primarily from the wisdom sphere. The reprimand (F. Horst, 220) in 15:2-16 is character- ized by rhetorical questions (vv. 2-3, 7-9, 11-14), ridicule (vv. 2-3, 7-11), and accusations (vv. 4-6, 15-16). Eliphaz then reads Job a lesson from the wisdom tradition that is intended to be a warning (or even, accusation): the fate of the wicked. The APPEAL TO ANCIENT TRADITION (vv. 17ff.) should be compared with 8:8-13. The (Semitic) myth of the primeval man underlies 13:7.

The second speech of Eliphaz is considerably sharper than the first. The author is heating the debate in deliberate fashion.

SPEECH OF JOB, 16:1 – 17:16

Structure

I. Introduction	16:1
II. Ridicule of opponent	2-6
III. Complaint	16:7–17:16
A. Description of attack by enemy (God)	7-14
B. Job does penance, though innocent	15-17
C. A cry for justice	18-21
1. Appeal to earth	18

Genre, Setting, Intention

The DISPUTATION SPEECH again is the genre. The ridicule of the opponent (vv. 2-6) is characteristic of any dispute, whether at court or among the wise. This is followed by a COMPLAINT (15:7–17:16) in which both the friends (17:10) and God (17:3) are addressed. The complaint largely draws on characteristic motifs: a description of the suffering inflicted upon Job (15:7-14), which serves as an accusation against God (Fohrer, 283); the description of his situation (16:1-17; 17:7-16); and reasons why God should intervene (16:22–17:2).

SPEECH OF BILDAD, 18:1-21

Structure

In 18:3 one should read "your" singular (not plural as in MT), and thus the lines are addressed to Job.

Genre, Setting, Intention

The DISPUTATION SPEECH is again the primary genre. Although the opening lines (vv. 2-4) are textually uncertain, it is clear that Bildad reads Job a lesson from traditional wisdom about the punishment in store for the wicked (vv. 5-21; on this theme see Westermann, 66-72). The implication, of course, is that Job is the wicked person. The tenor is not unlike Bildad's earlier speech (cf. 8:8-19), but now judgment has been passed upon Job.

SPEECH OF JOB, 19:1-29

Structure

III. Answer to opponents	4-6
IV. Accusatory description of God's unjust treatment of Job	7-12
V. Complaint	13-22
A. Description of reactions of neighbors	13-19
B. Description of Job's physical state	20
C. Appeal to friends for pity	21
D. Question to friends about their persecution of Job	22
VI. Job's affirmation of faith in his vindicator	23-27
A. Introduction: desire for a permanent record of his avowal	23-24
B. Avowal of faith	25-27
VII. Warning against the "friends" who persecute him	28-29

Genre, Setting, Intention

As might be expected, the genre is the DISPUTATION SPEECH. Again, elements from law and the Psalms appear. Job's words to the friends (vv. 2-6) are characteristic of a defendant replying to his accusers and affirming his innocence (v. 6). This leads him into an accusation (vv. 7-12) against God who has in effect become his enemy, and he lapses into a COMPLAINT (vv. 13-22). The famous lines in vv. 23-27 are a "confession of confidence" (Westermann, 81-82), typical of the complaint Psalms, but within them Job draws upon legal practice (gō'ēl, "vindicator" rather than "redeemer," v. 25). He ends with a WARNING (vv. 28-29).

SPEECH OF ZOPHAR, 20:1-29

Structure

I. Introduction	1
II. Description of Zophar's reaction to Job (introductory to vv. 4ff.)	2-3
III. Wisdom lesson describing the certain and complete destruction of the wicked	4-29

Genre, Setting, Intention

The primary genre is the DISPUTATION SPEECH. The heart of Zophar's speech is the APPEAL TO ANCIENT TRADITION that the joy of the wicked is fleeting (vv. 4-29). After the appeal (v. 4), the tradition is cited (v. 5), and then applied and expanded. Fohrer (p. 327) thinks that there are several originally independent sayings which are only loosely in context (vv. 10, 16, 24-25). The conclusion (v. 29) is the SUMMARY-APPRAISAL FORMULA. See also Job 8:8-13; 12:7-12; 15:14-18.

SPEECH OF JOB, 21:1-34

Structure

I. Introduction	1
II. Address to opponents, introductory to the poem in 7ff.	2-6

Genre, Setting, Intention

This section is another DISPUTATION SPEECH. The genre elements are all from wisdom teaching (Fohrer, 339). As Westermann (p. 54; cf. pp. 72-75) remarks, only here does Job argue in the same style as his friends. After the introductory remarks (vv. 2-6), he begins reading his lesson to the friends, starting with a rhetorical question (v. 7), and playing on the values so dear to the friends (progeny, home, possessions, vv. 8-10), but which are enjoyed by the wicked, even though they blaspheme (vv. 14-15). Rhetorical questions follow (vv. 17-18), and then Job attacks the objection that the wicked suffer at least in the punishment undergone by their progeny (vv. 19-26; v. 22 hardly fits here—cf. Skehan, 110). Again, he attacks their claim that the home of the wicked disappears (vv. 27-33).

SPEECH OF ELIPHAZ, 22:1-30

Structure

I. Introduction	1
II. Rhetorical questions, ridiculing and finally accusing Job	2-5
III. Body of Eliphaz's speech	6-30
A. Specific accusations against Job (v. 8 is errant, and probably belongs elsewhere; cf. Skehan, 111)	6-9
B. Threat ('al kēn ["therefore"]) to Job that present trials are due to his sinfulness	10-11
C. Accusation that Job claims God is ignorant	12-14
D. A warning for Job, derived from the "way" of the wicked	15-20
E. Instruction to Job, with (conditional) promise of restoration	21-30

Genre, Setting, Intention

Fohrer (p. 353) points out that the genre elements are taken from the prophets, Psalms, and wisdom, and the structural analysis above has given some indication of this. Fohrer suggests that the elements in vv. 6-14 derive from prophetic announcements that have been taken up into wisdom. He notes that in vv. 15-16 a WISDOM SAYING has been put in question form, and so transformed into a WARNING; the description of the triumph of the just (vv. 19-20) is a motif found in Psalms (52:8; 58:11; etc.), and serves here to strengthen the warning. For a warning with conditional promise, see also Job 8:5-7; 11:13-20. The conversion motif (v. 23) may derive from the prophetic warning (again, by way of wisdom; so Fohrer, 354). The description of the prayer in vv. 26-27 reflects the liturgical experience expressed in Psalms (cf. Ps 22:26 [RSV 25]; 61:6, 9 [RSV 5, 8]). The final verses appropriate wisdom teaching and here they flow from the warning.

SPEECH OF JOB, 23:1– 24:25

Structure

I. Introduction	23:1
II. Job's complaint	23:2–24:25
A. His wish for a meeting with God, and a process of vindication	2-7
B. But God is absent	8-9
C. Avowal of innocence	10-12
D. Job complains about God's arbitrary way	13-17
E. Job complains about God's failure to punish the wicked who oppress the poor	24:1-25
1. Introduction	1
2. Description of the actions of the wicked	2-4
3. Description of the fate of the poor	5-12
4. Description of rebels against the light	13-17
5. Vv. 18-24?	
6. Conclusion: rhetorical question, challenging the friends	25

Genre, Setting, Intention

Again the genre is the DISPUTATION SPEECH, although the tone is more reflective and less polemical than usual. The genre elements in ch. 23 are taken from legal procedure and the Psalms (Fohrer, 364). Although Job begins with a typical complaint (v. 2), he moves into a description of the litigation (vv. 3-7) he would have with God. This serves the function of an AVOWAL OF INNOCENCE, a motif that is clearly expressed in vv. 10-12. The complaint about God's absence (vv. 8-10) explores the reason why the desired litigation of vv. 3-7 cannot take place. A further reason is the arbitrariness of God (vv. 13-17).

Ch. 24 is a problem from many points of view; the text is very uncertain, especially vv. 18-24, which do not seem to be consonant with what Job has been saying all along. As far as form criticism is concerned, COMPLAINT dominates the chapter (vv. 1-17). See the commentaries for efforts to build the missing speech of Zophar from 24:18ff.

SPEECH OF BILDAD, 25:1-6

Structure

I. Introduction	1
II. A hymn (fragmentary?) commemorating God's power and justice	2-6

Genre, Setting, Intention

A HYMN in which affirmation (v. 2) is balanced by a RHETORICAL QUESTION (v. 3). These verses serve as a basis for God's justice and man's impurity (v. 4, a WISDOM SAYING cast in the form of a RHETORICAL QUESTION—so Fohrer, 375). This theme occurs also in 4:17 and 15:14 (Eliphaz) and in 9:2; 14:4 (Job). An a fortiori argument follows (vv. 4-5).

It is difficult to imagine that the text has been integrally preserved here. The chapter seems to be a fragment, and some commentators (e.g., Dhorme) find Bildad's speech continued in 26:5-14. The sharpness of the debate is not as evident as it was in previous speeches.

SPEECH OF JOB, 26:1-14

Structure

I. Introduction	1
II. Sarcastic reprimand	2-4
III. Hymn in praise of God's power	5-14
A. God's dominion over the underworld	5-6
B. His power reflected in creative activity	7-13
C. Conclusion	14

Genre, Setting, Intention

Once more the DISPUTATION SPEECH is the genre. The sarcasm of vv. 2-4 suggests a genre element from wisdom dispute and is addressed to "you" in the singular (!), hence to Bildad. What follows (vv. 5-14) is clearly in the HYMN genre (notice participial style in vv. 5-9). The state of the text and the unexpected hymn in praise of God by Job have led to various reconstructions of the speeches at this point; see the commentaries. As the text stands, Job seems to cut off Bildad's speech of 25:2-6, and he finishes it for him (cf. Skehan, 112).

SPEECH OF JOB, 27:1-23

Structure

I. Introduction (the formula, "again took up his discourse," differs from the usual introduction; cf. 29:1)	1
II. Job's affirmation of his integrity	2-6
III. Job's statement on the "enemy" or "godless," addressed (cf. vv. 11-12) to the friends	7-12
IV. Description of the fate of the wicked	13-23

Genre, Setting, Intention

The DISPUTATION SPEECH is again apparent. An OATH begins v. 2 (cf. Fohrer, 378, according to whom it is another preparation for the PURIFICATORY OATH of ch. 31; cf. also 21:6-34; 23:10-12), and it is expanded into a COMPLAINT against God, followed by an OATH of truthfulness (vv. 3-4). This serves to justify Job's affirmation of honesty (vv. 5-6; v. 5 is addressed to the friends). The following statements about the wicked (vv. 7-23) adopt traditional motifs found in wisdom and in the Psalms, and they do not fit in with Job's views, unless one interprets them (v. 7) as what he wishes for the three friends.

WISDOM POEM, 28:1-28

Structure

The meaning of the text and sequence of thought present problems. In its present form the MT seems to describe how man searches and finds precious items in the depths of the earth (vv. 1-11), but he is unable to find the incomparable but inaccessible wisdom (vv. 12-22). God alone knows wisdom and where it is (vv. 23-27), and he has told man that it is associated with fear of the Lord and avoidance of evil (v. 28). There is reason, however, to think that several verses in vv. 1-11 pertain to God's work (vv. 3, 9-11, appropriate after v. 24), or fit in with the inaccessibility of wisdom (vv. 7-8, appropriate after v. 21). The refrain-like character of vv. 12 and 20 suggests an original strophic structure (but Fohrer, 388-89, goes too far with this). The claim that v. 28 lies outside the thrust of the poem is true, but it ties the prologue (1:8; 2:23) in with the theme of wisdom's inaccessibility.

I. Man's pursuit of the earth's inner possessions	1-11
A. Earth, the source of precious metals	1-2
B. Man's underground search	3-4
C. Earth the repository	5-6
D. Locus unknown to animals	7-8
E. Man's worldwide search	9-11
II. Wisdom is inaccessible	12-22
A. Wisdom not to be found	12-14
B. Wisdom incomparable, not to be bought	15-19
C. Wisdom not to be found	20-22
III. Wisdom is with God	23-28
A. God alone knows wisdom	23-27
B. Wisdom is associated with fear of the Lord	28

Genre

The genre elements are almost all drawn from wisdom teaching (Fohrer, 393). Fohrer suggests that originally the question refrain (vv. 12, 20) may have been answered with a short saying, such as in vv. 21-23 (cf. Prov 23:29-30; Eccl 2:22-23; 8:1). Westermann (pp. 104-7) considers the poem as an expression of question (vv. 12-20) and answer (v. 23), hence a kind of riddle proposing a challenge and its solution. The motifs of nature, the incomparability and inaccessibility of wisdom, are stock themes of wisdom teaching.

Setting and Intention

Within the MT ch. 28 seems to be attributed to Job as part of his last speech to the friends, continuous with ch. 27. There is almost unanimous agreement, however, that ch. 28 is an independent poem inserted at this particular point, whatever the reason, and whoever the author. On this view, the poem serves as a rebuttal to the "wisdom" of the friends and even of Job himself. None of them have the wisdom to solve the questions that have been raised. For Westermann (pp. 106-7), ch. 28 is a "resting point" in the drama of Job and his friends, in which the reason for God's judgment on the three friends (42:7) is given: wisdom cannot be manipulated in the style which they have been guilty of. While the intention of the poem itself is clearly to underline the transcendent value of wisdom, which God alone (not any creature) knows, the intention of the poem within the book as it stands is to underscore the bankruptcy of the dialogue which has taken place, and plead for "fear of the Lord" (28:28; 1:8; 2:3).

JOB'S SOLILOQUY, 29:1–31:37

Text

Read 31:35-37 after 31:40a.

Structure

Chs. 29-31 are structurally and conceptually one; they are a soliloquy of Job with a single introduction in 29:1 (where "discourse" translates *māšāl*). The usual structural analyses recognize three parts, following the chapter divisions. An exception is P. W. Skehan (pp. 114-23), who recognizes a three-part speech of thirty-three plus twenty-two plus forty lines, reviewing the past (29:2–30:8; note that 30:1-8 is a continuation of the situation in ch. 29 because Job is still talking about his past prosperity, contrasting it with the situation of the parents of those who now revile him), the present (30:9-31), and the "negative confession" of ch. 31.

In ch. 31, there seem to have been some displacements; almost everyone recognizes that vv. 35-37, Job's challenge to God, should be at the end; hence vv. 38-40a are to be included among the series of PURIFICATORY OATHS, and v. 40b ("Job's words are ended") is an editorial addition.

I. Introduction	29:1
II. Job's desire for his former prosperity	29:2-25
A. A wish	2
B. An expansion of the wish, describing his former prosperity	3-25
1. God's blessing upon Job	3-6
2. The respect accorded to Job in public assembly (to be followed by vv. 21-25?)	7-10
3. Job's claim to being commended by his neighbors	11-17
a. The claim	11
b. The reasons: his social concern	12-17
4. Job's expectations of a happy reward (to be seen as conclusion, if vv. 21-25 are read after v. 10)	18-20
5. Job's prestige in the community (see above, 7-10)	21-25
III. Complaint	30:1-31
A. Job's description of his present ridicule	1
B. Job's description of the forebears of those who now revile him	2-8
C. Description of Job's present sufferings	9-19
D. An appeal to God, with accusation	20-23
E. Reasons why God should have shown Job sympathy	24-26
F. Description of Job's present suffering	27-31
IV. Job's "negative confession"	31:1-34, 38-40
A. Lust	1-4
1. His covenant with his eyes	1
2. Three questions indicating punishment to be expected in the light of traditional theology, had he done wrong	2-4
B. Purificatory oath relative to falsehood	5-6

The above outline has followed the MT closely, except for 31:38-40. However, 31:1-4 is problematical. Here v. 1 is specific (cf. Sir 9:3), whereas vv. 2-4 are a general introduction to the "negative confession." So Skehan (pp. 116-17), who places v. 1 before vv. 9-10, and also joins v. 6 after vv. 2-4, so that vv. 5, 7 (*'im* ["if "]) make good sense when joined with v. 8.

Genre, Setting, Intention

These chapters are a SOLILOQUY of Job that comes to a climax in his final challenge to God (31:35-37). They are not part of the dialogue, to which they form a kind of conclusion (just as ch. 3 formed an introduction). The soliloquy may be compared to a final statement before a judge. As Richter (p. 104) puts it, Job is seeking the resolution of the case by a divine decision.

The subgenres and motifs derive largely from the Psalms. Ch. 30 is clearly a COMPLAINT, and Westermann (pp. 33-39) explains Job's AVOWAL OF INNOCENCE (ch. 31) as corresponding to the same kind of motif in Psalms (Psalms 5, 7, 17, 26). Job's consideration of his past (ch. 29) would also correspond to the motif of "looking back at God's earlier saving activity" in the COMMUNAL COMPLAINT (Psalm 80; 40:2-10). The primary genre element in ch. 31 is the PURIFICATORY OATH which can be found at home in the liturgy (e.g., Ps 7:3-5) or in judicial process (Exod 22:7, 9-10). The oath is cast in the style of: if (the deed), then (the punishment), as in vv. 5-6, 7-8. The punishment may be merely implicit, and one is left only with the if-clause, e.g., vv. 29-30, 31-32. Fohrer (pp. 428-29) thinks that an original series of ten sins has been expanded to twelve (commentators do not agree on how many are in the text: Hölscher and Gordis agree on fourteen) to form a wisdom teaching. The genre of purificatory oath is here subordinated to the challenge which Job issues to God (31:35-37 are to be moved to the end). It is noteworthy that the challenge continues in the form of the purificatory oath; after expressing a wish in v. 35, Job invokes an implicit fate if he does not confront the Lord (vv. 36-37). The challenge is marked by legal terminology and practice, but there is not enough evidence that in Israel written depositions were used (*pace* Richter). It should be stressed that chs. 29–31 are outside the earlier debate; the dialogue with the friends is over, and Job never mentions them.

Extrabiblical parallels to ch. 39 are to be found in the Egyptian "negative confession" of the dead person before Osiris (*ANET*, 34-36).

SPEECHES OF ELIHU, 32:1–37:24

Structure

I. Narrative introduction — 32:1-5
  A. End of the debate recorded — 1
  B. Motivations for Elihu's intervention — 2-5
II. Elihu's first speech — 32:6–33:33
  A. Introduction — 6aα
  B. Elihu's preliminary remarks — 6aβ-22
    1. To the elders, Elihu expresses his fear — 6aβ-6b
    2. In a soliloquy ("listen" in v. 10 is singular), Elihu claims to be wise, despite youth (note repetition of "declare my opinion" in vv. 6, 10, and later in v. 17, and also the *inclusio* of *'āmartî* ["I say"] in vv. 7, 10) — 7-10
    3. Elihu "waited" (*hôḥaltî*, another *inclusio* in vv. 11 and 16); note that vv. 11-14 are addressed to the elders, while vv. 15-16 are a soliloquy — 11-16
    4. Elihu resolves to speak up, or "answer" (*'a'ăneh*, an *inclusio*, in vv. 17 and 20) — 17-20
    5. Elihu concludes: he is without flattery (note repetition of verb *knh* ["flatter"] and also of *nśh* ["bear"] in two meanings) — 21-22
  C. The speech (addressed to Job) — 33:1-30
    1. Summons to Job to hear — 1-4
    2. Renewed summons to Job to debate — 5-7
    3. "Quotation" of theses of Job — 8-11
      a. Introduction — 8
      b. "Quotation" — 9-11
        1) Job claims to be innocent (cf. 9:21; 10:7; 16:17; 23:11-12; 31:1-40) — 9
        2) Job claims God is hostile (cf. 10:16-17; 13:24-27; 19:11) — 10-11
  D. Elihu's arguments against theses — 12-30
    1. God warns (by dream) in order to save — 12-18
    2. God disciplines (by sickness), and man is saved by conversion to him — 19-30
  E. Appeal to Job to listen — 31-33
      (fits better before 35:2)
III. Elihu's second speech — 34:1-37
  A. Introduction — 1
  B. The speech (addressed to the "wise") — 2-37
    1. Summons to the wise to hear — 2-4
    2. "Quotation" of theses of Job — 5-9
      a. Job claims he is innocent and God has taken away his right (cf. 9:21; 13:81; 27:2) — 5-6
      b. Ridicule of Job — 7-8

On the remarkable structure of 32:6-22, see Skehan (pp. 85-87), who remarks: "Even within the Elihu chapters (32–37) this speech is unique; it offers 19 lines of verse in which, by way of introducing himself, the speaker says almost nothing at all, and with a seeming maximum of repetition. The character it creates for Elihu is so complete a caricature (in view of the substance and charm verifiable for instance in 33, or in 36:22–37:24) that one may perhaps more readily see in it the author of the dialogue poking fun at a son or a favorite pupil whose best efforts (chs. 33–37) he has decided to incorporate within his book, than any other situation. . . . The poem is therefore a formal rhetorical exercise, with a caricature of its ostensible protagonist inherent in its hesitations and its outbursts; if it has more words and more structure than the contents would seem to deserve, this is quite deliberate."

In the above outline, "quotations" is used broadly to indicate Elihu's understanding of Job's claims, and appropriate references are given.

For reconstructions of the Elihu speeches, see the commentaries, and also Westermann, 107-15.

Genre, Setting, Intention

The speeches of Elihu are in the same genre of DISPUTATION that characterized the speeches of Job and the friends. From the point of view of form criticism, several genre elements appear. Fohrer (p. 449) calls 32:6-22 the "self-introduction of a wise man in a dispute." The terminology and ideas derive from the wisdom sphere, as analyzed above; so does the structure. The disputatious character of the speeches can be seen from the common structure (cf. Westermann, 112): a quotation of a thesis of Job, followed by a refutation. H. Richter (*Studien*, 111ff.) has a slightly different view: Elihu speaks as a judge before a college of judges in a reprise of the dispute with Job.

The speech in ch. 34 has an even more pronounced lecture tone, if only because of the reference to the *ḥăkāmîm* ("wise," v. 2). Fohrer (p. 466) points to the hymnic elements in vv. 16-22, legal elements in vv. 23-29, and echoes of a COMPLAINT in vv. 31-37, but rightly considers the whole to be a DISPUTATION SPEECH of a wise man. Westermann describes the chapter as a "lecture of a wisdom teacher in a circle of wise men, to whom he addresses himself" (p. 108). In the fourth and final speech Fohrer (p. 484) sees a certain tie-in to the following Yahweh speeches. Thus, 37:14ff. imitate the divine questions, and the review of nature in 36:26ff. is reminiscent of 38:4ff.

The intention of the Elihu speeches is a moot question. As a "reply" to Job, they seem to add nothing new, despite Elihu's claims. Even his words about the medicinal or chastening effect of suffering (33:13-32; 36:8-15) are anticipated by Eliphaz in chs. 4–5. And the similarity of chs. 36–37 to the Yahweh speeches in 38:4ff. have just been indicated.

THE CONFRONTATION BETWEEN THE LORD AND JOB, 38:1– 42:6

Structure

I. Yahweh's first speech	38:1–39:30
A. Introduction	1
B. Opening challenge	2-3
1. Identity question	2
2. Invitation to "debate"	3
C. Ironic questions about creation and creatures	38:4–39:30
1. Establishment of earth	4-7
2. Taming of the sea (read *mî sak* ["who shut in?"] in v. 8)	8-11
3. Birth of day	12-15
4. Depth and breadth of creation	16-18
5. Light and darkness	19-21
6. Snow, hail, and wind	22-24
7. Rain even in desert	25-27

8. Rain/dew and ice/snow	28-30
9. The constellations	31-33
10. Clouds/rain	34-35, 37-38
	(v. 36 is problematical)
11. Feeding of animals	39-41
12. Births of animals	39:1-4
13. The untamed wild ass	5-8
14. The wild ox	9-12
15. The case of the ostrich	13-18
16. The case of the horse	19-25
17. The hawk and eagle	26-30
II. An exchange between the Lord and Job	40:1-5
A. The Lord challenges his critic	1-2
B. Job's humble reply: nothing to say	3-5
III. Yahweh's second speech	40:6–41:26
A. Introduction	6(=38:1)
B. Opening challenge	7-8
C. Ironic question and ridicule of Job's strength	9-14
D. Sarcastic challenge to Job concerning the control of two of God's creatures	40:15–41:26
1. Behemoth	40:15-24
2. Leviathan	40:25–41:16
	(*RSV* 41:1-34)
IV. Job's submission to the Lord	42:1-6
A. Introduction	1
B. Job's reply	2-6
1. Admission of divine power and purpose	2
2. Admission of his ignorance and presumption	3aβ-3b
3. Recognition of the fact that the Lord appeared to him	5
4. Submission to the Lord, and disowning of his words	6

Westermann (pp. 85ff.) bases his structure of these chapters on the theme of the praise of the creator (38:4–39:30), which is continued in the theme of the praise for the Lord of history (40:6–41:26: Behemoth and Leviathan are interpreted as earthly historical powers). Skehan (pp. 120ff.), following the pattern of speeches in the first cycle where Job always says more than his opponents, discovers three parts to Yahweh's intervention, each of which is deliberately longer than the respective speeches of Job's soliloquy in chs. 29–31, which of course Yahweh is answering: 38:2-38; 38:39–39:20; 40:7–41:26 (*RSV* 40:7–41:34). Each of these surpasses the three parts given to Job in 29:2–30:8; 30:9-31; 31:1-40. The strophic analysis provided by Skehan for chs. 38–41 is rather convincing.

It is best to omit 40:3aα (cf. 38:3) and 40:4 (cf. 33:31; 38:3; 40:7) as dittographies or adaptions of earlier verses. Otherwise one has to explain them as quotations (Gordis, 187-88) or reminiscences, and they do not fit in easily.

Genre, Setting, Intention

Basically, this is a DISPUTATION SPEECH (so also Westermann, 82, despite his emphasis of the motif of praise) as are so many of the speeches in the book, and this time it is the Lord intervening to present his side of the discussion. It can be likened to the Yahweh oracle of divine judgment in the liturgy, as Fohrer suggests, but it remains part of the debate. The imperatives and ironic questions are in the style of the sarcastic reply of the Egyptian Hori to the scribe Amenemope (Papyrus Anastasi I; *ANET*, 475-79). The display of knowledge about the items of creation probably owes something to the onomastica or name lists of the ancient world (Mesopotamia and Egypt) that contained the names of created things (cf. G. von Rad, 281-91).

The genre elements are drawn from wisdom teaching, legal procedure, and the Psalms (Fohrer, 498). Legal and wisdom background is evidenced in the opening challenge to Job to reply to the Lord's questions (note in 38:2-3 "counsel" and "knowledge," *'ēṣâ* and *da'at*), and again in 40:2, 8-10, 14. The far-reaching description of phenomena in the created order is due to the "nature wisdom" cultivated by the sages; at times this assumes a hymnlike quality as in the Elihu speeches (e.g., 36:24–37:13). But here it is characterized by first-person claims (38:9, 23; 39:6; 40:15) that are intrinsic to the Lord's reply to Job. Prime examples of this nature wisdom are of course the description of Leviathan and Behemoth. The whole is permeated with irony and sarcasm, effectively expressed in imperatives and questions, such as might be expected in a dispute among sages.

The intention of the Yahweh speeches is to convey the impact of a direct confrontation with the Lord, for which Job had yearned. The series of questions, ironic and unanswerable, is shaped to lead Job to his final submission. Yet these speeches, while they illustrate God's love for his varied creation, do not add anything significantly new to what had been expressed in earlier hymns (e.g., 5:10-16; 9:4-10; 26:5-14; etc.). No "answer" is given to Job; in fact, his problem is ignored. But the speeches are designed to give flesh to Job's experience (42:5, "Now my eye has seen you") of his encounter with God. Job's submission is not just an admission of defeat in an argument (42:2-3); it is an act of submission to the Lord, whom the vanquished has truly seen (v. 5); the vision of God is the reason for his disowning his own side in the debate (v. 6). (Cf. R. A. F. MacKenzie, "The Purpose of the Yahweh Speeches in the Book of Job," *Bib* 40 [1959] 435-45.)

EPILOGUE, 42:7-16

Structure

I. God's judgment on the friends	7-9
A. Introduction	7a
B. The Lord's words to Eliphaz	7b-9
1. The Lord's anger, and reason for it	7b
2. Commands for sacrifice and intercession of Job (with repetition of the reason given in v. 7b)	8
3. Carrying out of command, with the anticipated result	9

In its present position, v. 11 indicates that Job's visitors also contribute to his enrichment. Fohrer (pp. 543-44) interprets it as part of the original prologue, in which friends and relatives would have come to condole with Job. It was moved from this place when the condolences were assigned to the three friends (2:11-13).

Genre, Setting, Intention

This section clearly constitutes the epilogue to the book of Job. It is widely supposed to have been, in one form or other, part of the original Job story—a narrative about a God-fearer who endured his trials faithfully and was rewarded by God. The author of Job clearly found it to his purpose to provide this kind of ending. It does not go counter to the dialogue which rejected the traditional doctrine of reward. Rather, the author simply cannot just leave Job suffering in his agony; there has to be a resolution to the story. The author does accept the doctrine of the goodness of the Lord and he now expresses this concretely in the case of Job. To consider the epilogue as merely a "happy ending" and illogical is to mistake the intention, and neglect the sophisticated nature of the book.

PROVERBS

BIBLIOGRAPHY

J. N. Aletti, "Séduction et parole en Proverbes I-IX," *VT* 27 (1977) 129-43; L. Alonso Schökel, *Proverbios y Eclesiastico* (Madrid, 1968); A. Barucq, *Le livre des Proverbes* (SB; Paris, 1964); G. Boström, *Paronomasi i den aldre Hebreiska Maschallitteraturen* (LUÅ 29/8; 1928); G. E. Bryce, "Another Wisdom-'Book' in Proverbs," *JBL* 91 (1972) 145-57; idem, " 'Better'-Proverbs: An Historical and Structural Study," *1972 Proceedings of the Society of Biblical Literature* II (ed. L. C. McGaughey) 343-54; idem, *A Legacy of Wisdom: The Egyptian Contribution to the Wisdom of Israel* (Lewisburg, 1979); W. Bühlmann, *Vom rechten Reden und Schweigen* (OBO 12; Freiburg/Göttingen, 1976); B. Gemser, *Sprüche Salomos* (HAT 16; 2nd ed.; Tübingen, 1963); H.-J. Hermisson, *Studien zur israelitischen Spruchweisheit* (WMANT 28; Neukirchen-Vluyn, 1968); C. Kayatz, *Studien zu Proverbien 1-9* (WMANT 22; Neukirchen-Vluyn, 1966); B. Kovacs, "Sociological-structural Constraints upon Wisdom: The Spatial and Temporal Matrix of Proverbs 15:28-22:16" (Diss., Vanderbilt University, 1978); B. Lang, *Die weisheitliche Lehrrede* (SBS 54; Stuttgart, 1972); idem, *Frau Weisheit* (Düsseldorf, 1975); W. McKane, *Proverbs* (OTL; Philadelphia, 1970); O. Plöger, "Zur Auslegung der Sentenzensammlungen des Proverbienbuches," in *Probleme biblischer Theologie* (Fest. G. von Rad; ed. H. W. Wolff; Munich, 1971) 402-16; W. Richter, *Recht und Ethos* (SANT 15; Munich, 1966); A. Robert, "Les attaches littéraires bibliques de Prov. I-IX," *RB* 43 (1934) 42-68, 172-204, 374-84; 44 (1935) 344-65, 502-25; W. Roth, *Numerical Sayings in the Old Testament* (VTSup 13; Leiden, 1965); R. Scott, *Proverbs. Ecclesiastes* (AB 18; New York, 1965); P. W. Skehan, *Studies in Israelite Poetry and Wisdom* (CBQMS 1; Washington, 1971); U. Skladny, *Die ältesten Spruchsammlungen in Israel* (Göttingen, 1962); F. Vattioni, "Studi sul libro dei Proverbi," *Augustinianum* 12 (1972) 121-68; C. Westermann, "Weisheit im Sprichwort," in *Schalom* (Fest. A. Jepsen; AzT 1/46; Stuttgart, 1971) 73-85; R. N. Whybray, *Wisdom in Proverbs* (SBT 1/45; London, 1965); idem, *The Intellectual Tradition in the Old Testament* (BZAW 135; Berlin, 1974).

CHAPTER 1
The Book as a Whole

The following remarks deal only with the book; the discussion of various genres (sayings, etc.), and also of the pertinence of ancient Near Eastern wisdom, is to be found in the Introduction to the Wisdom Literature.

Structure

I. Title, "the proverbs of Solomon"	1:1
II. Introduction	1:2-7
A. Purpose	1:2-6
B. Programmatic saying	1:7
III. Series of instructions and speeches by wisdom	1:8–9:18
A. First instruction	1:8-19
B. Wisdom's speech	1:20-33
C. Second instruction	2:1-22
D. Third instruction	3:1-12
E. Fourth instruction	3:13-24
F. Fifth instruction	3:25-35
G. Sixth instruction	4:1-9
H. Seventh instruction	4:10-27
I. Eighth Instruction	5:1-23
J. Miscellany	6:1-19
K. Ninth instruction	6:20-35
L. Tenth instruction	7:1-27
M. Eleventh instruction: Wisdom's speech	8:1-36
N. Twelfth instruction: description of two banquets	9:1-18
IV. Collection of "proverbs of Solomon"	10:1–22:16
V. Collection of "the words of the wise" (restored title)	22:17–24:22
VI. Collection of "the words of the wise"	24:23-34
VII. Collection of "proverbs of Solomon" (men of Hezekiah)	25:1–29:27
VIII. Collection of "the words of Agur"	30:1-9
IX. Collection of (mostly) numerical sayings	30:10-33
X. Collection of "the words of Lemuel"	31:1-9
XI. An acrostic poem on the ideal housewife	31:10-31

There is general agreement among scholars that chs. 1–9 serve as a kind of introduction to the series of collections (most of which are clearly indicated as such by titles) in chs. 10–31. There is also a sharp difference in the genres (the

49

INSTRUCTION, in contrast to the discrete SAYING) that characterize these two main sections. Even if one does not adopt all the structural and stylistic claims of P. W. Skehan (pp. 1-45), several of his observations are compelling and deserve mention here.

First, the Solomonic collection in 10:1–22:16. There seem to be two collections here: chs. 10–15 are primarily in antithetic parallelism, while chs. 16–22 are primarily in synonymous parallelism. Is there any further evidence of a suture of two groups of sayings? Skehan analyzes in particular 14:26–16:15 and points to some unusual features that suggest that the suture is in this area and has been done with an eye to achieving a certain number of proverbs. The number of proverbs in the entire collection (10:1–22:16) is 375, which is the numerical equivalent of *šlmh* (Solomon) in the title, "the proverbs of Solomon," and the middle point of the 375 is at 16:4. Within 14:26–16:15 certain features are noticeable. At 14:26 there is a departure from antithetic parallelism (in the preceding proverbs, about 141, only nine lack this feature). In the forty-three verses between 14:26 and 15:33, eleven are without antithetic parallelism. Similarly, the mention of the Lord and the king in the previous verses was negligible; now both are mentioned frequently in 14:26ff.: eight successive sayings mention the Lord (15:33–16:7), and 16:10, 12-15 all treat of the king. Another observation: the sayings in 16:29-32 each contain a word for "hearing." These facts suggest that an editor has deliberately put together two collections and inserted certain proverbs in order to reach the total of the numerical equivalent of Solomon's name.

Second, there is the occurrence of the name of Hezekiah in 25:1. If one adopts a slightly different spelling than actually provided in the present MT (*yhzqyh* for *hzqyh*), the name spells out 140, the number of lines in the collection (25:1–29:27)!

Finally, if one adds the numerical equivalents of the key terms of the title in 1:1 ("The proverbs of *Solomon*, the son of *David*, king of *Israel*"), one comes up with the number of 930, which is only several digits off from the number of lines in the present (doubtless corrupt in many places) MT.

These data are too striking to be coincidental, and certainly tell us something about the scribal practices in Israel, as well as the structure of this particular book.

Genre

As a book, Proverbs belongs to the genre of collection. In fact, there are several genres to be found: SAYING, INSTRUCTION, ACROSTIC POEM, etc. But these are held together in a loose unity by means of the titles at 1:1; 10:1; 22:17 (emended text); 24:23; 25:1; 30:1; 31:1. Hence the book is a collection of wisdom pieces that presumably date from different periods and have various origins.

The genre of INSTRUCTION is found consistently in "the words of the wise" in Prov 22:17–24:22, that bear a resemblance to the Egyptian Instruction of Amenemope. The same genre receives a certain development in Proverbs 1–9, where the units are much longer than the customary prohibition and motive clause that characterize 22:17–24:22.

There is no unanimity in the determination of the precise characteristics of this genre. McKane (pp. 3, 19, 23, 369) sees the INSTRUCTION as having its Israelite setting in an educational context (court school) associated with the training of officials for public life. It is characterized by direct address ("my son") and consists of imperatives (an "essential" feature), prohibitions, motive clauses, etc. McKane's analysis, however, is more grammatical than form-critical, and underlying his approach to Proverbs is the thesis that there has been a Yahwistic (prophetic) interpretation of the vocabulary of old wisdom—a highly problematical position. Like McKane, R. N. Whybray (*Wisdom in Proverbs*) recognizes the similarity of Proverbs 1–9 to the Egyptian genre of INSTRUCTION. But he distinguishes between the discourses allegedly given by a wisdom teacher and the theological expansions (of these discourses) that deal with the concept of wisdom. Unfortunately he offers no satisfactory criteria for this dissection. For both of these scholars, a given setting seems to fit into their analysis: the court school.

In his two studies B. Lang has distinguished between the instruction (*weisheitliche Lehrrede*) and the wisdom speech (*Weisheitsrede*). He recognizes in Proverbs 1–7 ten instructions, each indicated by the address of the teacher to "my son." These are Prov 1:1-19; 2:1-22; 3:1-12; 3:21-35; 4:1-9; 4:10-19; 4:20-27; 5:1-23; 6:20-35; 7:1-27. They challenge the "son" to appropriate the lessons which the teacher has to offer; there are commands and prohibitions and aphorisms toward this end. Three major features of the teaching are the fate-working deed (wickedness works evil; goodness works good); motifs of personal piety that are similar to what one reads in Psalms; and the warning against the "strange woman." Lang is not the first to have discovered ten poems; Whybray did the same, but "the book of ten discourses" as reconstructed by Whybray does not agree with the ten instructions of Lang. So also with the ten discourses which R. Scott claimed to find. It seems as though the "my son" rubric is not a reliable division for units within these chapters.

The WISDOM SPEECH (Prov 1:20-33; 8:1-36; 9:1-6) is a public address uttered by personified wisdom. Lang interprets Lady Wisdom as the personification of Israelite school wisdom. The didactic style of the teacher is reflected in her discourses, and in ch. 8 she also assumes the privileges of a goddess (8:12-31), according to Lang (*Frau Weisheit*, 168).

C. Kayatz (*Studien*) has applied Egyptian models to Proverbs 1–9 from two points of view: form criticism and motif criticism. The form-critical results show similarity in structure between the Egyptian *Sebayit*, or instruction, and the didactic poems in Proverbs 1–9. There is a mixture of commands, motivations, purposes, descriptions (*Prädikation*, e.g., 3:13-20), casuistic introductions (e.g., 2:1,3,4), and questions (e.g., 5:16; 6:27). There is no rigid structure; the aforementioned elements are present in varying degrees in the units of Proverbs 1–9. Several motifs are common to both Egyptian and Israelite compositions, e.g., the emphasis on "hearing," and the role of the heart. The most unusual feature in Proverbs 1–9 is the (divine) speech in the first person, such as occurs in Proverbs 8 and 1:20-33. There is no suitable parallel for this in the rest of the OT. The divine speeches in the I-style (Exod 3:4-10; Isa 43:1-7; 44:24-28) differ, in that they make a claim for revelation in history and for the divine will. But in Proverbs the speeches are rather self-descriptive in a reflective, theological style. As Kayatz shows, the similarity to the motifs in Egyptian literature is too striking to be considered coincidence. Thus, the Egyptian divinity *Ma'at* ("justice, order"), like wisdom, is also preexistent. The Egyptian deity loves those who love her (Prov 8:17); *Ma'at* gives life and protection (Prov 1:33; 3:16,18; 8:35). An image of

51

Ma'at is worn by officials (Prov 3:3; 6:21) and in art she is represented with the *ankh* sign (=life) in one hand and a scepter, the symbol of honor and riches, in the other (Prov 3:16!). The cumulative effect of all these motifs is to establish beyond reasonable doubt the influence of Egyptian *Ma'at* upon the Israelite description of personified wisdom.

But the relationship of the wisdom speeches to the prophets is almost as striking. Prov 8:24-31 has affinities with the literary genre of the announcement of judgment, but in the context this has become a threat. The motifs are those of laughing and ridicule (Prov 1:26 and Ps 2:4), calling and not being heard (1:24 and Mic 3:4; Isa 65:12; 66:4), seeking and not finding (1:28 and Hos 5:6,15; Amos 8:12). The direction of the dependence is uncertain: A. Robert argues for prophetic influence upon the sages; C. Kayatz argues that the wisdom tradition has entered the prophetic stream. One should note, further, that the Egyptian motifs are to be found in ch. 8, and the prophetic motifs in ch. 1.

Another approach to Proverbs 1–9 is proposed by P. Skehan, who recognizes ALPHABETIZING POEMS (poems constructed with twenty-two or twenty-three lines, on the analogy of the number of letters in the Hebrew alphabet) in chs. 2–8. The emphasis is on the exterior form, which would have been cultivated by the sages, and on the inner connection of wisdom themes. Ch. 2 is a parade example. It is composed of twenty-two lines, the number of letters in the Hebrew alphabet. The exterior characteristics, first pointed out by Skehan, are unusual. The first stanza is signed by the letter *'aleph* (after the opening "my son" in v. 1, cf. *'im* in vv. 3-4, and *'āz* in v. 5). Stanzas two (vv. 5-8) and three (vv. 9-11) begin with *'aleph*, and with identical phrases ("then you will understand"). At the halfway mark (v. 12), the fourth stanza begins with *lamed*, the letter that begins the second half of the Hebrew alphabet. Both the fourth (vv. 12-15) and fifth (vv. 16-19) stanzas begin with the same words ("to save you from"). The final stanza (vv. 20-22) also begins with *lamed*. This external uniformity can hardly be disregarded; it fits into the alphabetizing concerns which are manifest elsewhere (acrostic and alphabetizing Psalms; Prov 31:10-31; Job 9; etc.). Skehan further argues that in Proverbs 2–7 there are seven columns of text (the "seven pillars" of 9:1), of twenty-two lines each, that develop the topics of ch. 2. The arguments in support of this structure are less convincing, although there are solid arguments for columns five (5:1-20), six (6:20–7:6), and seven (7:7-27) as separate units. The doubt about this analysis arises from the rearrangement which Skehan has to make of the units in columns two through four (chs. 3–5). Nonetheless, it must be said that the arguments rest on exterior features of the language rather than theological preconceptions (such as characterize McKane's and Whybray's proposals).

By way of conclusion, one may emphasize the positive elements discovered by Skehan and Kayatz: exterior signs of a unit poem, and the model of the Egyptian instruction for style and motifs. At the present time it seems safe to say that the author of Proverbs 1–9 wrote instruction poems that share in the Egyptian tradition, but are marked by alphabetizing considerations.

Setting

For a more detailed discussion of setting, →Introduction to the Wisdom Literature. Whatever may be the ultimate origins of the sayings and instructions (family or tribe, etc.), the collections in this book are attributed by title to "wise men" and kings (Solomon, Lemuel, perhaps Agur; cf. the mention of Hezekiah in 25:1). It is reasonable to conclude, therefore, that in this form they derive from the school associated with the royal court. There is evidence to support the inference that such a school existed in Jerusalem (against Whybray, *The Intellectual Tradition*; cf. H.-J. Hermisson, 113-36).

The editor (or editors) of the book in its final form put these collections in a given setting by the overall title, "the proverbs of Solomon" (1:1), and the purpose of the whole collection is indicated in 1:1-7. P. Skehan (pp. 27-45) has argued for further refinement of the setting: that the book is constructed in tripartite fashion (1–9; 10:1–22:16; 22:17–31:31) on the analogy of a tripartite house (front porch, nave, and rear private room) that corresponds proportionately to the dimensions of Solomon's temple. In this view the book is itself a house, the house of Wisdom (cf. Wis 9:8-11), in which the sayings and instructions, etc. have found an appropriate place.

This work would presumably have been a popular tool in the hands of the wise men and their students in the postexilic period.

Intention
Although each saying, instruction, etc. has its own intention, the book as a whole has a clearly stated purpose in 1:2-6, "that men may appreciate wisdom and discipline, may understand words of intelligence . . . the words of the wise and their riddles." The goal of the editor(s) is to pass on the traditional wisdom with a strong religious orientation. The message can be summarized: Wisdom brings life (cf. R. E. Murphy, "The Kerygma of the Book of Proverbs," *Int* 20 [1966] 3-4).

CHAPTER 2

THE INDIVIDUAL UNITS

TITLE AND INTRODUCTION, 1:1-7

Structure

I. Superscription, a title ("the proverbs of Solomon")	1
II. Introduction	2-7
A. Purpose	2-6
B. Programmatic saying	7

Genre

The SUPERSCRIPTION or title is swallowed up by the infinitives (vv. 2-6) of the introduction, which indicate the purpose of the "proverbs of Solomon." Vv. 2-7 form an introduction to the following instructions. The infinitival clauses are remarkably similar to the introductions of Ptahhotep (40-50; *ANET*, 412) and Amenemope (I,1-12; *ANET*, 421).

Setting

The origins of this kind of introduction doubtless are to be found in the oral tradition, in which a teacher would define the purpose of his instruction. Here the prolixity suggests a certain reflection and literary concern on the part of a writer (editor) who wishes to emphasize the value and importance of what follows. In the setting of the book as it now stands, these lines also serve as an introduction to all the collections that follow.

Intention

The verses underscore the purpose of the instructions and sayings that have been collected in the book. The saying about "fear of the Lord" in 1:7 is programmatic for the wisdom enterprise (cf. 9:10; 15:33; Ps 111:10; Job 28:28).

SERIES OF INSTRUCTIONS AND SPEECHES
BY WISDOM, 1:8–9:18
FIRST INSTRUCTION, 1:8-19

Structure

I. Admonition to heed parental teaching, with motive clause	8-9
II. Warning against enticement of sinners	10-19
A. Casuistic introduction	10-14
B. Admonition, with motive clause (v. 16 a gloss from Isa 59:7? cf. LXX)	15-16
C. Description of ways of sinners	17-19

54

Genre

The genre here is an INSTRUCTION. The admonition in v. 8 (cf. also v. 15), expressed both positively and negatively in antithetical parallelism, serves here as an introduction to the warning. The casuistic style of the warning is a pattern found already in Ptahhotep (*ANET*, 412-14).

Setting

The admonition suggests family origins, where parental authority is invoked. However, the relationship of father/son is also used to describe that of sage to student in the instructions (cf. "my son" throughout chs. 1–9, and also in Sirach).

Intention

The vivid quotation in vv. 11-14 concerning the machinations of the sinners emphasizes the point of the passage: parental instruction is to be followed, despite the enticement of wrongdoers.

WISDOM'S SPEECH, 1:20-33

Structure

I. Introduction to Wisdom's addressing the public	20-21
II. Wisdom's Speech	22-33
A. Plaintive address ("how long") to unwise audience	22
B. Command, with promise	23
C. Reproach (motif of calling/not heeding; cf. Isa 65:12; 66:4; Jer 7:23-27)	24-25
D. Threat (motif of mocking laughter, Ps 2:4; 59:9; motif of calling/not hearing, applied to God; cf. Mic 3:4; Isa 1:15; Jer 11:11; motif of seeking/not finding, Hos 5:6)	26-28
E. Reproach	29-30
F. Announcement of doom	31-32
G. Conclusion: promise to followers of Wisdom	33

Genre

This is a unique genre, which can be best termed a SPEECH of personified wisdom; the only parallels are Proverbs 8–9 and Sirach 24. The motifs show that Wisdom speaks in the guise of a prophet, and even as Yahweh.

Setting and Intention

Such a speech is a literary creation, and presumably composed by a sage, precisely to undergird the authority of the instructions. Wisdom's authority is in fact put on the same level as that of the prophets. The intention is to persuade the listener to follow wisdom.

SECOND INSTRUCTION, 2:1-22

Structure

I.	*'Aleph* stanza, laying down the condition, "if"	1-4
II.	*'Aleph* stanza, indicating the promise or result, "then": achievement of fear of the Lord, with motive clauses	5-8
III.	*'Aleph* stanza, reprise of the promise ("then you will understand", vv. 5, 9), with motive clauses	9-11
IV.	*Lamed* stanza, stating purpose: to deliver from bad company, whose ways are described	12-15
V.	*Lamed* stanza, stating purpose: to deliver from the "strange woman," whose ways are described	16-19
VI.	*Lamed* stanza, stating purpose: to walk in justice, with motive clauses about the fate of the just and the wicked	20-22

The alphabetical signs (twenty-two lines, *'aleph* and *lamed* stanzas) are as important for the structure as the logical development. Kayatz (p. 65) points out that the absence of any imperative is striking, and for this reason McKane (p. 278) hesitates to consider this section as an instruction.

Genre

This is an INSTRUCTION (see the parallel promises in 3:21-26; 4:10-19; 6:20-35). The identification of the genre as instruction cannot be made to depend merely on the presence of an imperative (contra McKane).

Setting

In itself, a conditional promise seems to be part of any teaching. In this case, the literary dress suggests that the whole has been composed in view of a written composition, namely the following chapters (3–7; cf. Skehan, 9-14).

Intention

Kayatz (p. 66) notes that the conditional promises bring the Lord and wisdom together: "He who seeks wisdom finds fear of the Lord and knowledge of God, because the Lord gives the wisdom that leads to him." Hence to seek the Lord and to seek wisdom is the same thing—the Lord is the master of wisdom.

THIRD INSTRUCTION, 3:1-12

Structure

I.	Prohibition and jussive command to heed sage's teaching, with motive clause (promise of benefits)	1-2
II.	Prohibition and imperative commands about kindness and truth, with motive clause (in form of imperative!) indicating benefit	3-4
III.	Command, prohibition, and command about relying on the Lord, with motive clause in v. 6b	5-6
IV.	Prohibition and command about fear of the Lord, with motive clause about its benefits	7-8

V. Command to worship the Lord, with motive clause about
   the benefits   9-10
VI. Prohibitions concerning attitudes, with a motive clause   11-12

The structure is basically six couplets, consisting of commands or prohibitions
with motive clauses. Hence 3:3b (=7:3) should probably be omitted with LXX[B].
Skehan (pp. 10-11, 33 n. 11) points out that the section on wisdom (3:13-24)
interrupts the style established in 3:1-12, and he puts 3:1-12, 25-34 together as
an alphabetizing poem of twenty-two lines.

Genre

This is another INSTRUCTION. In contrast to the more prolix examples (e.g.,
1:8-19), the commands and motive clauses so characteristic of this genre are set
out here in successive couplets.

Setting and Intention

The variety of topics suggests the hand of an editor who may have collected
traditional advice. In such a succession of commands and prohibitions, each unit
makes its own point. One can see that the general advice in vv. 1-4 becomes
specific in vv. 5-12.

FOURTH INSTRUCTION, 3:13-24

Structure

I. Hymn in praise of Wisdom   13-18
   A. Introduction, using "happy the man" formula ('ašrê
      of v. 13 finds *inclusio* with mĕ'uššār of v. 18)   13
   B. The benefits of Wisdom   14-18
II. Wisdom's association with the Lord in creation   19-20
III. Prohibition and command to keep wisdom, with motive
     clauses (promise of benefits, vv. 22-24)   21-24

The play on the root 'šr indicates that vv. 13-18 constitute a self-contained unit,
expanded by vv. 19-20. Thus, I and II serve as bases for III.

Genre

The genre is INSTRUCTION, as vv. 22-24 clearly shows. As a lead into his commands, the writer has included a song in praise of Wisdom that may have existed
as an independent poem.

Setting

The loose structure suggests that the whole is a literary composition for its present
appearance in these chapters. Skehan (p. 33) suggests that this composition would
blend nicely after 4:1-9, which is also in praise of Wisdom, and the whole would
yield a poem of twenty-two lines.

Intention

The primary intention is to urge the student towards Wisdom, and the praise of Wisdom is to be seen in this light. For the significant parallelism between Wisdom and Egyptian *Ma'at* in vv. 16 and 22, see C. Kayatz, 105, 116-17.

FIFTH INSTRUCTION, 3:25-35

Structure

I. Prohibition against fear, with motive clause	25-26
II. Series of five prohibitions concerning ethical conduct	27-31
III. Series of sayings about the Lord's dealings with the good and the evil	32-35

It is possible that v. 32 is a motive clause (*kî* ["because"]) for the prohibition in v. 31. In general, this section bears some similarity to vv. 1-12, with its prohibitions.

Genre, Setting, Intention

See the discussion in 3:1-12.

SIXTH INSTRUCTION, 4:1-9

Structure

I. Introduction	1-4a
A. Appeal to accept sage's teaching	1-2
B. Reason: his teaching was received from his father	3-4a
II. The traditional advice, handed down from the father	4b-9

The body of this unit consists of a series of commands and prohibitions about the acquisition of wisdom, with motive clauses describing her benefits (for v. 9, see Kayatz, 116-17 on the Egyptian motif of *Ma'at*'s granting a crown to the king).

Genre, Setting, Intention

This is an INSTRUCTION, and evidence of family origin is reflected more strongly here than in any other section of chs. 1–9. The text aims to convince a student of the centrality of wisdom. The description of the benefits of wisdom is reminiscent of 3:12-24.

SEVENTH INSTRUCTION, 4:10-27

Structure

I. Introduction: teacher's command to youth, with promise	10
II. Way of wisdom described and urged upon the youth	11-13
III. Way of the wicked described and warned against	14-19
IV. Reprise of introduction; cf. v. 10	20-22
V. Series of commands and prohibitions relative to various organs of body: heart, mouth, lips, eyes, feet	23-27

Genre, Setting, Intention

This INSTRUCTION betrays a flavor of training within the family (cf. 4:1ff.). The introduction of the theme of the two ways serves to strengthen the teacher's urgent appeals on behalf of wisdom.

EIGHTH INSTRUCTION, 5:1-23

Structure

I. Introduction: appeal to accept teacher's wisdom	1-2
II. Description of the "strange woman" (adulteress) and her ways	3-6
III. Reprise of introduction	7
IV. Series of commands and prohibitions, with motive clauses, that concern avoidance of the strange woman	8-14
V. Series of commands and prohibitions, with motive clauses concerning fidelity to one's wife (6:22 is best read after 5:19; cf. Skehan, 1-8)	15-20
VI. Conclusion: statement of retribution for the wicked from the Lord	21-23

Genre, Setting, Intention

This is an INSTRUCTION on the avoidance of the "strange woman." This theme was already announced in 2:16-19, and is developed here; cf. also 6:24-29 and 7:5-27.

MISCELLANY, 6:1-19

Structure

I. Advice in case one has gone surety for another	1-5
II. Warnings against laziness	6-11
A. Command to learn wisdom from the ant and its ways	6-8
B. Threat to the sluggard; cf. 24:33-34	9-11
1. Rhetorical questions	9
2. Quotation of words of the sluggard	10
3. Fate of the sluggard	11
III. Description of a man of "belial" and his fate	12-15
IV. A numerical saying about what is an "abomination to the Lord" (note parts of body)	16-19

Genre, Setting, Intention

This is a collection of disparate pieces which interrupt the sequence of lengthy instructions in chs. 1–9. In themselves, these short units are instructional and designed to alert the student to the values concerned, but there is no connection among them.

NINTH INSTRUCTION, 6:20-35

Structure

I. Introduction: encouragement to accept parental command and teaching	20-21
A. Command to obey	20
B. Binding on heart and neck; cf. 3:3; (Kayatz, 107-8, points out that Egyptian officials wore an image of *Ma'at* around their necks)	21
II. Reasons for obedience	22-24
A. MT does not make grammatical sense (hence 6:22 to be read after 5:19?). As the text stands, v. 22 can be construed as describing the good effects secured by the teaching	22
B. Reprise of theme of commandment and teaching (v. 20), culminating in claim that they preserve one from the pitfall of the evil woman	23-24
III. Warning against involvement with another's wife	25-35
A. Prohibitions and motive clause	25-26
B. Motivation further developed by two rhetorical questions (vv. 27-28) and statement of punishment for adulterer	27-29
C. Another motivation: if even a thief is punished, although hunger drove him to thievery, how much more will the adulterer be punished!	30-35

Genre, Setting, Intention

This INSTRUCTION is characterized by COMMANDS and PROHIBITIONS with motivations, as the above outline shows; it betrays considerable reflection and thought in establishing the motivation. Cf. 5:1-23. It is obvious that the youth is being warned against adultery.

TENTH INSTRUCTION, 7:1-27

Structure

I. Introduction: a series of commands by teacher to youth	1-5
A. Obey his teachings	1-2
B. Interiorize the teachings	3
C. Have a correct attitude to wisdom (chiasmus)	4
D. Purpose of the commands: preservation from the "strange" woman	5
II. An example story	6-23
A. Sage's observation of a youth "without sense"	6-9
B. The youth encounters the woman	10-13
C. The woman entices him to adultery	14-20
D. The youth yields to her blandishments	21-23
III. Conclusion	24-27
A. Call for attention	24

B. Prohibition   25
C. Motive clauses   26-27

Genre, Setting, Intention

The INSTRUCTION incorporates here an EXAMPLE STORY as part of its teaching. The obvious point is to deter young men from yielding to the temptations of adultery.

ELEVENTH INSTRUCTION: WISDOM'S SPEECH, 8:1-36

Structure

Genre

This is a WISDOM SPEECH. Lang (*Frau Weisheit*, 57-111) has emphasized the sapiential language and motifs with which Wisdom presents herself. In vv. 1-11 and 32-36, "it is always the teacher who speaks—only, the words of the teacher sound more majestic in the mouth of Lady Wisdom" (p. 62). There are macarisms (v. 34), appeals to become wise, the "finding of wisdom" (vv. 17, 35; cf. Prov 2:25; 3:13). But the image which Wisdom draws of herself goes beyond that of a teacher. She assumes the role of royalty (v. 15) and even of divinity, to speak with the prerogative of Yahweh (v. 17, the relation of Yahweh to the king is taken over by wisdom); cf. Lang, *Frau Weisheit*, 74-85. The claim has been made that vv. 22-31 give a preexistent description of Wisdom that was incorporated into the speech, and in particular that it betrays Canaanite influence (cf. M. Dahood, "Proverbs 8,22-31. Translation and Commentary," *CBQ* 30 [1968] 512-21). But convincing evidence is still wanting.

Setting and Intention

In the broad sense this is a teaching situation. The author has departed from the instruction genre to use the WISDOM SPEECH in order to convince the student, and offer inspiration and encouragement in the pursuit of wisdom.

The wisdom speech in ch. 8 can be best evaluated against the deceitful speeches and promises made by all forms of non-wisdom in Proverbs 1-9 (cf. J. N. Aletti, "Séduction et parole," 129-43, esp. 142-43). The adulteress speaks deceitful words in 7:14-20, with commentary in 7:21-27. Her "smooth words" (Prov 2:16; 5:2-3; 6:24; 7:5,21), the invitation of sinners (Prov 1:11-14), and the invitation and aphorism of Dame Folly (Prov 9:16-17) are balanced by the wisdom speeches of 1:22-33; 9:4-6, and especially that of ch. 8. But the extraordinary claims made for personified wisdom are tantalizing. She is feminine without being a woman, since she existed before creation (8:22-31). She speaks in "the gates," but she embraces the world (8:27-30). The paradoxical nature of this wisdom, both human and divine, makes it very difficult to answer the question of identity. She has been commonly understood as a divine attribute (e.g., Whybray, *Wisdom in Proverbs*, 78). G. von Rad (*Wisdom in Israel*, 156-57) has instead seen personified wisdom as immanent in nature. In any case, she is given by the Lord (Prov 2:6), and is to be the object of Israel's quest.

TWELFTH INSTRUCTION: DESCRIPTION OF TWO BANQUETS, 9:1-18

Structure

I. Wisdom's banquet	1-6
A. Introduction	1-3
1. Wisdom's preparation of house and·banquet	1-2
2. Wisdom's issuance of invitation	3
B. Wisdom's speech	4-6
1. Her address to the simple (read "I say" with Peshitta)	4
2. Invitation to dine	5-6
II. Miscellany of sayings and directions	7-12
III. Folly's banquet	13-18
A. Introduction	13-15
1. Characterization of Folly	13
2. Folly's issuance of invitation	14-15
B. Folly's speech	16-17
1. Her address to the simple (read "I say" with Peshitta; cf. v. 4)	16
2. A proverbial saying	17
C. The verdict of the writer	18

Section II is out of place in Wisdom's speech; it deals with the correction of the arrogant (*lēṣ*) and with the wise (vv. 7-8, 9, 12). Within it, v. 10 is another programmatic statement on fear of the Lord (cf. 1:7; 2:5). Although v. 11 is consonant with the promises of Wisdom (3:16) and the teacher (3:2; 4:10), its address is in the singular and hence it does not fit with vv. 5-6 (plural). The basic structure is a contrast between Lady Wisdom and Dame Folly.

Genre, Setting, Intention

This chapter is made up of several genres, locked together in the main theme, a description of the banquets provided by Lady Wisdom and Dame Folly (vv. 1-6, 13-18), which is separated by a miscellany of sayings and directions. Within the descriptions are a speech by Wisdom (vv. 4-6) and by Folly (vv. 16-17). For the motifs that may lie behind these scenes, cf. B. Lang, *Frau Weisheit*, 115-44, and J. N. Aletti, "Séduction et Parole." In the last chapter which the writer has prepared before the collections of discrete sayings in chs. 10ff., the intention to steer the youth toward wisdom, as opposed to folly, is clear.

COLLECTION OF "PROVERBS OF SOLOMON," 10:1–22:16

It is not feasible to treat each of the discrete sayings in chs. 10ff., according to the fourfold aspect of structure, genre, setting, and intention. This would involve much repetition, and in many instances lead to fruitless speculation (e.g., about possible settings). The reader of Proverbs is better served by an indication of some guidelines on structure and genre, a discussion of certain stylistic details, and a characterization of the main collections insofar as this is possible. The reader is referred to the fundamental statements about sayings which are to be found in the Introduction to Wisdom Literature.

Structure

Prov 10:1–22:16 (and indeed in the other collections that follow) has no real structure; it is essentially a collection (probably formed from earlier collections) of discrete SAYINGS. But if no structure can be pointed out, the catchwords which often account for the present sequence of the sayings can be indicated. Despite the acknowledgment that these chapters contain separate sayings, can one claim that true *contexts* are formed, out of which the individual saying is to be interpreted? Two scholars have made this difficult claim: H.-J. Hermisson (pp. 171-83) for Proverbs 10–15, and O. Plöger for Proverbs 11.

The approach is suggestive, but is not to be exaggerated. It does illustrate the concrete gathering of the sayings; they were not put together in a haphazard way. But it is a delicate task to determine a shift in meaning, as "context" implies, simply because one saying is juxtaposed to another. Rather, the evidence suggests that the sages were aware of the inherent limitations of a saying. That is why they put certain sayings back to back—to balance them off, as it were. An example of this would be Prov 26:4-5:

> *Answer not the fool according to his folly,*
> * lest you too become like him.*
> *Answer the fool according to his folly,*
> * lest he become wise in his own eyes.*

Each saying retains its meaning, according to its original intentionality. But all sayings have limitations and can be relativized by juxtaposition without a change in meaning. Hermisson gives the example of Prov 10:15-16:

> *A rich man's wealth is his strong city;*
> * the poverty of the poor is their ruin.*
> *The wages of the righteous leads to life,*
> * the gain of the wicked to sin.*

One may readily grant that these sayings complement each other, but Hermisson claims that v. 16 provides the context in which v. 15 is to be understood; it "corrects" v. 15. On the contrary, v. 15 retains its point (the *only* point that it makes): the presence or absence of possessions is determinative of life—of strength or weakness. This is an observation about the difference that possessions (or the lack of them) make in this life. It has no moral thrust of itself. Presumably it had a context in the life of the wise man, a context of other values (to which v. 16 speaks). But one cannot invoke v. 16 to determine the meaning of v. 15. Any proverb is of its nature limited in what it can say. It should also be noted that the catchwords are against joining vv. 15 and 16: v. 15 is bound to v. 14 by the repetition of *měḥittâ* ("ruin"), and v. 16 is bound to v. 17 by the repetition of *lěḥayyîm* ("life").

In his study of Proverbs 11, O. Plöger attempts a contextual interpretation of the sayings. Thus, vv. 3-8 pivot about the just/wicked contrast; vv. 9-14 (even vv. 9-17) deal with the effects of conduct upon the environment (neighbor, society). In vv. 18-20 and in the final verses of the chapter there is a return to the topic of the just and wicked. But Plöger fails to show how any one saying receives meaning from the context. What he explains is a feature that has long been noted about proverb collections: sayings that deal with the same area, specific or general, tend to be put together. Catchwords are the guide to the arrangement of the sayings, but a general "theme" is not an adequate interpretative guide to the particularities of the individual sayings.

We should recall here some of the aspects of the structure of the book which were indicated above. First of all, most of the sayings in chs. 10-15 are in antithetical parallelism, (163 out of 183 verses according to Skladny, 23 n. 141). In the second part (16:1-22:16), the distribution in kinds of parallelism is more even (according to Skladny, 41 n. 115, the count is synonymous 52, antithetic 47, synthetic 37 among the total of 190 sayings). Second, there is a marked shift from the prevailing antithetic parallelism at 14:26 as Skehan has pointed out (p. 18). Of the 43 verses between 14:26 and 15:33, a total of 11 lack antithetic parallelism. This fact leads to a third observation: there appears to be a suture, as Skehan suggests, between the collections in chs. 10-15 and chs. 16-22. The following peculiarities in 14:26-16:15 support this view: (1) a substantial number of duplications occur just here (e.g., 15:20 and 10:1; 14:27 and 13:14; etc.); (2) the only mention of the king in chs. 10-15 occurs here at 14:28,35; (3) beginning with 14:26 the Lord is mentioned, and the divine name occurs in 11 of the 43 verses to the end of ch. 15, whereas it occurred in only 9 of the 141 sayings in chs. 10-14; (4) the pattern of the sayings in 15:29-32 and 15:33-16:7: the first group is characterized by the word "hear"; the second group by the word "Yahweh."

As Skehan remarks, this type of procedure "is best accounted for by supposing that here he [the editor] was working to join together two collections of approximately equal length, in view of the definite number (375) which he had set himself as his goal" (p. 19). It would appear that we are dealing with a deliberate editorial move; the entire collection (10:1-22:16) consists of 375 sayings, a number that corresponds to the numerical value of the Hebrew name Solomon in the title "proverbs of Solomon." It should be noted that the number of proverbs in chs. 25-29 approximates 130, which is the numerical value of the name Hezekiah, and 25:1 refers to the activity of the "men of Hezekiah" in copying out this collection (cf. earlier remarks on the book as a whole, p. 50).

This evidence of editorial work strengthens the impression that chs. 10ff. are to be integrated with the introduction in chs. 1-9. Corresponding to the fact that chs. 1–9 are addressed mainly to "my son," is the appearance of the saying about the wise and foolish son in 10:1. The contrast between the just and the wicked, so steadily apparent in chs. 1–9 (2:20-22; 3:32-34; 4:14-19; 5:21-23) appears four times in 10:1-7.

Stylistic Observations

H.-J. Hermisson has pointed out several important features of the literary style of the wisdom sayings that deserve notice here. The actual style is often obscured in English translation, but the following examples will attempt to remain as literal as possible.

1. Juxtaposition. The poetic line merely puts together two persons or things in a nominal sentence, without a verb:

> *One who loves wrong—one who loves strife*
> *One who makes his gate high—one who seeks destruction* (17:19).

Here four participles, designating general categories, are paired in a chiastic AB-B'A' arrangement.

> *Hope deferred—a sick heart*
> *and (=but) a tree of life—desire fulfilled* (13:12).

Four items, set in a chiastic AB-B'A' format, are paired off.

> *The path of the upright—avoidance of misfortune* (nouns)
> *One who preserves his life—one who marks his way* (participles)
> (16:17).

Again there is a chiastic AB-B'A' arrangement, in synonymous parallelism. See also 12:1; 14:2. Also the juxtaposition can be simply between two objects:

> *One who keeps his tongue and mouth—*
> *one who keeps his soul from troubles* (21:23).

Here there are two participles in synonymous parallelism.

The juxtaposition may leave the subject-predicate relation in doubt, and one must rely on the content to determine it (cf. 13:12 above). As H.-J. Hermisson remarks, the association should be rendered as "belong together," rather than "is." The sayings are classifying and comparing various phenomena, rather than identifying them.

Juxtaposition is found also in the so-called priamel, a listing of different objects, with the characteristic common to all receiving explicit mention:

> *Heavens for height and earth for depth,*
> *and the heart of kings—unsearchable* (25:3).

Some of the "deed-consequence" sayings are expressed by simple juxtaposition of terms:

> *A wicked man—one who reaps empty profit; One who sows justice—sure*
> *reward* (11:18).

But more often, finite forms of the verb appear:

> *The house of the wicked—(it) will be destroyed;*
> *and (=but) the tent of the just—(it) will flourish* (14:11).

The juxtaposition serves to emphasize the (inevitable) final result in each case. The course of action can receive emphasis by the use of the prepositions "to," "after" (21:17), or "before" (16:18):

The thoughts of the diligent—only to abundance;
and (=but) everyone who is in a hurry—only to want (21:5).

2. *Comparison*. In the case of juxtaposition the comparison is merely implicit. Often a simple *waw* ("and" or "but") serves as an implicit comparative particle:

Cold water upon an exhausted soul—
and [=like] good news from a distant land (25:25).

But the simile, in which the comparison is made explicit by such particles as *kĕ* ("like") or *kēn* ("so"), is very frequent, especially in Proverbs 25–27:

Like snow in summer and like rain in the harvest,
so honor is out of place for a fool (26:1).
Like a bird that is far from its nest,
so is a man who is far from his home (27:2).

Obviously, the use of "like" and "so" assures clarity, though sometimes at the expense of pungency of expresssion. The challenge of juxtaposed terms is greater than explicit comparisons.

3. *The "Good" Saying*. The majority of these sayings are in fact "not-good" sayings:

Without knowledge, even zeal is not good (Prov 19:2).

Such round judgments are to be found in 17:26a; 18:5a; 20:23b; 24:23b; 25:27a; 28:21a: *lō' ṭôb*—"not good." The positive of this is not simply "good," but "how good" (15:23).

A milder form of "not good" is *lō' nā'wâ* ("unseeming," "unfitting"), as in Prov 17:7; 19:10; 26:1. Reprobation is also expressed by the phrase, "abomination (to the Lord)":

False scales are an abomination to the Lord,
but a full weight is his delight (Prov 11:1).

The antithesis to abomination (*tô'ăbat*) is "delight" (*rāṣôn*), as 11:1 shows. For examples of "abomination," see Prov 3:32; 11:1,20; etc. The phrase "abomination to the Lord" occurs only in Proverbs (eleven times) and Deuteronomy, and some have argued for a cultic derivation, but the equivalent also occurs in Amenemope (13:16; 15:21; *ANET*, 423).

4. *The "Better" Saying*. The simplest form of this saying is in the style of "this is better than that":

Two are better than one (Eccl 4:9).
The gain from it is better than gain from silver
and its profit better than gold (Prov 3:14).

He who is slow to anger is better than the mighty,
   and he who rules his spirit than he who takes a city (Prov 16:32).
A good name is to be chosen rather than great riches,
   and favor is better than silver or gold (Prov 22:1).

In these instances the idiom usually consists of *ṭôb min* ("better than"), although it is possible to express the same idea simply by the use of the comparative *min* (see 22:1a above).

The more sophisticated form of the "better" saying has been described by G. E. Bryce (" 'Better'-Proverbs, " 349) as "a binary opposition in which a paradox is achieved by the transformation of elements compared through the addition of a set of middle terms." The general formula is: a, in view of b, is better than a', in view of b', and a paradoxical claim can be made:

Better is a little with righteousness
   than great revenues with injustice (Prov 16:8).

Thus, in this saying, the contrasting middle terms, "righteousness" and "injustice," transform the negative ("little") into a positive, and the positive ("great") into a negative. Bryce lists the transformational elements for the "better" sayings in chs. 12–27 as follows:

12:9, work—as opposed to lack of bread (the negative element)
15:16, fear of the Lord—as opposed to trouble
15:17, love—as opposed to hatred
16:8, righteousness—as opposed to injustice
16:19, low of spirit—as opposed to proud
17:1, quiet—as opposed to strife
19:1, integrity—as opposed to perverseness
27:5, openness—as opposed to hiddenness
27:10b, nearness—as opposed to distance

(Omitted from this list are 16:32 and 22:1, in which Bryce claims the middle term is implied; both instances seem to be simple preferences.) The remaining examples in Proverbs (3:14; 8:11, 19; 25:7) are direct evaluations, such as wisdom is better than precious metals.

5. The Numerical Saying. The numerical pattern is found in various parts of the Bible (e.g., Amos 1–2), and is particularly characteristic of the sayings in ch. 30 (see also 6:16-19). The opening line usually gives the number, and this may be graded (three things, four; x, x plus one), and the list of items intended are then given. See below on ch. 30.

Setting and Intention

It would be pure speculation to attempt to specify the original setting of the various sayings (→ Introduction to Wisdom Literature). They could have originated in the tribe or family, in daily intercourse or court school. Suffice it to say that they are clearly in a teaching context, and are being handed down as representative of Israel's wisdom tradition.

The sayings obviously intend to inculcate certain values and patterns of conduct. Even where a saying is a mere observation about reality, it receives a certain didactic quality from its association with moral recommendations. The wise person is expected to be "aware" as well as obedient to the injunctions.

CHAPTER 10

V. 1. To the first saying is prefixed a title by the editor that serves for 10:1–22:16. It is not insignificant that the first saying of the collection deals with a "wise son," in view of the frequent repetition of "my son" in chs. 1–9.

Vv. 2-3. These sayings are bound together by common features: (1) righteous/wicked contrast; (2) chiasmus; (3) both begin with the negative particle (*lō'*) and verb.

Vv. 4-5. Both sayings have to do with diligence; v. 4 is characterized by chiasmus, v. 5 by alliteration and nominal juxtaposition.

Vv. 6-7. Both are contrasts between righteous and wicked; "blessing" serves as a catchword.

V. 9. Striking alliteration in v. 9a (*hōlēk battōm yēlek beṭaḥ*).

Vv. 11-12. The verb *ksh* ("conceal, cover") is the catchword for these chiastic sayings.

Vv. 13-15. "Wisdom" and "wise men" bind vv. 13-14 together, and "ruin" ties v. 14 with v. 15, a striking example of juxtaposition of nouns.

Vv. 16-17. "Life" is the catchword which binds these sayings together.

Vv. 18-21. These sayings deal with "lips" (v. 20, "tongue"); the catchwords for vv. 20-21 are *ṣaddîq* ("righteous") and *lēb* ("mind, sense").

Vv. 24-25. The catchwords are "wicked/righteous."

Vv. 27-32. These are bound together by the catchwords, "wicked/righteous" (but v. 29: "upright/evildoers"); in vv. 31-32, two specific catchwords appear: "mouth" and "perverse."

CHAPTER 11

V. 1. The saying is formed by a simple juxtaposition of subjects and predicates. *Rāṣôn* ("delight," "acceptable") is the catchword for 10:32 and 11:1.

V. 2. There is striking alliteration in v. 2a: *bā' zādôn wayyābō' qālôn*.

Vv. 3-11. The themes of integrity and righteousness are treated in these verses, as the upright are contrasted with the wicked. Most of the verses begin with either *bĕ* (vv. 7,9-11) or a form of *ṣdq* (vv. 5-6,8).

V. 4. On v. 4b see 10:2b and also 11:6a. "Righteousness" is the catchword in vv. 4-6, and also "deliver."

V. 5. The root *yšr* ("straight," "upright") is the catchword for vv. 5-6; cf. v. 3.

Vv. 8-11. Tying two or more of these verses are several catchwords: "righteous, wicked, city, deliver"; vv. 9-12 all begin with the letter *beth*.

V. 15. The onomatopoeia in v. 15a is noteworthy: *resh* (four times) and *'ayin* (three times); v. 15b is formed by juxtaposition of participles.

Vv. 18-19. The catchword is "justice," and the theme of the good and the evil is continued in vv. 20-21.

Vv. 23-24. These two sayings, which concern quite different things, find a catchword in "only" ('ak).

Vv. 25-26. The verses are tied together by bĕrākâ ("blessing," "liberal").

Vv. 29-30. As the MT stands, "wise" is the catchword. However, in v. 30 most modern translations read "lawlessness" (RSV), or something similar, with the LXX. "Righteous" is the catchword for vv. 30-31.

CHAPTER 12

Vv. 1-3. The catchword is rš' ("condemn," "wickedness").

Vv. 5-7. The catchwords are "righteous" and "wicked."

Vv. 9-11. These verses deal with the laboring class. "Bread" is a catchword for vv. 9 and 11.

Vv. 12-13. "Righteous" is the catchword; cf. v. 10 also.

Vv. 13-23. The general theme of speech ("lips," "mouth," "truth," etc.) is treated in these verses.

Vv. 15-16. The catchword is "fool."

Vv. 18-19. The catchword is "tongue."

Vv. 20-21. There is the usual contrast between the righteous and the wicked; the catchword is rā' ("evil," "trouble").

V. 22. One of several "abomination" sayings (there is a very close parallel to this verse in Amenemope, X, 13:15-16; ANET, 423).

Vv. 26, 28. The catchwords are derek ("way") and the root ṣdq ("righteous," "righteousness").

CHAPTER 13

Vv. 2-4. These lines are tied together by the catchword nepeš ("desire," "life," "soul"), which occurs four times. There is a pithy juxtaposition in v. 3: "he who guards his mouth, he who preserves his life" (alliteration: nōṣēr pîw šōmēr napšô); "he who opens wide his lips—ruin to him."

Vv. 5-6. The roots ṣdq ("righteous") and rš' ("wicked") are the catchwords.

Vv. 7-8. The catchwords are the roots rwš ("poor") and 'šr ("rich"). The yēš-saying in v. 7 is a paradox, with no moral implication.

V. 12. The saying is formed by the juxtaposition of four terms. "Desire fulfilled" is taken up again in v. 19.

Vv. 13-14. A common motif unites these verses: adherence to the word/instruction is beneficial.

Vv. 15-19. Boström has pointed out modest paranomasia in these verses, e.g., v. 15 begins with śēkel ("sense") and v. 16 with kol ("everything"); v. 18 speaks of mûsār and v. 19 has the phrase sûr mērā'.

V. 20. There is a play on the roots r" (the catchword in vv. 19-21: "evil," "harm," "misfortune") and r'h ("companion").

Vv. 21-22. The catchwords are ṭôb ("prosperity," "good man"), and ṣaddîq ("righteous").

Vv. 23-25. These sayings seem quite disparate, but 'ōkel ("food") may be a catchword reflecting back to v. 23.

CHAPTER 14

Vv. 1-3. These verses are united by the motifs of wisdom and fear of the Lord (emended text in v. 1, reading "wisdom" with most modern translations, except the *NEB*). The style in v. 2 is juxtaposition of four participles.

V. 5. The repetition in v. 5b and 6:9a illustrates how certain lines were reused in the formation of new sayings; see also 12:17; 14:25; 19:5.

Vv. 6-8. The root *yd'* ("knowledge") is the catchword for vv. 6-7, and *kĕsîl* ("fool") for vv. 7-8.

Vv. 11-14. The catchwords are *yšr* ("[up]right") for vv. 11-12, *'aḥărît* ("end") for vv. 12-13, and *lēb* ("heart," "perverse" [*sûg lēb*]) for vv. 13-14.

Vv. 15-18. These verses lay down characterizations of the simple and the prudent (vv. 15,18) the wise and the foolish (vv. 16-17).

Vv. 19-22. Both vv. 19 and 22 have the root *r''* ("evil"), which is similar to the root *r'h* ("neighbor") occurring in vv. 20-21, which deal with the poor (*rāš/'ănîyîm* [*Kĕtîb; Qĕrê, 'ănāwîm*]).

Vv. 26-27. "Fear of the Lord" is the catchword for these verses. Synonymous parallelism appears in v. 26, and from this point on to 15:33 it becomes relatively frequent (Skehan, 18).

Vv. 28-29. The root *rbb* ("great," "multitude") is the catchword for these verses. Juxtaposition characterizes vv. 29-30, both of which deal with similar attitudes ("slow to anger," "tranquil mind").

CHAPTER 15

Vv. 1-4. With the exception of v. 3, these sayings all deal with speech, but the root *ṭôb/yṭb* ("good") is the catchword for vv. 2-3.

Vv. 5-9. Sayings about wise/fools and just/unjust alternate in vv. 5-8, while "abomination" and "wicked" are catchwords uniting vv. 8-9.

Vv. 13-15. *Lēb* ("heart, "mind") is the catchword. In the consonantal text of vv. 13-14, the words *pānîm* and *pĕnê* serve as catchwords, although the *Qĕrê* reading is to be preferred in v. 14b ("mouths"). *Ṭôb* ("cheerful") in v. 15 is a catchword for the "better" (*ṭôb*) sayings that follow in vv. 16-17.

Vv. 16-17. These are "better" sayings, which find a striking parallel in Amenemope VI, 9:5-8; *ANET*, 422.

Vv. 20-21. The root *śmḥ* ("glad," "joy") is the catchword binding these verses; cf. also v. 23 ("joy").

V. 22. The thought is similar to 11:14, and both have chiastic structure.

Vv. 25-26. These are two "Yahweh" sayings; cf. vv. 29,33.

Vv. 28-32. A series of catchwords lock these sayings together: "righteous" in vv. 28-29; *šm'* ("hear," "heed") in vv. 29, 31-32; "admonition" in vv. 31-32; "instruction" in vv. 32-33.

CHAPTER 16

Vv. 1-7. These are all "Yahweh" sayings, and give evidence of editorial arrangement at this point (see above).

V. 1. Cf. v. 9.

V. 2. See the variant in 21:2; "the ways of a man" appears also in v. 9.

V. 3. This is a rare appearance of a command in the midst of the sayings.

V. 4. Skehan (p. 18) counts this as the middle saying of the 375 proverbs in the Solomonic collection.

V. 5. A variant for v. 5b appears in 11:21.

V. 8. Cf. 15:16.

Vv. 10-11. The catchword is *mišpāṭ* ("judgment," "just").

Vv. 12-13. The root *ṣdq* ("righteousness," "right") is the catchword.

Vv. 13-15. A group of "king" sayings; cf. v. 10.

V. 17. The alliteration and juxtaposition in v. 17b (*šōmēr napšô nōṣēr darkô*) is reminiscent of 13:3.

Vv. 18-19. Catchwords ("spirit," and "pride/proud") and content unite these sayings. The "better" saying in v. 19 introduces *ṭôb* ("prosper" of v. 20), which ties vv. 19 and 20 together.

Vv. 21-24. These sayings deal with a common wisdom theme: speech. There are several catchwords: *mtq* ("pleasant," in vv. 21 and 24); *śkl* ("wisdom," "judicious" in vv. 22-23).

V. 25. This repeats 14:12.

Vv. 27-29. "Man" is the catchword for these verses, which have a common wisdom theme: evil speech. This is perhaps in contrast to vv. 21-24. "Perverse" (v. 28) is repeated in v. 30.

CHAPTER 17

V. 1. A "better" saying.

V. 3. The first line is repeated in 27:21; the pithiness of the expression is secured by the use of *lĕ* ("for").

V. 4. The style is juxtaposition; synonymous parallelism increases in chs. 16ff.

V. 9. In each line two participles are placed in juxtaposition.

V. 11. There is striking alliteration: *'ak mĕrî/'akzārî*.

V. 12. The style is unusual; v. 12a gives an example of danger, only to be surpassed by the example in v. 12b; the total effect is one of comparison.

V. 13. Again the style is unusual; v. 13a is an absolute nominative, or *casus pendens*.

V. 14. In fact, the command in v. 13b is a commentary upon v. 13a.

V. 15. Participles are juxtaposed in v. 15a; an "abomination" saying.

V. 16. The unusual style is best seen in a literal translation of this rhetorical question: Why money in the hand of a fool/to buy wisdom, and (he has) no mind?

Vv. 17-18. The catchword is *rēa'* ("brother," "neighbor").

V. 19. In each line two participles are in juxtaposition.

Vv. 21-22. The catchword is *śmḥ* ("joy," "cheerful").

CHAPTER 18

Vv. 4-8. These verses (if v. 5 refers to judgment) have to do with speech; vv. 6-7 are virtually identical.

Vv. 10-11. The catchwords for these lines are *'ōz* ("strong") and the root *śgb* ("safe," "high"); v. 11a=10:15a. The back-to-back positioning of these two sayings is another example of antinomies (cf. 17:27-28); God and wealth are compared with regard to the security they offer.

V. 12. The first line compares with 16:18; v. 12b is exactly the same as 15:33.

V. 13. Another example of nominative absolute, or *casus pendens* (cf. 17:13).

Vv. 18-19. *Midyān* ("disputes," "quarreling") is the catchword for these lines; the text of v. 19 is uncertain. For content, v. 18 is related to v. 17; both deal with disputes.

Vv. 20-21. Both these verses are concerned with speech, and the catchword is *pěrî* ("fruit").

V. 23. Chiasmus is used effectively here.

CHAPTER 19

Vv. 1-2. The catchword is *ṭôb* ("better," "good"); the "better" saying in v. 1 resembles 28:6, in the light of which many emend the text.

V. 5. Cf. v. 9, and 6:19; 14:5,25.

Vv. 6-7. "All" and "friend" serve as catchwords in sayings that continue the theme of v. 4. The third line in v. 7 cannot be translated meaningfully, and is probably corrupt; but v. 7ab makes good sense as an a fortiori saying.

Vv. 11-12. Both sayings deal with anger.

Vv. 13-14. "Father" and "wife" are the catchwords for these verses, which deal with the family; cf. 10:1; 27:15.

Vv. 15-16. The catchword is *nepeš* ("person," "life").

V. 18. This saying is unusual in form here: an imperative followed by a prohibition. The verb *nāśā'* ("pay," "set") serves as a catchword for vv. 18-19.

Vv. 20-21. Again, there is unusual form in that v. 20 contains two imperatives; *'ēṣâ* ("advice," "purpose") is the catchword.

V. 24. The saying is really a description of the conduct of a lazy man, who is pointed out as a bad and hopeless example.

V. 25. Although the saying is in the imperative form, the emphasis is not on following the advice ("strike," "reprove"), but on the way in which one learns prudence and knowledge.

Vv. 26-27. "Son" is the catchword.

V. 27. As with v. 25, the imperative is practically equivalent to an if-clause.

Vv. 28-29. The roots *lyṣ* ("mocks," "scoffers") and *špṭ* ("justice," "condemnation") are the catchwords for these lines, although some emend "condemnation" to "rods" (*šěbāṭîm*).

CHAPTER 20

V. 1. The catchword of 19:28-29 appears again ("mocker").

Vv. 5-6. The catchword is *'îš* ("man"), repeated four times.

Vv. 7-9. Each verse begins with the letter *mem* (cf. 11:9-12).

V. 10. Cf. v. 23, and also 11:1; another "abomination" saying, and the style is juxtaposition.

V. 11. Note the onomatopoeia in v. 11a (*yitnakker/nā'ar*); *gam* ("also") is the catchword for vv. 10-12, and *gam šĕnêhem* ("them both," "both alike") ends vv. 10,12.

Vv. 12-13. The catchword is "eye," and the form in v. 13 is made up of prohibition and command.

V. 14. The saying is rather a description of human activity that contains its own lesson; cf. 19:24.

V. 16. Repeated in 27:13; this is an instruction about giving surety, a common topos in Proverbs. There is a play on words between *'rb* ("surety") and *'rb* ("sweet") in v. 17.

Vv. 18-19. The form is instructional: a command in v. 18b, a prohibition in v. 19b. Compare v. 19a with 11:13.

V. 22. The form is instructional: a prohibition, followed by a command. *Yhwh* is the catchword for vv. 22-24.

V. 24. This verse, and also vv. 25-26, begin with the letter *mem* (cf. vv. 7-9). "Man" (*'ādām*) is the catchword for vv. 24-25.

V. 29. Each line presents terms in juxtaposition.

V. 30. "Innermost parts" may be a catchword with v. 27; note also the "king" sayings in vv. 26,28.

CHAPTER 21

Vv. 1-3. These are "Yahweh" sayings; the catchwords in vv. 1-2 are "every" and "heart."

Vv. 5-6. Both sayings deal with acquisition of possessions.

Vv. 7-8. Both sayings are characterizations of the unjust; note the onomatopoeia in *hăpakpak derek 'îš wāzār wĕzak* in v. 8.

V. 9. A repetition of 25:4.

Vv. 11-12. These verses are united by the catchword *śkl* ("instructed," "observes").

V. 17. The repetition of a word within the saying is characteristic also of vv. 21, 23.

V. 23. There is a play on the word "keep" (*šmr*).

Vv. 25-26. The root *'wh* ("desire," "covet") is the catchword for these verses.

Vv. 28-29. "Man" is the catchword.

Vv. 30-31. These verses are related in meaning, as well as by the catchword "Yahweh."

CHAPTER 22

Vv. 1-2. "Rich" is the catchword for these verses, the first a "better" saying, and the second a "Yahweh" saying in which the juxtaposition of the half-lines is striking.

V. 3. This is repeated in 27:12; the onomatopoeia is striking: *'ārûm rā'â rā'â wĕyistār*. The letter *'ayin* begins vv. 2-4.

Vv. 5-6. "Way" is the catchword.

V. 7. The saying is an observation without moral evaluation; note the onomatopoeia in v. 7b: *lōweh lĕ'îš malweh*.

V. 10. As in v. 6, the imperative is equivalent to a conditional clause.

V. 13. Compare 26:13, and also 19:24; the saying is a description of the conduct of the lazy person.

COLLECTION OF "THE WORDS OF THE WISE," 22:17 – 24:22

If there is no title in the MT at 22:17, it is because it seems to have been incorporated into the verse itself as "(hear) the words of the wise." As many scholars propose, this phrase should be prefixed to the unit, and 22:17a should read: "Incline your ear and hear my words" (cf. LXX). The end of this unit at 24:22 is clearly indicated by the appearance of a title in 24:23.

Another important change in the MT is at 22:20: the revocalization of *šlšwm* ("day before yesterday," or as the *Qĕrê* has it, *šlyšym*, "officers") as *šĕlōšîm* ("thirty"). The widely acknowledged dependence of this section upon the Instruction of Amenemope (*ANET*, 421-24), which is divided into thirty "houses" (=chapters), is thus further indicated by "thirty" (sayings) in v. 20. Despite the efforts of various commentators (e.g., McKane, Gemser, Scott), however, there is no certain division of the biblical material into precisely thirty sayings. The topical similarity with Amenemope's work does not seem to extend beyond 23:11, although the editor of 22:17 – 24:22 could have had thirty units in mind.

Scholarly opinion favors the dependence of the author-collector of 22:17 – 24:22 upon the work of Amenemope. For the scholarly discussion see G. Bryce, *A Legacy*, 15-87. However, the Israelite writer is remarkably independent. Only a third of this collection corresponds to the sayings of Amenemope, and then in an order differing from the Egyptian work. He has freely imitated and reworked the material, rather than simply taken it over. As W. Richter (p. 27) remarks of 24:24, the title hardly designates authorship, but rather the group (wise men) that was associated with these "words."

Contrary to the consecutive logical style of the instructions in Proverbs 1–9, this collection is made up of separate and disparate COMMANDS (note the frequency of motive clauses), PROHIBITIONS, and even SAYINGS (24:3-9, 24-26). It purports to provide "instructions" (*mō'ēṣôt*, 22:20) for a single person ("my son," 23:15,19,26; 24:13,21). They are offered by one person (22:19-20; not by the wise men). The style is almost exclusively synonymous parallelism (antithetic in 24:16). Thus, the genre for the unit is that of INSTRUCTION; the setting is that of a sage who wants to provide guidance for a youth; the intention is indicated in 22:20-21.

Structure

I. Title (emended text: "the words of the wise")	22:17a
II. Introduction	22:17-21
A. Commands to pay attention	17
B. Motive clauses, giving reasons	18
C. Writer's declaration of purpose	19-21
III. Body of the instruction	22:22– 24:22
A. Prohibitions, with motivation, relative to oppression of the poor	22-23

B. Prohibitions, with motivation, relative to association
with the hot-tempered (note chiasmus in v. 24)   24-25
C. Prohibitions, with motivation (in conditional and
question form), relative to going surety   26-27
D. Prohibition against changing boundary line
(dittography of 24:10?)   28
E. Question (29a) introducing a saying about the
"skillful"   29
F. Advice (commands and prohibition) relative to
conduct at table of ruler   23:1-3;
v. 3a=6b
G. Advice (prohibition and command) about attitude
toward wealth   4-5
H. Prohibitions, with motivation, relative to conduct at
table of stingy man   6-8
I. Prohibition, with motivation, against speaking before
a fool   9
J. Prohibition, with motivation, relative to boundaries
(chiasmus in v. 10; cf. 22:28)   10-11
K. Invitation to listen to wisdom (a new beginning
here?)   12
L. Prohibition and command, with motivation, relative to
disciplining youth   13-14
M. Encouragement to "my son," with motivation (note
chiasmus)   15-16
N. Prohibition against envy of sinners, with motivation   17-18
O. Commands and prohibition, with motivation, relative
to gluttony and drunkenness   19-21
P. Commands and prohibitions relative to acquisition of
wisdom, with motivation (parents)   22-25
Q. Commands to follow the teacher's example and avoid
the harlot, with motivation   26-28
R. Instruction concerning intoxication   29-35
    1. Question-answer lesson (reminiscent of riddle
    style)   29-30
    2. Prohibition against intoxication   31
    3. Motivation: a description of effects of intoxication   32-35
S. Prohibitions against envy of evil man, with motivation
(v. 1 begins with 'aleph)   24:1-2
T. Wisdom sayings about the house that wisdom builds
(v. 3 begins with beth)   3-4
U. Wisdom sayings about the strength of the wise (cf
11:14; 20:18), and weakness of the fool (v. 5 begins
with gimel)   5-7
V. Wisdom sayings (united by catchword, zmm
["mischief," "devising"]) about intrigue   8-9
W. Wisdom saying about perseverance (play on word ṣar
["adversity," "small"])   10

X. Commands relative to concern for victims of
violence, with motivation (causuistic style and
question)   11-12

Y. Command to eat honey (i.e., wisdom, as food to be
consumed), with motivation   13-14

Z. Prohibition against oppression of just, with motivation   15-16

AA. Prohibition against rejoicing in the downfall of one's
enemy, with motivation   17-18

BB. Prohibition against being envious of the wicked, with
motivation (cf. 23:17-18; 24:14)   19-20

CC. Advice (command and prohibition) to honor authority
(God and king), with motivation   21-22

Genre, Setting, Intention

See above on structure.

COLLECTION OF "THE WORDS OF THE WISE," 24:23-34

This short collection is found in the LXX after the sayings of Agur (30:1-14).
The title in v. 23 is, literally: "also these to the wise men" (cf. 22:17, emended
text, above). Skehan (p. 21) argues that it really belongs to the previous collection
(22:17–24:22) and should be rendered: "These also belong to the [collection of
'Sayings of] wise men.' "

Structure

   I. Title   24:23a

   II. Wisdom sayings about just judgment   23b-25

      A. A "not good" (*bal ṭôb*) saying, condemning partiality
(has a half-line been lost here?)   23b

      B. Motivation: two wisdom sayings in antithetic
parallelism   24-25

  III. A saying about honest speech   26

  IV. A command which urges priorities in establishing a house   27

   V. A prohibition against malicious witness   28

  VI. A prohibition forbidding one to take revenge   29

VII. An example story about a sluggard, followed by sayings   30-34

      A. The example story   30-32

      B. The lessons drawn by the sage: sayings repeated from
6:10-11   33-34

Genre, Setting, Intention

The structure indicates the various genres in this section. This is in fact a miscellany (cf. 6:1-19) of various lessons which the sages wished to inculcate.

COLLECTION OF "PROVERBS OF SOLOMON" (MEN OF HEZEKIAH), 25:1–29:27

Structure

See the introductory remarks to ch. 10. Like the first collection of the "proverbs of Solomon" (10:1–22:16), this collection is made up of discrete sayings, with the exception of 27:23-27. Skladny (pp. 46-67) separates chs. 25–27 from chs. 28–29. Chs. 25–27 display a remarkable interest in nature: the products of creation, the animal world, etc. He calls these chapters a "vademecum" or mirror for peasants and laborers. Although there are many sayings about the proper use of speech, the portrait of the fool reveals less moral than intellectual emphasis; the fool is simply dumb, and the contrast between the righteous and the wicked, so frequent in Proverbs, is rarely presented. The attitude to the king is distant, but respectful. There is a remarkable difference in style as well. About one-fourth of the section contains prohibitions, and parallelism is to be found in less than half of the verses. About two-thirds of the sayings are comparisons, very often made explicit with *kĕ* or *kēn* ("so"). Chs. 28–29 have as their significant themes judicial and social problems, especially the poor, and the conduct of the king. Skladny suggests that these chapters are a mirror or program for rulers. Antithetic parallelism predominates (82%) in these sayings. Skladny's observations are helpful, whether or not one agrees that there is sufficient evidence that two collections have been combined here.

G. Bryce ("Another Wisdom-'Book' in Proverbs") has claimed that 25:2-27 is a literary unit, comparable to 22:17–24:22, and to the wisdom of the Egyptian Sehetepibre (*ANET*, 431). His arguments are drawn from content and structure. The first four verses announce the two topics of the instruction: the king (vv. 2-3) and the wicked (vv. 4-5). Then vv. 6-15 develop the first topic (v. 6, *melek*, "king"; v. 15, *qāṣîn*, "ruler"), while vv. 16-26 deal with the wicked (*rāšā'*). However, the topics cannot be divided as neatly as this. In vv. 8-14 one is confronted with disparate sayings that have little if any relationship to "kings." Similarly, the content of vv. 16-26 is too diversified to be characterized as dealing with the "wicked" (cf. vv. 18,20,23-25). Bryce also points to composition "rubrics" in the structure: "glory" appears in vv. 2 and 27b, while "honey" occurs in vv. 16 and 27a. But this evidence is too fragile to support the existence of an original wisdom book in this chapter.

CHAPTER 25

V. 1. The title of the collection. This attributes the collection of the sayings to the "men of Hezekiah," and thus points to the court as the responsible agent for the work.

Vv. 2-7. These all have to do with the king, and there are many deliberate repetitions within them.

V. 2. The remarkable form of the Hebrew deserves to be quoted: *kĕbōd 'ĕlōhîm hastēr dābār; ûkĕbōd mĕlākîm ḥāqōr dābār*. The style is juxtapositional. Tying vv. 2-3 together is *ḥqr* ("search," "searchable").

Vv. 4-5. There is an implicit comparison between these verses, and the catchword is "take away." The imperative (in Hebrew, infinitive absolute) is equivalent to an if-clause.

Vv. 6-7. An admonition with motivation. The final clause, "what your eyes have seen," belongs with v. 8.

V. 8. An admonition with motivation. Catchwords with v. 9 are provided: *rîb* ("court," "case") and *rēa'* ("neighbor").

Vv. 9-10. An admonition with motivation; the topic unites these lines with v. 8.

Vv. 11-12. The metaphors indicate the value of the right word (cf. 15:23) and of wise reproof.

Vv. 13-14. Both use comparisons from nature, and there is a play on *qāṣîr* ("harvest") and *ṣîr* ("messenger").

Vv. 16-17. The catchword is *śb'* ("sated," "weary"). Both verses are in the genre of INSTRUCTION.

Vv. 18-20. Boström points to onomatopoeia in these verses, all of which have unusual metaphors. Compare, e.g., *běyôm ṣārâ* ("in time of trouble"), *běyôm qārâ* ("on a cold day").

Vv. 21-22. An admonition with motivation.

V. 24. Identical with 21:9.

CHAPTER 26

Vv. 1-12. These sayings (except v. 2) are grouped around a common topic: the fool (*kěsîl*). The form consists mainly in comparisons.

V. 1. The alliteration (especially with the *k*-sound) is noteworthy; v. 1a is a variant of 19:10a.

V. 3. 10:13b and 19:29b are variants of v. 3b.

Vv. 4-5. A striking form of antinomies.

V. 8. Compare v. 1; the *k*-sound is repeated here also.

V. 9. Compare v. 7b.

Vv. 13-16. These sayings all deal with the sluggard (*'āṣēl*).

V. 13. A variant of 22:13.

V. 15. A variant of 19:24.

Vv. 18-19. These verses belong together; a complex comparison.

Vv. 20-28. The topic common to these verses is the use of the tongue: whispering, lying, etc.

V. 22. This is repeated from 18:8.

V. 27. The metaphors here are classical; cf. Ps 7:16 (*RSV* 15); Eccl 10:8; Sir 27:26-27.

CHAPTER 27

Vv. 1-2. The root *hll* ("boast," "praise") is the catchword.

Vv. 3-4. The style of each saying is similar: *a minore ad majus* ("from the less to the greater"), although v. 4 ends in a rhetorical question.

Vv. 5-6. These sayings are concerned with the value of reproof.

V. 7. The style of juxtaposition is striking; note also the repetition of *nepeš*, ("he who," "one who") and alliteration with *nōpet* ("honey").

V. 8. The Hebrew is characterized by noticeable alliteration.

V. 11. The address "my son" is not frequent outside of chs. 1–9, but cf. 23:15, 26.

V. 12. Practically identical with 22:3.

V. 13. A repetition of 20:16.

Vv. 15-16. These are united by a common theme.

V. 19. The succinctness of expression makes this saying difficult to understand.

V. 20. Cf. 30:15-16.

V. 21. 17:3a is repeated here in v. 21a.

Vv. 23-27. This instruction for a farmer is unique in the OT (but cf. Isa 28:23-29). The address begins with an imperative, and the perspective remains in the singular. One can only speculate about a possible setting, but the sages show a fairly wide acquaintance with farm life (10:5; 12:10-11; 14:4; 24:27; 28:19).

CHAPTER 28

L. Alonso Schökel has remarked that most of the sayings in ch. 28 have a strong moral bent. The frequent participle form ("he who") facilitates the emphasis upon the conduct of the good and the wicked.

Vv. 4,7,9. The frequent mention of the "law" (*tôrâ*) is unusual in Proverbs, and it is generally understood to refer to "instruction," such as the sayings of the wise. However, there is a strong religious coloring to v. 9, and one must assume that the will of the Lord stands behind the "law" which is referred to here; note also the phrase in v. 5, "those who seek the Lord."

V. 10. The last line may be a gloss.

V. 13. Contrast Psalm 32.

V. 14. This "blessing" (*'ašrê*) may be contrasted with v. 1.

Vv. 15-16. Both sayings deal with leaders of the people (*mōšēl, nāgîd*).

V. 19. A variant of 12:11.

V. 21. V. 21a is a variant of 24:23.

V. 22. "Hastening" after riches is a common topos; cf. v. 20.

V. 28. See v. 12.

CHAPTER 29

L. Alonso Schökel rightly observes that in this final chapter of the collection almost all the sayings are repetitious or variations of proverbs that have appeared previously; there is little concern on the part of the collectors to unify them in a thematic way.

V. 1. The second part of the verse is identical with 6:15b.

Vv. 2-3. The catchword is *śmḥ* ("rejoice," "glad").

Vv. 6-7. The righteous/wicked contrast, so frequent in chs. 10–15, makes one of its infrequent appearances in this collection; cf. vv. 16,27.

Vv. 8-9. The catchword is the root *ḥkm* ("wise").

Vv. 13-14. The "poor" (*rāš, dallîm*) are the theme common to both verses.

Vv. 15,17. Both verses deal with the theme of correction (*ysr, tôkaḥat*).

Vv. 19-20. The catchword is *dābār* ("word").

Vv. 19,21. Both verses have the "servant" as theme.

Vv. 25-26. These are "Yahweh" sayings.

COLLECTION OF "THE WORDS OF AGUR," 30:1-14

There is no certainty among commentators as to the length of Agur's discourse (end at v. 4, or v. 6, or v. 14?). In the LXX this chapter is divided, with 30:1-14 following 22:17–24:22, and vv. 15-33 following 24:23-24. It is certain that the MT of v. 1b ("Ithiel," "Ucal") has to be emended, and probably it is part of Agur's oracle, however it may be translated ("there is no god," "I am not god," etc.). In the current text one can recognize some grouping by reason of topics: lie (*kzb*, vv. 6,8), blasphemy and curse (vv. 9-11), generation (*dôr*, vv. 11-14).

According to Roth (pp. 7,38), vv. 11-14 contain a numerical saying from which the title line (three kinds of men Yahweh hates, and four are abhorrent to him) has fallen out. McKane (p. 651) regards the lines as condemnatory rather than reflective. Roth (pp. 69-70) classifies vv. 7-9 as a reflective numerical saying. Skehan (pp. 42-43) asks the question, who is Agur? He then analyzes Agur's saying in vv. 1-4: Agur says that he is not really wise and suggests (v. 4) that the almighty, God the creator, is truly the wise one. By ending with a request for his name and his son's name (v. 4), Agur seems to be proposing a riddle. Where is the data to answer this riddle? The only names provided are "Agur son of Jakeh." If Agur is taken as "I am a sojourner" (as it literally means), he is to be associated with the Jacob of Gen 47:9 who speaks of his sojourn to Pharaoh, and with the Jacob of 28:12-13 (ladder and angels; cf. v. 4, "who has ascended to heaven and come down?"). In other words, Agur is the people of Israel, and then Jakeh must be Yahweh himself. The Hebrew of Jakeh is *Yqh*, i.e., an abbreviation of *Yhwh qādôš hû'* ("the Lord, blessed is he")—an antecedent to the well-known *haqqā-dôš, bārûk hû'* ("the Holy one, blessed is he") of a later era.

Structure

I. Title		1a
II. Agur's oracle (*nĕ'ūm*; *RSV* "says to")		1aβ-4
A. Agur describes his ignorance		1aβ-3
B. Agur raises ironic questions about man's distance from God the creator		4a
C. Agur (rather than God) invites answers to his questions (a riddle?): what (is his name. . .)?		4b
III. An instruction about God's word		5-6
A. Saying about the word of God (cf. Ps 18:31 [*RSV* 30])		5
B. Prohibition against adding to God's word (cf. Deut 4:2)		6
IV. Prayer		7-9
V. Prohibition against slander, with motivation		10
VI. A fourfold characterization of wicked men (each verse repeats *dôr* ["generation"])		11-14

Genre, Setting, Intention

The introduction above and the structure indicate the various genres to be found in this collection. The setting is, as usual, that of instruction. If Skehan's analysis of Agur son of Jakeh is correct, there is no reason to see here non-Israelite wisdom, and in fact the sayings are consonant with the general tenor of Israelite wisdom.

COLLECTION OF (MOSTLY) NUMERICAL SAYINGS, 30:15-33

Structure

I.	Saying about the two daughters of the leech	15a
II.	Graded numerical saying (3/4) about insatiability	15b-16
III.	Saying about punishment awaiting those who show disrespect to parents	17
IV.	Graded numerical saying (3/4) about marvels in nature	18-19
V.	An interpretation (probably a gloss) of vv. 18-19	20
VI.	Graded numerical saying (3/4) about intolerable things	21-23
VII.	Numerical saying about four small but wise creatures	24-28
VIII.	Graded numerical saying (3/4) about stately creatures	29-31
IX.	Command against pride, with motive clause	32-33

Genre, Setting, Intention

The various genres are indicated in the structure above. There is no certainty as to the origins of the numerical sayings (the riddle? magic?). Their main concern here is nature and its phenomena, an area that formed part of the wisdom tradition; thus the setting and intention is that of instruction.

COLLECTION OF "THE WORDS OF LEMUEL," 31:1-9

Structure

I.	Title	1
II.	Instruction	2-9
	A. Call for attention	2
	B. Series of commands and prohibitions regarding women (v. 3), strong drink (vv. 4-7), and justice (vv. 8-9)	3-9

The enigmatic "what, my son" of v. 2 is construed here as equivalent to "listen, my son."

Genre, Setting, Intention

This is a typical instruction for royalty, which finds its counterpart in the Egyptian Instructions of Amenemhet and Merikare, which are directed to kings (*ANET*, 414-19), and also in the Babylonian "Advice to a Prince" (as Lambert, 110-11, terms it). It is unusual, however, in that the instruction is given by a woman. If one translates "Lemuel, king of Massa," the unit may be taken as an appropriation of non-Israelite wisdom (perhaps Edomite?), and the Aramaic forms in vv. 2-3 suggest foreign origin. The situation is that of parental instruction of a young monarch. In the context of the book of "proverbs of Solomon," it purports to have some association with that king. The advice deals with royal conduct, but the ideals are "democratized" by the very fact that they are included in this book, and hence are applicable to the conduct of any wise man.

AN ACROSTIC POEM ON THE IDEAL WIFE, 31:10-31

Structure

I. Introduction: rhetorical question	10a
II. Description of her value to her husband	10b-12
III. Description of her activities	13-22
IV. Description of her effect upon her husband	23
V. Description of her activities	24-27
VI. Praise of the woman, from her family	28-29
VII. Wisdom saying, which is applied to her	30
VIII. A command of the poet that she be duly recognized	31

Genre, Setting, Intention

This is a WISDOM POEM, created by the sage on the pattern of an acrostic, i.e., each verse begins with the successive letters of the Hebrew alphabet. The setting is of course instructional. The wisdom accents are explicit in vv. 26, 30. Like wisdom herself (significantly, personified as a woman), the woman of the poem is more precious than jewels (v. 10; cf. Job 28:10-15; Prov 3:13-16; 8:11,19). The intention is at least twofold. The poem describes the ideal wife from the husband's vantage point; these were qualities a man should look for in his beloved (see Canticles as offering a complementary point of view). On the other hand, the poem also holds out an ideal which Israelite society held up for the woman herself.

RUTH

BIBLIOGRAPHY

S. Bertman, "Symmetrical Design in the Book of Ruth," *JBL* 84 (1965) 165-68; E. F. Campbell, "The Hebrew Short Story: A Study of Ruth," in *A Light Unto My Path: Old Testament Studies in Honor of J. M. Myers* (ed. H. Bream et al.; Philadelphia, 1974) 83-101; idem, *Ruth* (AB 7; New York, 1975); W. Dommershausen, "Leitwortstil in der Ruthrolle," in *Theologie im Wandel* (Munich, 1967) 394-407; G. Gerleman, *Ruth* (BKAT XVIII/1; Neukirchen-Vluyn, 1960); H. Gunkel, "Ruth," in *Reden und Aufsätze* (Göttingen, 1913) 65-92; R. Hals, *The Theology of the Book of Ruth* (Facet Books—Biblical Series 23; Philadelphia, 1969); H. Hertzberg, *Das Buch Ruth* (ATD 9; Göttingen, 1954); P. Humbert, "Art et leçon de l'histoire de Ruth," *RTP* 26 (1938) 257-86 (repr. in *Opuscules d'un Hebraïsant* [Neuchâtel, 1958] 83-110); P. Joüon, *Ruth* (Rome, 1924); O. Loretz, "Das Buch Rut," in *Gotteswort und menschliche Erfahrung* (Freiburg, 1963) 38-68; J. Myers, *The Linguistic and Literary Form of the Book of Ruth* (Leiden, 1955); D. F. Rauber, "Literary Values in the Bible: The Book of Ruth," *JBL* 89 (1970) 27-37; W. Rudolph, *Das Buch Ruth* (KAT XVII/1; Gütersloh, 1962) 23-72; J. Sasson, *Ruth* (Baltimore, 1979); H. E. Witzenrath, *Das Buch Rut: Eine literaturwissenschaftliche Untersuchung* (SANT 40; Munich, 1975); E. Würthwein, *Die Fünf Megilloth* (HAT 18, 2nd ed., 1969) 1-24.

CHAPTER 1

THE BOOK AS A WHOLE

Structure

The structure proposed by Hermann Gunkel has been followed, with only slight variations, by a large number of recent commentators, such as R. Hals, P. Humbert, E. Würthwein, etc. Some (G. Gerleman, O. Loretz) are satisfied to recognize the chapter divisions as indicative of the main scenes.

The structural outline below follows Gunkel:

This structure is determined largely by the change of scenes and the course of action within the story. In addition, a significant use of catchwords holds the units together: *šûb* ("return") in 1:1-22; *lqṭ* ("glean") in 2:1-17; *g'l* ("redeem") in 3:6-15; *qnh* ("acquire") and *g'l* ("redeem") in 4:1-12. These and other structural details will appear in the analysis of each unit. For another division, based upon balancing sections (ABC, CBA), see Bertman, 167.

Genre

Many commentators have followed Gunkel in his choice of novelle as the genre of the book of Ruth. However, Gunkel makes no effort to define the genre which he applies to Ruth. He merely says (p. 85): "It is through such a broad development of dialogues that finally a new genre emerges, which we can best term 'novella.' The Italian novelle of the Renaissance (the starting point for the modern novelle) also arose out of the materials of *Märchen* and saga, which came to be highly developed from an interest in the depiction of characters." This is rather a definition of the unknown by the more unknown. E. Würthwein does not accept the term novella (for which he adopts a definition from Goethe—it deals with an "unheard-of event"), and proposes the term "idyl" (pp. 3-4). This he defines as a "striving for an ideal and innocent condition. . . . and for patriarchal conditions, such as the appearance of a few, simple, mostly model-type characters" (p. 4). As regards both of these characterizations, it should be said that the definitions are wanting.

It seems better to accept the genre of Ruth as a "Hebrew historical short story," as proposed by E. F. Campbell. In his commentary on Ruth (pp. 5-6) he points out the characteristics that make up this genre: (1) the work is composed in a distinctive literary style (cf. Genesis 24, the Joseph cycle, Genesis 38, the court history of 2 Sam 9–20, the prose framework of Job 1–2; 42:7-17); (2) an interest in typical people is combined with an interest in mundane affairs; (3) the purposes are several: both entertaining and instructive; and (4) an impression of the artistry and creativity of the author is made upon the reader. Campbell regards the Hebrew SHORT STORY as probably a new form, a new literary creation, and he dates the work to the early part of 950-700 B.C.

As far as the historicity is concerned, we do not have the evidence available to answer this question, although the individual scenes themselves are historically plausible. The story dominates the entire book up to the genealogy of 4:18-22, and here the story is subordinated to the background of the history of the Davidic line.

Setting

The canonical setting of the book of Ruth (cf. 1:1, "in the days of the judges") indicates that the book gives the family background of David. This is clearly shown by the ending in 4:18-22. There is no real evidence for the setting(s) the story might have had in its preliterary days. J. Myers has argued for the poetic base in the book, and it may very well have been handed down in oral tradition. But both the genre and the setting at this stage remain hypothetical; cf. Campbell, *Ruth*, 7-8.

Intention

W. Dommershausen (pp. 394-95) has given a convenient summary of the views of the meaning of Ruth proposed in the 19th and 20th centuries. It was seen as a recommendation of the levirate marriage (A. Bertholet), or a justification for the Davidic succession (E. Reuss). E. Reuss claimed that it was a presentation of the earlier family history of the house of David, in which figures such as Tamar, Rahab, and Ruth suggest the implicit divine direction. P. Cassel saw in it "the power of love." For C. F. Keil, the pious and virtuous ancestors of David are pictured. Many commentators have followed the position of A. Kuenen and A. Bertholet that the book is a protest against the rigorous measures taken by Ezra and Nehemiah against mixed marriages. In this century, there were some new wrinkles on old theories. Thus, W. Staples found in the book certain relationships to the fertility cult. A. Jepsen interpreted it as a book of consolation for the Israel that returned home from exile. Both H. Hertzberg and W. Rudolph emphasize the work as a portrayal of the providence of the God of Israel, who rewards everyone who takes refuge under his wings. O. Loretz thinks that the central point of the Ruth story is the preservation of the name of the family, and the work is written to the glory of David (the "last word" in the story, 4:17). G. Gerleman claims that the principal theme of the book is the incorporation of Ruth into a Jewish family.

This résumé of Dommershausen's summaries can be extended further. The position of Gerleman is actually more subtle. The Judaizing of Ruth the Moabitess is the story, but it has been given another direction by the secondary addition in 4:17b-22, which refers it to David. This is an attempt to soften and to make palatable the harmful Moabite tradition which was associated with David's origins. But it is also a story of Providence; the divine direction is a hidden power behind the events; hence one cannot object to the Moabite origins of David. R. Hals (p. 6) describes the book as a story about the providence of God, but of a special kind. It is the hidden God at work here. There is no direct reflection concerning the meaning of the events on the part of the author; instead, he "portrays God's guiding hand as totally hidden in normal causality" (p. 18) in tracing out the background of David. E. Würthwein characterizes the story as an "idyl," in which the themes of *hesed* (loyal faithfulness), family and tribal fidelity, are celebrated, as is also the divine direction of events. It is from wisdom circles, he claims, that this emphasis on *hesed* (Ruth 1:8; 3:10; cf. Prov 21:21) derives. P. Humbert (p. 110) argues that the lesson of Ruth underlines the value of *pietas* in the eyes of God—the religious duty of fidelity to family and people. This secures the blessing of God; although the story began with human misery, it ends with blessing.

From this survey of opinions one may conclude that some distinctions are necessary. First, the intention of the Ruth story (1:1–4:17) is not necessarily the same as the intention given to the book in the light of 4:18-22. Second, within the story itself, more than one theme (such as fidelity, or providence) is illustrated, and these deserve to be considered as part of the intention of the book. Many derive the intention from a context outside the book, but into which the book is nevertheless placed. Thus, a postexilic date for the book prompts one to see it as a kind of polemic against the mixed marriage legislation of Ezra. But the telling argument against this is that the book is entirely too bland, too weak an argument, to be conceived as an answer to this legislation. Here the alleged context, or setting, is allowed to determine the intention.

A full reading of the text will allow several intentions to appear as part of the meaning.

1) As many commentators have pointed out, this is a story of providence, or *Führungsgeschichte*. R. Hals is correct in his discernment of the manner in which providence is portrayed: it is hidden, and it works through the all-pervading causality of God; it does not become a topic itself for reflection. Part of the concern is the preservation of the name and the family, as O. Loretz has urged. This is within the total concern of the story, but it is hardly the dominant theme. The concern for the preservation of the name, the continuation of the family, is not possible, the story shows, without family loyalty (the emphasis of Würthwein).

2) As the book stands in its entirety, the intention is to present the providential care that was working behind the choice of David. Gerleman is correct in seeing a parallel between Ruth and the patriarchal narratives; both have the same theological direction—leading into the primary saving institutions of Israel: the covenant with Israel at Sinai, and the covenant with David.

THE INDIVIDUAL UNITS

SETTING THE SCENE, 1:1-5

Structure

I. Elimelech's family leaves Judah for Moab	1-2
A. Time (period of the judges) and reason (famine)	1a
B. Identification of persons concerned	1b-2a
C. Reprise: inclusion with v. 1b, "fields of Moab"	2b
II. A history of disaster	3-5
A. Death of Elimelech	3
B. Marriage of two sons to Orpah and Ruth	4
C. Death of two sons—bereavement of Naomi	5

Gunkel's "Exposition" or setting of the scene is followed widely by commentators, but Würthwein takes vv. 1-7a as a unit that leads up to the conversation which follows.

Genre, Setting, Intention

This is a REPORT about the movement of the family of Elimelech and Naomi to Moab during the period of the judges, and the consequent calamity that afflicted them in this land. The data supplied here is to set up the dialogue which ensues between Naomi and her daughters-in-law. The names of her sons, if one grants the traditional etymology, are in themselves ominous: Mahlon (*ḥlh* ["sick"]), and Chilion (*klh* ["come to an end"]).

NAOMI RETURNS HOME, 1:6-18

Structure

I. Naomi and the daughters-in-law begin the return to Judah	6-7
II. The farewell scene	8-18
A. First phase: refusal of a farewell	8-10
1. Naomi's farewell	8-9bα
a. What she says (order to return, and blessing)	8-9a
b. What she does (kiss)	9bα
2. Reaction of the women	9bβ
a. What they do (crying, weeping)	9bβ
b. What they say (refusal)	10

B. Second phase: Naomi again orders them to return and
   gives reasons   11-13
   1. The order   11aα
   2. Reason: she has no husbands to provide   11aβ-11b
   3. Another order   12aα
   4. Reason: because she cannot produce husbands,
      even in reasonable time   12aβ-13a
   5. Final prohibition and reason   13b
C. Third phase: Orpah departs, but Ruth goes with
   Naomi   14-18
   1. Naomi urges Ruth to return with her sister to her
      people and gods   14-15
   2. Ruth refuses and identifies Naomi's home, people,
      grave, and God as her own; in a formula of
      imprecation (v. 17b) she swears that only death
      will separate them   16-17
   3. Naomi ceases arguing   18

Würthwein ends this scene with v. 19a, the arrival in Bethlehem. The three phases of the scene are dominated by the catchword, *šûb* ("return") (Dommershausen, 396-98), which occurs twelve times in ch. 1: six times in the sense of return to Moab (vv. 8, 11, 12, 13, 15, 16) and six times as a return to Bethlehem (vv. 6, 7, 10, 21, 22 twice). The word is also supported by synonyms: "go" (ten times), "come" (three times), "go forth" (twice), etc. The orders of Naomi are full and sonorous in vv. 8-10, but terse in vv. 11-13. The total effect of ch. 1 owes as much to the style as to the tender expression of the farewell scene. Gunkel (p. 67) finds here an instance of the "delay factor" (*retardierendes Motiv*) in that Naomi at first refuses to accept the sacrifice of her daughters-in-law, but eventually permits Ruth to accompany her. As he remarks, generosity is arrayed against generosity. Orpah serves as a counterpoint to Ruth, to make Ruth's unusual generosity stand out.

Genre, Setting, Intention

This is a description of a farewell scene that reveals the tender love and mutual loyalty of the three women. It is almost entirely in dialogue (of the eighty-five verses in the book, Joüon notes, fifty-five contain dialogue). The author has prepared the reader to expect only goodness from two such noble women, and he has raised the question of divine retribution ("the hand of the Lord," v. 13), which appears again in v. 21. The scene is dominated by the idea of homecoming (*šûb*).

INTERLUDE: ARRIVAL OF NAOMI AND RUTH IN BETHLEHEM, 1:19-22

Structure

I. A description of the reaction to their arrival in Bethlehem   19
II. Naomi's reply to the women of the town   20-21
III. Reprise of the action in vv. 6-19   22

In a few verses of effective dialogue the writer has brought alive the home-coming scene: the wondering and surprise behind the question, "Is that Naomi?" and the play on her name ("pleasant").

Genre, Setting, Intention

This is a description of another scene in the development of the story. The reaction of the women of Bethlehem gives the opportunity to further underline the tragedy that has come upon the émigré. Würthwein remarks that the author makes Naomi overlook deliberately that she has a daughter such as Ruth ("better than seven sons," 4:15), and she does not realize that Ruth is the key to a happy future. The summary sentence in v. 21 is a kind of resting point in the action: what will happen to this stricken couple now that the homecoming (see on this theme above) has taken place?

RUTH, THE MOABITESS, FINDS FAVOR IN THE FIELD OF BOAZ, 2:1-17

Structure

I. Boaz is introduced into the narrative and identified	1
II. With Naomi's leave, Ruth "happens" to glean in the field of Boaz	2-3
III. Boaz's conversation with his reapers and servant	4-7
IV. Boaz's conversation with Ruth	8-13
V. Boaz and Ruth at mealtime	14
VI. Boaz's orders to his reapers concerning Ruth	15-16
VII. Ruth at work, gleaning	17

Dommershausen (pp. 398-402) has pointed out the catchwords of ch. 2: *lqt* ("glean," twelve times); "Moabite" (three times); "find favor in the eyes of" (three times). All three occur in the very beginning in vv. 2-3. The whole section is artfully articulated in changing scenes and significant dialogue. The introduction of Boaz in v. 1, who has never been mentioned by Naomi, is deliberate in view of v. 20; he is to solve the problems of Naomi and Ruth (Loretz). The gleaning of the barley harvest (thus v. 2 connects with 1:22) provides the opportunity to underscore Ruth's practical solicitude for Naomi. The scenes in the field are manifold: Boaz greets his workers; the conversation with his servant reveals the identity of Ruth ("a fine artistic touch," according to Würthwein, that the servant should be the one to convey the information, thus indicating her status as one of the poor who gleans behind the reapers in accordance with Deut 24:19, and echoing the community news about the foreign girl); the conversation of Boaz with Ruth; mealtime, etc. The conversation with Ruth in vv. 8-13 reveals the "basic thought" (Gunkel, 73) of the story when Boaz wishes for her recompense (*šlm*, twice in v. 12) from the Lord under whose wings she has sought refuge. Dommershausen points out that the key phrase, "find favor in the eyes of" forms an inclusion to Ruth's brief replies (vv. 10-13) to Boaz; in v. 10 she plays on the word *nkr* ("take notice" and "foreigner"). The warmth of Boaz's reception is heightened by his sharing food with her and even serving her (v. 14), and ensuring for her special treatment from his workers (vv. 15-16).

Genre, Setting, Intention

This is a description of several scenes at harvest which are conveyed largely through dialogue that moves the story forward. The third principal figure of the story, Boaz, is introduced, and with him (and his kindness towards Ruth) there is an air of anticipation of the eventual solution of the problems of Naomi and Ruth. The goodness of both Boaz and Ruth shines forth in the actions and conversations; Gunkel (p. 73) speaks of Boaz's friendliness and Ruth's humility as motifs that are echoed several times.

INTERLUDE: RUTH REPORTS TO NAOMI, 2:18-23

Structure

I. Introduction: Ruth's plentiful supply prompts a conversation	18
II. The conversation between Ruth and Naomi	19-22
A. First phase	19-20
1. Naomi asks where Ruth worked, and blesses her patron	19a
2. Ruth's reply: she has worked with Boaz	19b
3. Naomi again blesses Ruth's patron, and identifies him as a *gō'ēl* ("redeeming kinsman")	20
B. Second phase: a reprise of the motif sounded in vv. 8-9, Naomi agrees that Ruth should stay with Boaz's workers	21-22
III. A summary description of Ruth's work until the end of harvesting	23

Genre, Setting, Intention

This is a report of a conversation which sets up an important motif, that of the redeeming kinsman. Before Naomi even knows that Ruth's patron is a kinsman, she has blessed him (v. 19; a blessing that forms a pendant to Boaz's blessing of Ruth in v. 12). The blessing is expanded because of the *ḥesed* ("kindness") of the Lord that has been concretized in Boaz's conduct. Although Naomi has never mentioned Boaz, she now appears well informed about his identity as kinsman (just as in 2:5 Boaz appears to be ignorant of Ruth's identity and then seems to be remarkably well informed in 2:11). The conversation serves to introduce the theme of the *gō'ēl*, which will dominate the rest of the story. The final verse creates some tension. It says nothing about any deepening of the relationship between Boaz and Ruth; she simply keeps on working till the harvesting is over. What will happen now?

NAOMI'S PLAN, 3:1-5

Structure

I. Introduction	1a
II. Naomi's directions to Ruth concerning the visit to Boaz	1b-4
III. Ruth's obedient response	5

Commentators note that ch. 3 contains the main scene (vv. 6-15) between two conversations of Naomi with Ruth, and Würthwein points out a certain concatenation: the later scene will take up traits of the earlier scene. Although nothing is said about levirate marriage in vv. 1-5, it is obvious that Naomi's plan is predicated upon Boaz's recognition of his duty as kinsman (although "acquaintance," not "kinsman," is used in v. 2, Naomi clearly has marriage in mind). According to Dommershausen, two of the three catchwords appear in vv. 1-5: *gōren* ("threshing floor") and *škb* ("lie down"). It is oversubtle to adopt for *škb* with Dommershausen and Gerleman the meaning of "the gesture of one who is making a request" in vv. 4, 7, 8. The word occurs in its normal sense here and also in vv. 4 (twice), 7, 13, 14. It is true that Ruth's action is ultimately understood by Boaz as a request. Campbell ("The Hebrew Short Story," 97) points out that *mānûaḥ* ("rest," or *RSV*, "home") in 3:1 resumes 1:9, *mēnûḥâ*: "the wish connected to Yahweh's activity becomes fulfilled by the human protagonist."

Genre, Setting, Intention
This is a report of a dialogue that serves to set up the main scene, in which Ruth will carry out the directions of Naomi. Gunkel (p. 76) claims that the author attributes whatever is clever and sophisticated in the plan to Naomi, and leaves the obedience and fidelity to Ruth.

BOAZ PLEDGES HIMSELF TO RUTH AT THE THRESHING FLOOR, 3:6-15

Structure

I. The discovery at the threshing floor	6-8
II. The agreement between Boaz and Ruth	9-13
A. Ruth claims Boaz for *gō'ēl* and future husband by the request that he cover her with his robe	9
B. The reaction of Boaz	10-13
1. Blessing upon Ruth because of her kindness (*ḥesed*)	10
2. Boaz swears to exercise the right of *gō'ēl* in the morning, if the next of kin foregoes his right	11-13
III. Ruth's departure	14-15

The catchwords of "threshing floor" and "lie down" continue in this section, that is also dominated by the term *g'l* (redeem, vindicate, perform the right of kinsman or *gō'ēl*), which occurs seven times in ch. 3.

Genre, Setting, Intention
This is a description of the manner in which Naomi's plan is realized. The pace of the narrative is fast until the moment that Boaz is surprised by Ruth's presence. Then the dialogue betrays his reaction and his determination to take action in the morning. At issue is the levirate marriage (Deut 25:5-10; cf. also Lev 25:5). Boaz is to exercise the right of *gō'ēl* and raise up seed and preserve the name for his dead relative. In Ruth's request that Boaz spread his garment *(knp)* there is an allusion to 2:12, the "wings" of the Lord under which she sought refuge. Boaz's

reply to Ruth in 2:11 is exactly the same as Ruth's reply to Naomi in 2:5. Würthwein is correct in saying that sexual intimacy is not envisioned in the episode: Ruth is praised for her *ḥesed*, and her claim that Boaz is her *gōʾēl* is the reason for her coming and her symbolic action. The ambiguity of her night visit is properly resolved by Boaz's concern to protect her reputation (v. 14). The use of "gate" in v. 11 ("all the gate of my people," or "all my fellow townsmen") is proleptic for ch. 4.

INTERLUDE: RUTH REPORTS TO NAOMI, 3:16-18

Structure

I. Naomi's tense question of Ruth	16a
II. Ruth's answer, singling out the gift of barley	16b-17
III. Naomi's analysis of the situation	18

Genre, Setting, Intention

This is a description of Naomi's reaction to the execution of her plan. To the anxious question, the author provides a summary answer and chooses to emphasize the gift of barley with the words of Boaz, "you must not go back to your mother-in-law empty-handed" (*rêqām*, the word used by Naomi to describe her "empty" situation in 1:21). This gesture of Boaz emerges as a kind of "hidden message" (Würthwein) to Naomi. The scene ends with tension, as is so often the case in this very short narrative: how will the next morning's affair be resolved?

REPORT OF THE TRANSACTION AT THE BETHLEHEM GATE, 4:1-12

Structure

I. Boaz takes the initiative at the gate	1-2
A. With the *gōʾēl*	1
B. With the witnesses, ten elders	2
II. Boaz discusses the redemption of Naomi's land with the *gōʾēl*	3-6
A. Boaz explains the right of the *gōʾēl* to redeem the land	3-4b
B. The *gōʾēl* agrees to redeem the land	4b
C. Boaz further points out that acquisition of land involves the acquisition of Ruth	5
D. The *gōʾēl* declines in favor of Boaz's right	6
III. The agreement between the two men is ratified	7-12
A. A historical note explaining the sandal exchange	7
B. Execution of the exchange ceremony	8
C. Boaz makes public his acquisition to elders and people as witnesses	9-10
D. The witnesses acknowledge the acquisition, and offer good wishes for posterity and prosperity	11-12

93

According to Dommershausen (405-7), the catchwords in this section are "gate" (occurring by way of anticipation in a phrase in 3:11), "redeem/redeemer" (g'l/gō'ēl), and "acquire" (qnh). There are several characteristic touches of the author in the narrative: the name of the gō'ēl is not even given (Mr. So-and-so, 4:1). Tension is achieved by the clever bargaining of Boaz: at first the gō'ēl chooses to exert his right to acquire Naomi's field, until Boaz plays his trump card: with the field goes Ruth as well. The gō'ēl declines because this would mean expending capital for property that legally belongs to Ruth's dead husband Mahlon.

Genre, Setting, Intention

This is a vivid REPORT of a transaction at the town gate. The author has brought his story to a neat and effective ending by joining two motifs, the redemption of land and levirate marriage. The note about the sandal exchange (v. 7) is designed to make the days of the judges (1:1) seem to belong to the distant past. The blessings invoked for Boaz are traditional: fertility of wife, prosperity and perpetuation of a name. This does not quite fit the case at hand, where Boaz will be perpetuating the name of the dead Mahlon. The reference to Tamar and Perez (Genesis 38) is a reference to a levirate marriage. (For this whole scene, see esp. E. F. Campbell, *Ruth*, 154-61.)

CONCLUSION: THE BIRTH OF A SON, 4:13-17

Structure

I. Note concerning birth of son to Boaz and Ruth	13
II. The bearing of this upon Naomi	14-17
A. The women extend good wishes to Naomi	14-15
B. Naomi's reaction	16
C. The women neighbors give the name	17

Genre, Setting, Intention

This is a record of the birth of a son, and the consequent reaction thereto. Due to the story line (a deliberate contrast with the Naomi of ch. 1), the emphasis is placed upon Naomi. She is portrayed in the ritual of adoption as she places the child on her bosom (v. 16), and the good wishes of the women (v. 14, "next of kin") refer to the catchword, gō'ēl, which this son now is. Just as Naomi's return home (šûb) was empty (1:20), now the child is described as "a restorer of life" (literally, "the one who brings home life"—mēšîb nepeš). The praise of Ruth in v. 15 also reflects back on 1:20, for Naomi did not return home empty; Ruth was with her, "better than seven sons." What was impossible (1:12-13) has turned out to be possible.

It is unusual for women neighbors to give the name to the child; normally it is done by the mother. And the name itself is suspect; one would have expected from the phrase in 4:17 (yullad ben lĕno'ŏmî, "a son is born to Naomi") a name that is derived from that phrase, and commentators have suggested Jibleam, Ben-Noam, etc. The presence of the name Obed seems to be a later addition, dependent upon the genealogical appendix which was added to the story of Ruth (compare vv. 17 and 22).

APPENDIX, 4:18-22

Structure

I. Genealogical formula, introducing the line of Perez   18a
II. The descendents of Perez, extending down through Obed
    to David   18b-22

Genre, Setting, Intention

This is a GENEALOGICAL LIST that agrees with 1 Chr 2:9-12. This genre is at first sight unusual in the book of Ruth, and it immediately becomes suspect when one recalls that the concern of the author was to show how Ruth became the mother of a child who was accounted to the dead Mahlon, son of Elimelech, whereas this genealogy deals with Boaz and goes back to Perez. Perhaps the mention of Perez in 4:12, even if in passing reference to a levirate marriage, served to justify the addition of the genealogy. Certainly, the identification of Boaz with the Boaz in the list of 1 Chronicles 2 is the reason for adding this list, and it probably also led to the insertion of the name of Obed in 4:17. The intention of this appendix is discussed above in the Introduction (under Intention).

Canticles
(Song of Songs)

Bibliography

W. F. Albright, "Archaic survivals in the text of Canticles," in *Hebrew and Semitic Studies* (ed. D. W. Thomas and W. D. McHardy; *Fest*. G. R. Driver; Oxford, 1963) 1-7; J. Angénieux, "Structure du Cantique des Cantiques," *ETL* 41 (1965) 96-142; J.-P. Audet, "Love and Marriage in the Old Testament," *Scr* 10 (1958) 65-83; idem, "Le sens du Cantique des Cantiques," *RB* 62 (1955) 197-221; J. C. Exum, "A Literary and Structural Analysis of the Song of Songs," *ZAW* 85 (1973) 47-79; G. Gerleman, *Das Hohelied* (BKAT XVIII/2-3; Neukirchen-Vluyn, 1965); A. Gonzalez, "El lenguaje de la naturaleza en el Cantar de los Cantares," in *Naturaleza, Historia Y Revelación* (Madrid, 1969) 321-62; R. Gordis, *The Song of Songs* (New York, 1954); F. Horst, "Die Formen des althebräischen Liebesliedes," in *Gottes Recht: Gesammelte Studien* (TBü 12; Munich, 1961) 176-87; L. Krinetzki, *Das Hohe Lied* (Düsseldorf, 1964); F. Landsberger, "Poetic Units Within the Song of Songs," *JBL* 73 (1954) 203-16; O. Loretz, "Das Hohelied," in *Gotteswort und menschliche Erfahrung* (Freiburg, 1963); idem, *Das althebräische Liebeslied* (AOAT, Studien zur althebräischen Poesie 1; Neukirchen-Vluyn, 1971); R. E. Murphy, "Form-Critical Studies in the Song of Songs," *Int* 27 (1973) 413-22; idem, "Towards a Commentary on the Song of Songs," *CBQ* 39 (1977) 482-96; M. Pope, *Song of Songs* (AB 7C; New York, 1977); H. Ringgren, *Das Hohe Lied* (ATD XVI/2; Göttingen, 1958) 1-37; A. Robert, A. Feuillet, and R. Tournay, *Le Cantique des Cantiques* (EBib; Paris, 1963); W. Rudolph, *Das Hohe Lied* (KAT XVII/2; Gütersloh, 1962) 77-186; H. Schmökel, *Heilige Hochzeit und Hoheslied* (Wiesbaden, 1956); M. Segal, "The Song of Songs," *VT* 12 (1962) 470-90; R. N. Soulen, "The *Waṣfs* of the Song of Songs and Hermeneutic," *JBL* 88 (1967) 183-90; W. Staerk, "Das Hohelied," in SAT III,1 (Göttingen, 1911) 291-306; M. A. van den Oudenrijn, *Het Hooglied* (BOuT 8/3, Roermond, 1962); John B. White, *A Study of the Language of Love in the Song of Songs and Ancient Egyptian Poetry* (SBLDS 38; Missoula, 1978); E. Würthwein, *Die Fünf Megilloth* (HAT 18, 2nd ed., Tübingen, 1969) 25-71.

For ancient Near Eastern parallels, the following have been consulted: J. Cooper, "New Cuneiform Parallels to the Song of Songs," *JBL* 90 (1971) 157-62; M. Held, "A Faithful Lover in an Old Babylonian Dialogue," *JCS* 15 (1961) 1-16; A. Hermann, *Altägyptische Liebesdichtung* (Wiesbaden, 1959); W. Herrmann, "Gedanken zur Geschichte des altorientalischen Beschreibungsliedes," *ZAW* 75 (1963) 176-96; S. N. Kramer, *The Sacred Marriage Rite* (Bloomington, Ind., 1969); S. Schott, *Altägyptische Liebeslieder* (Zürich, 1950); W. K. Simpson, *The Literature of Ancient Egypt* (New Haven, 1972); R. Tournay, "Les parallèles non-bibliques," in the commentary of Robert, Feuillet, and Tournay (see above), 339-426.

The Book as a Whole

Structure

The positions concerning the structure of Canticles (leaving aside the question of its being a "drama") are clear and they are twofold. Either the eight chapters as they stand are a unit, composed of a relatively small number of poems, or the chapters are an anthology of disparate poems (even of a verse in length) that have been assembled with only the slightest unity. On both sides there are difficulties. There is no agreement among the experts concerning the demarcation of the units that constitute the whole work (e.g., Angénieux, 8; Exum, 6; Robert, 5; etc.). On the other hand, those who recognize that Canticles is basically an anthology of love lyrics (the predominant view today) do not agree as to the number of poems that have been collected in the loose unity of the eight chapters.

Arguments have been advanced in support of these opposing views. Many rely upon "logical" analysis, or the development of thought. This may often seem less than compelling, but frequently it is inevitable. The reader can test this by considering the example of 8:5-11, which should probably be broken up into the following units: vv. 5, 6-7, 8-10, 11-12, 13-14. There is no intrinsic connection between these lines, and such a phenomenon occurs many times throughout the eight chapters. Thus, the description of the parade of Solomon and his entourage (3:6-11) does not seem to have anything to do with the man's description of the physical beauty of the woman in 4:1ff. The longest unit proposed in the analysis below is 5:2–6:3, and even here the unity may seem contrived.

In favor of the recognition of Canticles as a unit is the presence of refrains and repetitions. These can be best seen in the following block (adapted from Loretz, 60):

	1	2	3	4	5	6	7	8
I. Daughters of Jerusalem	1:5a	2:7a (=III)	3:5 (=III)		5:8b, 16d			8:4b (=III)
II. Embrace		2:6						8:3
III. Adjuration		2:7	3:5					8:4
IV. Mutual Possession		2:16				6:3	7:11 (*RSV* 10)	
V. Mountain		2:17		4:6				
VI. Eat, friends					5:1e-f			
VII. Turn, gazelle		2:9a-b 17 (=V)						8:14
VIII. Mountain/hill				4:6 (=V)				

Angénieux (pp. 96-142) has attempted to analyze the whole into eight poems, with the help of primary refrains (e.g., the adjuration), the secondary refrains (e.g., "how beautiful," 1:15; 4:1, 7; 7:7 [*RSV* 6]), but the result is a very hypothetical reconstitution of the poem. The efforts of J. C. Exum have greater respect for the text, but the arguments are not really convincing. The primary difficulty is that the refrains do not yield a significant pattern. Even if they are editorial insertions, it is not clear how they bond the unity of the whole. On the other hand, the atomization of the work into the smallest units (e.g., Landsberger, 202-16) is to be avoided. There seems to be no doubt that several catchwords connect various poems, and these are pointed out in the analysis below. While the entire eight chapters do not give the impression of deriving from one hand, or of being written to form a unified work, it must be admitted that there is a remarkable homogeneity and a puzzling number of repetitions that seem to be signs of an effort to strive for unity.

The interpretation of Canticles as a drama labors under the difficulties of both of the above theories, in addition to the fact that very arbitrary stage instructions have to be supplied by the proponents of this view. The genre of drama does not seem to have been known to the Hebrews. Canticles is a dialogue, but not a drama; it lacks any real conflict. The dialogical character was recognized as long ago as the Codex Sinaiticus (ca. A.D. 400), in which the terms "bride" and "bridegroom" were supplied by a copyist to delineate the course of the dialogue. But it is not always easy to determine who the speaker is. The most difficult passages in this respect are: 1:2-4 (note the puzzling change of persons); 1:7-8 (contrast *NAB* with *NEB*); 2:7 (which some, like *NEB*, attribute to the man); 2:15 (=3:4; 8:4, which some, like *NEB*, attribute to the companions; cf. also 3:6-11); 6:10; 6:11-12 (by the man or by the woman?); 7:1-6 (*RSV* 6:13–7:5); 8:5a; 8:6-7 (by the woman, yet *NEB* attributes this to the man). The commentaries should be consulted for various opinions.

The following structure of Canticles is proposed for this study. It is based upon the recognition of various genres which succeed each other, changes in the identity of the speaker, the appearance of refrains, and the abrupt transitions which appear within the body of the work. These details will be pointed out in the analysis of the individual units.

I.	Superscription	1:1
II.	Love's desires	1:2-4
III.	Black but beautiful	1:5-6
IV.	An inquiry	1:7-8
V.	Song of admiration, by the man	1:9-11
VI.	Song of admiration, by the woman	1:12-14
VII.	Song of admiration, in dialogue	1:15-17
VIII.	Song of admiration, in dialogue	2:1-3
IX.	Love sickness	2:4-7
X.	Invitation to the tryst in the spring	2:8-13
XI.	Tease	2:14-15
XII.	Invitation	2:16-17
XIII.	The beloved seeks and finds her lover	3:1-5

Genre

The commonly accepted view is that Canticles is made up of lyric love poems or songs (for practical purposes, poem and song are interchangeable). The eight chapters may be called an anthology, but this term prejudges the structure (see above) as a collection rather than as a unity. The term "love song" is more of a general category than a specific genre. Within this category the following genres, based primarily upon the basic study of F. Horst, should be noted: SONG OF YEARNING; SELF-DESCRIPTION; the TEASE; ADMIRATION SONG; DESCRIPTION OF AN EXPERIENCE; DESCRIPTIVE SONG or *waṣf*, a description of the physical charms of the loved one; BOAST (e.g., 6:8-10; 8:11-12).

The validity of these various genres of love songs rests upon the analysis of the content, but it also receives strong support from similar Egyptian poems which date in the main from a period of a few centuries before the conquest. There are four substantial collections. The Chester Beatty I Papyri (late Ramesside period, ca. 12th century B.C.) contain seven "Songs of the Great Joy of the Heart," in which the speaking roles alternate between a man and a woman, and three "wishes." The Papyrus Harris 500 (end of the Amarna period, ca. 14th century B.C.) features a collection of eight poems, and a group of eight more entitled "Beginning of the pretty and joyous songs for your beloved when she returns from the fields," and also three "flower songs." The Turin Papyrus (a cycle written down in the 20th Dynasty, ca. 1100 B.C.) has three "tree" poems. Finally, Ostracon 25218 of the Cairo Museum (18th-19th Dynasties, ca. 1400?) contains ten short poems, mostly love poems from the point of view of the man. The most extensive English translations are to be found in Simpson.

Like Canticles, all of these poems are anonymous; the attribution of Canticles to Solomon at the time of editing is due, among other reasons, to the presence of his name in 1:5; 3:7, 9, 11; 8:11. Again like Canticles, the Egyptian poems present dialogues between the lover and beloved. Even more importantly, they illustrate the *atmosphere* which is found in Canticles: gardens, animals, fruits, flowers, perfumes, trees. The study of A. Hermann *(Altägyptische Liebesdichtung)* has pointed out the literary fictions or TRAVESTIES that are characteristic of this kind of literature in the ancient and the modern world. There is the "knight" fiction, whereby the lover assumes a role above the social class to which he normally belongs. Thus, the man is compared to a "king's agent" (Simpson, 321), or to the falcon, the royal bird of Egypt; the woman is garbed in "royal linen" (Simpson, 298, 310). The "servant" fiction corresponds to the figure of the shepherd in western literature. In Egypt this is expressed by the man's wish to be the doorkeeper at the girl's house (Simpson, 300), or to be her maid, washerman, or even (cf. Cant 8:6) the seal ring on her hand (Simpson, 311). The "shepherd" fiction is manifest in the guises assumed by the woman as a bird-catcher or one who fishes (Simpson, 302, 310). In a similar way one must understand the portrayal of the man in Canticles as king and as shepherd. This literary fiction represents the human desire to occupy another and different role, while at the same time remaining one's self; it is characteristic of the "make-believe" language of love. The following list is representative (not exhaustive) of the many literary topoi which occur both in Canticles and the Egyptian love songs (the page reference is to Simpson):

1. *Wasf*, or description of the physical charms of the one loved (Cant 4:1-7; 7:1-5 [*RSV* 6:13-7:4]; 5:10-16; cf. pp. 299, 316).

2. The one loved is unique (Cant 6:9; "fairest among women" in 1:8; 6:1; cf. pp. 305, 315-16).

3. Love sickness (2:5; cf. pp. 300, 316, 320).

4. Kissing in public (8:2; cf. p. 320).

5. The name (1:3; cf. p. 321).

6. Gazelle (2:9, 17; 8:14; cf. p. 322).

7. Captivation by the hair and eyes of the beloved (7:5; 4:9; 6:5; cf. pp. 324, 309).

8. A tease at the door (5:3; cf. p. 325).

9. Love under the trees (1:15-17; cf. pp. 312-15).

10. Voice of the dove (2:12; cf. p. 304).

11. Embrace (2:6; 8:3; cf. pp. 304, 309-11).

12. Sister and brother terminology (4:9-12; cf. pp. 301-3 and passim).

13. Obstacles to love (8:7; cf. p. 310).

14. Voice of the one loved (2:14; 8:14; cf. p. 309).

15. Breasts of the female (7:7-8 [*RSV* 7:6-7]; cf. pp. 298-99).

From the Egyptian poetry we learn something of the nature of the love language current in the ancient Near East—the genres and topoi that were common—and this is a valuable insight into the style, language, and genres of Canticles. It seems reasonable to assume that the earlier love poetry of Egypt had some influence upon the love songs that came to be assembled in Canticles. But it would be an exaggeration to claim, with Gerleman (pp. 69-71), that the influence is so far-reaching that the *"wasf"* or descriptive poem is a reflection of the pictorial art of Egypt.

The Mesopotamian literature has not been as helpful for Canticles as the literature of Egypt. Only the two publications of Cooper and Held deal with love between two humans. However, there is a considerable literature concerning the sacred marriage rites (Tammuz-Ishtar cult), and alleged parallels have been pointed out especially by H. Schmökel and S. N. Kramer. The so-called cultic interpretation claims that Canticles is dependent upon the Tammuz-Ishtar rites. This view is losing ground, and it raises more problems than it solves (cf. the judgment of E. Würthwein, 30). It is reasonable to suppose that there was mutual influence between the love language of ancient Israel and that of the pagan fertility rites with which Israel was often involved, but there is no evidence that portions of Canticles were originally composed for or modelled upon these rites.

Throughout the analysis below, care has been taken to point out the salient stylistic features of Canticles—an item which more recent commentators (Gerleman and especially Krinetzki) have well illustrated. A question relating indirectly to genre still remains. Are the poems in Canticles "popular," or are they the work of (a) sophisticated author(s)? Opinion on this is divided. To attribute the poems wholesale to an unknown *Volkspoesie*, or folk poetry, seems to neglect the fact that we are dealing with highly sophisticated poetry. The wealth of symbolism, the large number of hapax legomena, and the high literary quality would suggest that this is *Kunstdichtung*, poetry produced by an educated class. Not much more can be said, for we have as yet no clear criteria for judging and factoring out "popular" from "artistic" poetry.

Setting

Two different settings are immediately obvious: the original setting that the various poems would have had before they were collected and assembled into the loose unity of the eight chapters of Canticles, and the setting within the final work, the setting that emerged when they were made into the "Song of Songs." Roughly, these two steps correspond to the *oral* (even if in these periods some of the songs were written down) and the *literary* (when the whole was edited as literature) stages of the work.

1. Original setting. Many commentators have claimed that the original setting for several if not most of the poems is a marriage feast. Würthwein holds that twenty-four of the thirty-nine units into which he divides Canticles certainly refer to aspects of an Israelite wedding. Krinetzki recognizes almost as many, although he holds that no marriage ritual is present here, and he finds many love songs. W. Rudolph is more cautious: some units refer to marriage (e.g., 3:6-11 refers to a wedding procession), but others need not have such a reference. On the other hand, Gerleman takes a firm position and rules out altogether the setting of marriage, and argues that we are dealing with love songs that simply extol love between the sexes. The position of Rudolph seems to be the most reasonable. The *sole* reference to marriage in Canticles is in 3:6, and the rest of the poems are equally possible outside such a presumed setting. They are love poems which can be uttered in the innumerable settings which are associated with the relationship of lovers.

2. The setting of the book. Once these poems became literature and were edited as "the Song of Songs by Solomon," a new setting is indicated. The title suggests that these chapters were attributed to Solomon in the spirit of the description of his multitudinous harem (1 Kgs 11:3). J.-P. Audet ("Love and Marriage," 80-83), has proposed that the new setting is the work of postexilic sages who recognized here a betrothal song (to which they added 8:6b-7), which deserved to be preserved because of the lessons of mutual love and fidelity that it inculcated.

Intention

From what has already been said above, the primary intention of Canticles deals with human sexual love—the experience of it, its delights, and its power. It is an expansion of the wonder perceived in Prov 30:19, "the way of a man with a maiden," and expressed also in Prov 5:18-19. The text itself offers no basis for the traditional Jewish and Christian interpretation (influenced by the prophetic marriage theme, as in Hosea 1–3) which recognized here the marriage relationship between the Lord and his people, or Christ and the church, whether by way of parable or allegory (see the treatment in the valuable commentary of A. Robert). It would be extravagant, however, to claim that the literal historical sense exhausts the meaning of Canticles. The history of interpretation in both Jewish and Christian traditions shows that the communities in which the book was received found other levels of meaning.

CHAPTER 2
THE INDIVIDUAL UNITS

SUPERSCRIPTION, 1:1

Structure

I. Title	1:1a
II. Claim of Solomonic authorship	1:1b

Genre, Setting, Intention

"The Song of Songs," an idiomatic expression for the superlative in Hebrew ("the greatest song"), is clearly an editorial title given to this work. The ascription of the work "to" (*lamed* of authorship) Solomon is in accord with the tradition of the literary activity and wisdom of that king (1 Kgs 4:29-34). The designation of "song" *(šîr)* is only a very general and superficial indication of genre, but it serves to give a certain unity to the eight chapters as a whole. The unity which the editors tried to ensure is helped by the ascription to Solomon, whose name occurs in 1:5(?); 3:7-11; and 8:11-12.

Could there have been an original title that was lost by the addition of this rubric of "Song of Songs"? J.-P. Audet ("Love and Marriage," 81-82) has argued that the superscription is "appreciative" and therefore derives from the editor, not from the author. He has suggested a title, "Song of the Kiss of the Betrothed," based upon the opening words ("let him kiss me . . ."). It should be noted that many of the collections of Egyptian love songs have been provided with titles, such as "the beginning of the songs of excellent enjoyment" and "beginning of the songs of entertainment" and "the beginning of the songs of extreme happiness" (cf. Simpson, 302, 308, 315).

What does such an editorial superscription mean for these eight chapters? Whatever may have been the history of the preliterary stage of this poetry, it is now put forth as a unity (or "song") and associated with Solomon.

LOVE'S DESIRES, 1:2-4

Structure

I. The beloved expresses her yearning	1:2-4aα
A. The beloved desires to receive her lover's kisses	2a
B. Reasons for the desire	2b-3
1. His love better than wine	2b
2. His fragrance	3aα
3. His person ("name")	3aβ
4. Conclusion: hence the maidens love him	3b

C. An appeal to him to draw her to himself   4aα
II. An interjection (by the daughters of Jerusalem) indicating
    a resolve to pursue him   4aβ
III. The beloved acknowledges that he (the king) has brought
    her to his chamber   4bα
IV. An interjection (by the daughters of Jerusalem) expressing
    joy in and adulation of the lover   4bβ

Although the structure is doubtful because of the bewildering change of persons speaking in the dialogue, the length of the unit is assured by the new theme in 1:5-6, and the inclusion (*'ăhēbûkā* ["they love you"]) in vv. 3 and 4. Many commentators (Würthwein, Rudolph, Loretz) interpret the plural forms in v. 4 as referring to the man and woman ("let us run") or to the man ("we will rejoice"). Gerleman attributes some lines to the "poet," a very hypothetical approach.

Note the play on words in v. 3, *šemen* . . . *šĕmekā* ("your name is [like] oil") Assonance and alliteration are striking features of all eight chapters and have been worked out in detail by L. Krinetzki. In this section there are several repetitions: *ṭôbîm* ("better," "fragrant"); "your love" compared to "wine" (cf. 4:10).

Genre
With Horst (pp. 185-86) and many others, this unit is to be characterized as a SONG OF YEARNING; motifs from the ADMIRATION SONG (comparisons with wine, oil) also appear.

Setting
Because of the reference in v. 4 to the king's bringing the woman to his chambers (either as statement of fact as in the MT, or as an imperative as in the LXX), it has been suggested that the setting is marriage (Staerk, 294), when the bride is brought to the home of the bridegroom (Krinetzki, Würthwein), and the plural forms would indicate that wedding guests participate in the dialogue. There may be an allusion to the bride's coming to the groom's house, but this is not sufficient to determine a particular setting.

The "king" is the lover, and such a designation derives from the well-known literary fiction according to which he is acclaimed as king, shepherd, etc. (cf. Hermann, *Altägyptische Liebesdichtung*, 111ff.).

Intention
The poem expresses woman's longing for her lover. This feeling is heightened by the admiration and love which others feel for him, and by the affirmation of the excellence of his person and his love.

BLACK BUT BEAUTIFUL, 1:5-6

Structure
I. The beloved affirms her beauty to the daughters of
   Jerusalem   5

II. She prohibits their staring at her blackness	6aα
III. She explains the reasons for her blackness	6aβ-6b
A. The sun has burned her	6aβ
B. Her brothers appointed her caretaker of the vineyards but she has not cared for her own vineyard	6b

The structure is governed by the play on the word *šḥr/šḥrḥrt* ("dark," "swarthy") that gives an inner unity to the lines. For the first time the "daughters of Jerusalem" are explicitly introduced. They serve as a foil to the girl in the development of the dialogue (cf. 5:9; 6:1). There is an important wordplay on *kĕrāmîm* ("vineyards") in v. 6. Although a caretaker of vineyards, she has neglected her own vineyard, which is herself. That is why she is burnt, but there is also the implication that "her own vineyard" is hers to dispose of, despite her overanxious brothers (cf. 8:8-9), and that she belongs to her lover (cf. 1:14; 2:15; 7:13 [*RSV* 12]; 8:11-12 for vineyard). The MT reading of "Solomon" instead of "Salma" (a bedouin tribe known from Nabatean inscriptions) in v. 5 is due to the traditional understanding of the work as associated with Solomon. The chiastic structures in vv. 5-6 should be noted.

Genre
Although this is basically a SELF-DESCRIPTION (Horst, 182), it is also a justification and defense of herself that the beloved offers to the daughters of Jerusalem. The reason given in v. 6 provides the opportunity for broadening the self-description into the perspective of the entire work in which the girl is the "vineyard" of her lover.

Setting
The positioning of this piece at the beginning of the work seems to be deliberate: the daughters are introduced, the theme of the vineyard appears for the first time, and the mention of the brothers finds a sort of *inclusio* in 8:8. There is not enough evidence to postulate an original setting in marriage celebration, as is done by Krinetzki and Würthwein. Rudolph derives the poem from conflict between a peasant girl and city maidens over the issue of color. The situation seems to be a contrived one, not a real setting, that is reminiscent of the Cinderella motif (Gerleman).

Intention
The beloved claims that she is beautiful and defends her claim, at the same time that she hints that she is reserved for her lover.

AN INQUIRY, 1:7-8

Text
Read with the LXX and OL "one who wanders" in v. 7 in place of "one who is veiled."

Structure

I. The girl requests of the shepherd (=lover) knowledge as to his whereabouts	7a

II. The reason for the request: lest she miss him   7b
III. The reply of the lover: follow the tracks of the flock   8

A repetition frequent in Canticles occurs here: "whom my soul loves" (e.g., 3:1, 3), and "where" ('*êkâ*) is repeated twice. "Follow" (*sĕ'î*) resembles "flock" (*ṣō'n*), and "pasture" (*rĕ'î*) resembles "shepherds" (*rō'îm*). Not all agree that the lover replies in v. 8; according to Krinetzki the words belong to the bridegroom's companions; Gerleman ascribes them to the poet.

Genre

This dialogue illustrates the genre of teasing which is characteristic of the language of lovers (so Horst, 183-84, and Staerk, 305). The TEASE consists in his reply to her—that she should pursue the way she feared to pursue. The underlying motif is the presence/absence of the one who is loved.

Setting and Intention

As with 1:5-6, the positioning of these verses near the beginning seems deliberate. The fiction of the lover as "shepherd" (cf. "king" in 1:4) is introduced and the ever recurring theme of presence/absence makes its first appearance. The shepherd motif is comparable to that of the king (1:4); it is poetic fiction, and not to be considered as pointing to a given setting. Moreover, teasing is frequent enough among lovers in all situations.

The text bespeaks the understanding and love that binds the man and the woman, and it underlines her need to know where he is, in order to enjoy his presence.

SONG OF ADMIRATION, BY THE MAN, 1:9-11

Structure

I. The lover compares the beloved to Pharaoh's steed   9
II. The reasons for comparison: cheeks and neck are adorned   10
III. The lover declares he will provide more ornaments   11

Both Loretz and Rudolph take vv. 9-17 as a unit in which the lovers express their admiration of, and joy in each other.

Genre

This is an ADMIRATION SONG (*Bewunderungslied*, Horst, 176), rather than a mere description. The accent is on her adornment, not upon her physical parts, which are the object of a *waṣf*, or description. However, descriptions and admiration songs differ only slightly from each other; admiration is never absent from description.

Setting and Intention

Such a song could fit many situations in which lovers find themselves. The extravagance of the finery (royal steeds, jewels, etc.) is in the mood of a lover's imaginative description, and it also fits into the king fiction—he will provide her with more precious adornments. The intention of the text is to express admiration of the woman, resplendent in her finery.

SONG OF ADMIRATION, BY THE WOMAN, 1:12-14

Structure
I. Indication of place: the king's "couch" or table   12a
II. The woman makes comparisons with nard, myrrh, and
     henna, in praise of her lover's fragrance   12b-14

The repetitions (*dôdî lî*, "my beloved to me" in vv. 13-14) are striking; they are repetitions, not refrains. Nearly all commentators understand "my nard" (v. 12) as referring to the girl's scent, although the poem goes on to speak of the man's fragrance. The fragrance of the one who is loved is an acknowledged topos in love poetry.

Genre, Setting, Intention
Compare the remarks on 1:9-11; here, too, is another ADMIRATION SONG, but now on the lips of the woman. Although Krinetzki separates v. 12 from vv. 13-14, he characterizes them as possibly in the genre of "table-song," specifically at the wedding feast. However, *bimĕsibbô* ("on his couch") is a very obscure reference. Krinetzki points out the beautiful assonance in these lines: *m, n, r,* in v. 12, and *m, n, l, d,* in vv. 13-14. The text expresses the beloved's admiration for her lover—his presence and delight—in metaphors that suggest fragrance and tenderness.

A SONG OF ADMIRATION, IN DIALOGUE, 1:15-17

Structure
I. The lover acclaims the beauty of the beloved   15
II. In return, the beloved returns the compliment to her lover   16a
III. The beloved describes their rustic trysting place   16b-17

Verse 15 is repeated in 4:1, where it begins a description of the physical beauty of the beloved. "Behold you are beautiful" is uttered twice by the man, and she picks it up (v. 16) to return him the compliment.

Genre, Setting, Intention
The genre is the same as in vv. 12-14, an ADMIRATION SONG, except that this is a dialogue of mutual admiration. It is not easy to see how the description of their trysting place fits into the dialogue, except that it does give the concrete setting. It should be noted that frequently there are specifications of time and place throughout the entire book. Horst (p. 177) sees the second part of an admiration song as dealing with the "effects" of the beauty that is admired. Thus one is led to express a wish for union or joy over union; he refers explicitly to 1:17, 16b *(sic)*.

A SONG OF ADMIRATION, IN DIALOGUE, 2:1-3

Structure

I. The woman describes herself in flower metaphors	1
II. The lover heightens this description by referring to her uniqueness	2
III. She returns the compliment to him	3a
IV. She records her delight in his presence	3b

The entire unit is set in a striking chiasmus: statement, comparison, comparison, statement (vv. 1, 2, 3a, 3b). In 2:2 the man takes up the woman's metaphor (cf. 1:15-16) of the lily.

Genre, Setting, Intention

This is an ADMIRATION SONG (Horst, 176, Würthwein, Gerleman) in dialogue form (cf. 1:15-16). The dialogue (which incorporates a "self-description" in v. 1) ends on the note of her yearning for him (v. 3). It is suitable for almost any meeting of lovers. The text begins with a coquettish tone (so Gerleman): the girl is just one among many; then the feeling intensifies as the comparisons make each of them unique in each other's eyes.

LOVESICKNESS, 2:4-7

Structure

I. The beloved records a rendezvous ("banqueting house") with her lover	4
II. Because of lovesickness, she gives orders (to many) for sustenance	5
III. She describes her lover's embrace, which apparently serves to sustain her	6
IV. She adjures the daughters of Jerusalem concerning love	7

Verse 6 is better understood as a statement (*NAB, NEB*) than as a wish (*RSV*). There is no agreement concerning the identity of the speaker(s) of v. 7, nor of the meaning of *'ahăbâ* (love? lover?) in this verse. Vv. 6-7 form the most striking refrain in the work, being repeated in 8:3-4. The adjuration (v. 7) appears in 3:5 (cf. 5:8!). Rudolph and Gerleman see *tappûaḥ* ("apple[tree]") as the catchword uniting this section with the previous unit (vv. 3, 5).

Genre, Setting, Intention

This section is difficult to classify. Horst (p. 185) recognizes a SONG OF YEARNING in vv. 4-5. This seems to be a song about love and its delights, from the point of view of the effects (lovesickness) and its nature ("do not stir up"). It is attached to no particular setting; lovesickness is a fairly universal phenomenon (in Egyptian songs, cf. Simpson, 316, 320). Würthwein overreaches himself in detailing the setting. This is supposedly the wedding day: the "house of wine" or banqueting house points to the marriage feast, and sexual union is allegedly indicated in v. 6. The wedding companions are the ones who adjure the daughters not to disturb the lovers. While such a setting can make sense, it is merely one of several possible settings which can be hypothesized for these lines, such as Gerleman's suggestion of a rendezvous in the wine-house.

AN INVITATION TO A TRYST IN THE SPRING, 2:8-13

Structure

I. The beloved describes the approach and presence of the beloved at her window		8-9
II. The lover addresses the beloved		10-13
A. Introduction		10a
B. Invitation to depart with the lover		10b
C. Description of spring (which serves as a motivation for her leaving with him)		11-13a
D. A reprise of the invitation		13b

Both Loretz and Würthwein include v. 14 in this poem, presumably because of the emphasis on singing in vv. 10-13. There is a clear *inclusio* in vv. 10b and 13b. "Gazelle" and "hind" serve as catchwords to associate this section with the previous unit (vv. 9a and 7a). V. 9a is echoed in part in v. 17. The chiasmus with "face" and "voice" in v. 14 is striking.

Genre, Setting, Intention

It is difficult to determine the genre of this unit. It begins as a DESCRIPTION OF AN EXPERIENCE (*Erlebnisschilderung*, Horst, 184) that issues in an invitation—and perhaps the invitation should determine the whole unit. Horst (p. 186) classifies vv. 10-13 as a song of yearning in which the "spring song" (vv. 10b-13) provides the motivation for the yearning. Würthwein understands vv. 10b-14 as a *Werbelied*, or courtship song, in the concrete setting of a spring feast, replete with singing (vv. 12, 14). Gerleman compares the unit to the *Türklage (Paraklausithyron)*, or "complaint at the door" of the beloved, but he is forced to admit that the poem does not issue in a complaint!

A TEASE, 2:14-15

Structure

I. The lover invites the beloved, who is apparently inaccessible, to reveal her presence and let her voice be heard	14
II. She responds with a song about the little foxes	15

Although some commentators treat the enigmatic v. 15 as an independent unit (Horst, 179: "an allegorical song"; Krinetzki, Würthwein), it seems less enigmatic if one takes it as a reply to the lover's request in v. 14. The catchword, joining this with the previous section, is *sĕmādar* ("blossom," vv. 13, 15). Albright (pp. 2-3) calls attention to the repetitive parallelism of the single-word type in v. 15.

Genre, Setting, Intention

If the above understanding of these verses is correct, they may be classified as a TEASE (*Scherzgespräch*). The dialogue is built around the theme of presence: she reveals herself to him in answer to his request. But the reply is a coquettish one. It cannot refer to real foxes and vineyards. Rather, it is an allegory, in which the foxes are the young men who lay siege to the women (the metaphor of the vineyard again; cf. 1:6). The fact that "catch us" is both spoken by and addressed to a plurality suggests that the verse may be a line from a song or a ditty.

AN INVITATION, 2:16-17

Structure

I. The beloved proclaims the formula of mutual possession   16
II. Yearning, she invites him to hasten to the mountains
   (=herself)   17

Genre, Setting, Intention

The genre of this small unit is indicated by the invitation, which indicates a SONG OF YEARNING (Horst, 186), and it is in such a vein that the cry of mutual possession (v. 16) should be understood. This formula occurs with slight variations in 6:3 and 7:11. It is clear from v. 17 that the lover is absent, and she yearns for his presence and invites him, in language of poetic symbolism (cf. 2:9a), to come to enjoy herself. The comparison to the gazelle is found also in the Chester Beatty Cycle of Three Songs (Simpson, 322). Once again, the theme of presense/absence is at the heart of the feeling that is expressed. The words are appropriate for any situation in which lovers find themselves parted from each other.

THE BELOVED SEEKS AND FINDS HER LOVER, 3:1-5

Structure

I. The woman describes a search by night for her lover   1-4
  A. A search at night, and failure to find him   1
  B. A search for him in the city   2-4
    1. The resolve to search for him   2a
    2. Failure of the effort   2b
    3. Encounter with the city watchmen   3a
    4. Her interrogation of the watchmen concerning her
      lover   3b
    5. Discovery, and return with the lover to her
      mother's house   4
II. Adjuration to the daughters of Jerusalem about love
  (=2:7; cf. 5:8)   5

The frequent repetitions should be noted: seek and find, four times; "whom my soul loves," four times. There is an "ironic contrast" (Exum, 56) between the woman's failure to "find" the man and the fact that the watchmen "find" her.

Genre, Setting, and Intention

This is a DESCRIPTION OF AN EXPERIENCE (*Erlebnisschilderung*, Horst, 194), similar to 5:2-6, in which the theme of the absence and presence of the lover is celebrated. Commentators (e.g., Würthwein, Rudolph, Krinetzki) generally interpret the section as a dream of the beloved. Exum (pp. 56-59) subsumes 3:1-5 under the motif of seeking and finding (cf. 5:6–6:3) and as part of a larger unit (2:7–3:5), but such a structure seems to disregard form-critical considerations. The eventual discovery of the lover blends with the aphoristic saying about love in v. 6 (refrain; cf. 2:7). The story of the dream illustrates the intensity of the woman's love and the necessity of the presence of her lover.

A WEDDING PROCESSION, 3:6-11

Structure

I. The procession of Solomon's litter	6-8
A. Announcement of the procession	6aα
B. Description of the procession	6aβ-6b
C. Identification of the procession: Solomon's litter	7aα
D. Description of the "mighty men" accompanying the procession	7aβ-8
II. The procession of Solomon's palanquin	9-10
III. Invitation to daughters to gaze upon King Solomon on his wedding day	11

Although Gerleman separates vv. 6-8 (the "princess") from vv. 9-11 (the "king"), he admits that these verses have been deliberately put together. They are spoken by no character in particular, perhaps by the "poet," the author himself (Rudolph, Gerleman). The threefold repetition of Solomon's name (vv. 7, 9, 11; "king" occurs twice) is noteworthy, and there are other minor repetitions ('*śh* ["made"] vv. 9-10; "mighty men," v. 7; "day," v. 11).

Genre, Setting, Intention

Horst (p. 182) regards vv. 6-11 as a mixed genre of DESCRIPTIVE and ADMIRATION SONGS. The only clear reference to marriage in the entire work is in v. 11. The setting clearly is a wedding procession (perhaps as the bride is brought to her new home? so Würthwein, Staerk [p. 294], Rudolph, Loretz, Krinetzki). The mention of Solomon, within the context of the entire poem, is to be interpreted in line with the king fiction (cf. 1:4, 12; 6:8-9; 7:5 [*RSV* 4]). The song captures the glory and celebration of a wedding procession.

THE BEAUTY OF THE BELOVED, 4:1-7

Structure

I. Introduction (cf. 1:15): acclamation of her beauty	1aα
II. Description of parts of the body	1aβ-5
A. Eyes	1aβ
B. Hair	1b
C. Teeth	2
D. Lips	3a

This unit is clearly separate from the description of "King Solomon" and his entourage in the previous verses. It finds a suitable ending in the inclusion (v. 7; cf. v. 1), and before the invitation which begins v. 8. The sequence in the description of the body is from the top down. V. 6 is not properly part of the description. It is a repetition (or refrain?) that is found partially in 2:17 (cf. 2:9). There is a play on words in *šklm* and *šklh* ("all of which," "bereaved") of 4:2.

Genre

This is a description of the physical beauty of one's beloved. Such a description, which enumerates parts of the body in sequence, has become known by the Arabic term *waṣf*. It has a long history in the Near East, and especially within Hebrew culture, as shown by the recently discovered Genesis Apocryphon (cf. W. Herrmann, "Gedanken"). The genre can be used by the lover of his beloved as here and in 6:4-7, or by the girl in reference· to the lover, 5:10-16; see also 7:1-6 (*RSV* 6:13–7:5).

Setting

There is no one setting for this kind of description. All that is needed is the love and admiration on the part of a lover. Within Canticles these descriptions provided motivation for the mutual love of the man and the woman.

Intention

The *waṣf* is clearly direct praise of the physical beauty of another person. Are the images to be taken as presentational or representational? R. N. Soulen has argued in favor of understanding them as presentational, i.e., they convey the subjective delight of the spectator, the effect of the vision, and hence do not represent what is seen. But this seems to imply that *any* pleasurable comparison would do; on this premise, the teeth could be just as easily compared to the pomegranate halves (v. 3, where they refer to cheeks) as to the washed lambs (v. 2). These figures of speech seem to have a representational quality as well as the presentational, even if these comparisons are strange to Western taste.

AN INVITATION, 4:8

Structure

  I. The lover invites the beloved to come to him from
      Lebanon   8a
  II. A description of the inaccessible places she inhabits   8b

Most commentators separate this verse from the preceding description and the following song of admiration, perhaps as a fragment of a larger piece. Gerleman points out the catchwords: "Lebanon" (vv. 11, 15). In addition, *lĕbônâ* ("frankincense") in vv. 6 and 14 sounds like "Lebanon," and the *libbabtinî* ("you have ravished my heart," twice in v. 9) is also similar. The term *kallâ* ("bride") is another catchword (vv. 8-12).

Genre, Setting, Intention

Horst (p. 186) regards this verse as a SONG OF YEARNING, in which the reason for the yearning has fallen away. No setting can be specified, but the emphasis seems to be on the inaccessible place in which she finds herself; the reference to Lebanon, etc. would thus be metaphorical. This is a topos in love poetry; the loved one is frequently to be found in a place difficult of access (cf. 2:8, and the Cairo Ostracon 25218, in which the lover is separated from the beloved by a crocodile [Simpson, 310]).

SONG OF ADMIRATION, 4:9–5:1

Structure

I. The lover describes the effect the beloved has upon him	4:9
II. The lover expresses his admiration of her	10-15
A. Various admiration formulas	10-11
1. Comparison of love to wine (cf. 1:2b)	10abα
2. Scent of her ointment	10bβ
3. Comparison of lips to honey	11abα
4. Comparison of garment scent to that of Lebanon	11bβ
B. Garden theme	12-15
1. Comparison of beloved to garden and water source	12
2. Description of the fruits of the garden	13-14
3. Comparison of beloved to water source	15
III. Invitations	4:16–5:1a
A. A summons to the wind to blow upon the garden	16a
B. The beloved invites her lover to enjoy his garden	16b
C. The lover accepts the invitation by affirming his possession of the garden	5:1a
IV. Conclusion: invitation to "friends" to enjoy love	1b

This unit can be separated from the lover's invitation (4:8) to the beloved to come from Lebanon; however, in its present position v. 8 might be intended as a prelude to the admiration song that follows. Where does this unit properly end? Many commentators separate vv. 9-11 from vv. 12ff., and thus two separate units, 4:9-11 and 4:12–5:1, are recognized. F. Horst (p. 178) agrees with this separation, but he also admits that vv. 12ff. "as a whole come extraordinarily close to the genre of admiration song." In our judgment it is a continuation of the ADMIRATION SONG begun in v. 9. Albright (p. 4) calls attention to the repetitive parallelism in vv. 9-12. The entire unit is characterized by several repetitions ("how!" twice in 4:10; "garden" in vv. 12, 15, 16), and plays on words (*lbb* ["ravish the heart"]; *lĕbônâ* ["incense"]; *lĕbānôn* ["Lebanon"]). The admiration song comes to a climax with invitations. He (or possibly she?) summons the wind to blow on the garden; she invites him to the garden and he accepts. The final invitation, presumably to the couple ("friends"), is variously attributed to the bridegroom (*NEB*), the daughters (*NAB*), or to the poet himself (Gerleman, Würthwein). "Sister" and "bride" are repeated over and over in this unit.

Genre, Setting, Intention

As the above remarks on structure indicate, this section is an ADMIRATION SONG which culminates in dialogue. It praises physical aspects of the girl, as well as her exclusive ("enclosed garden") fidelity to her lover. It is possible that this section is built up from originally independent poems (vv. 9-11, and the garden theme in vv. 12-15). No given setting can be specified; the admiration of the beloved is a constant theme in love poetry. The text underscores the satisfaction which the lover feels for the beauty and delights of the woman who has given herself exclusively to him. In the context of Canticles, the note of fidelity receives emphasis here; the same theme is treated from a slightly different point of view in Prov 5:15-20.

THE BELOVED LOSES AND FINDS HER LOVER, 5:2–6:3

Structure

I. The beloved describes a (dream?) experience (cf. 3:1-5) with her lover	5:2-8
A. Indication of dream at night	2a
B. The lover appears at the door and seeks entrance	2b
C. The beloved replies in a teasing manner	3
D. The beloved describes the "door" sequence	4-6
1. His hands on the lock	4a
2. Her reaction	4b
3. Her approach to the door	5a
4. The myrrh at the lock	5b
5. She opens the door and finds the lover gone	6a
6. Her reaction: distress and fruitless search	6b
7. She is discovered and beaten by the watchers of the city	7
E. Adjuration to the daughters	8
II. The beloved describes her (lost) lover to the daughters	5:9-16
A. Introduction: the daughters, taking up the adjuration of v. 8, ask for a description of the lover	9
B. The beloved describes her lover	10-16
1. Color	10
2. Head and hair	11
3. Eyes	12a
4. Teeth (insert *šinnāw*)	12b
5. Cheeks and lips	13
6. Arms and torso	14
7. Legs	15
8. Jaws (=kisses)	16a
9. Conclusion	16b
III. A dialogue in which the presence of the lover is revealed	6:1-3

A. Attracted by the description of the lover, the
daughters question the beloved as to his whereabouts   1

B. The beloved replies: he is in his garden partaking of
its fruits (i.e., he was never really lost)   2

C. The beloved reiterates the formula (cf. 2:16; 7:11) of
mutual possession   3

There is wide agreement among recent commentators that this structure is a secondary composition, firmed up by the questions in 5:9 and 6:1, and by the conclusion in 5:16b. As the above outline indicates, the continuity is created by the theme of the absence of the lover; this leads to the question of the daughters, "what does he look like?" In reply the beloved launches into a description. When the daughters then evince considerable interest in the lover, the beloved is able to make her triumphant claim that he was never really lost (formula of mutual possession, 6:3). While one may grant that originally discontinuous pieces have been molded into a unity here, Würthwein goes too far in suggesting that the composition was destined for dramatic presentation at a marriage celebration. The catchword 'ăḥōtî ("my sister") serves to tie 5:2ff. with 5:1; Rudolph points also to "awake" in 4:16 and 5:2.

Genre

Although the entire unit might be called a dramatic composition, it is doubtful if the editor saw it precisely this way. But one can distinguish various subgenres. There is a DESCRIPTION OF AN EXPERIENCE (Horst, 184, and he goes on to characterize it more closely as a *Traumerlebnis*, or experience of a dream) in 5:2-6, in which several motifs appear: the night visit of the lover, the seeking and (not) finding, the encounter with the watchmen of the city, and finally the adjuration (a SONG OF YEARNING) to the daughters. The similarity to 3:1-5 is obvious, but again the influence of the "complaint at the door" seems farfetched (against Gerleman).

A *waṣf*, or description of the physical beauty of the lover, is found in 5:9-16, framed by the introductory question of the daughters (v. 9), and the concluding presentation (v. 16b) by the beloved. The concluding dialogue in 6:1-3 presents the garden theme on the lips of the beloved in vv. 2-3. While Gerleman grants that this section is loosely connected with the preceeding, he argues perhaps rightly that vv. 2-3 are a reply to v. 1 in only a very secondary way; their original thrust is to describe the erotic pleasures which the lover can find in his beloved. He points to the catchwords "beds of spices" and "lilies" in 5:13 and 6:2.

Setting and Intention

The various genres cannot be pinned down to specific settings; they all fit into the situations and emotions of lovers. The editor has put them together in an artful way so as to achieve a certain movement from absence to presence, from loss to discovery. The whole section is dominated by the expressions of love, admiration, and devotion that the beloved feels for her lover.

PRAISE OF THE BELOVED, 6:4-7

Structure

I.	The lover acclaims the beauty and terror of his beloved	4-5a
	A. He compares her beauty to that of Tirzah and Jerusalem	4a
	B. He compares the terror she evokes to that of a bannered army (cf. 6:10) and requests her to avert her eyes	4b-5a
II.	The lover launches into a description (=4:1-3) of her physical beauty	5b-7
	A. Hair	5b
	B. Teeth	6
	C. Cheeks	7

Genre, Setting, Intention

This unit appears to be a mixed genre. There is clearly a *wasf*, or DESCRIPTIVE SONG in vv. 5b-7; Horst (p. 176) recognizes an ADMIRATION SONG in vv. 4b and 5b. The difference between these two genres is rather slight, as has already been seen in Canticles. This is the only occasion in the work in which the motif of fear is added to that of love in connection with the woman. Würthwein remarks that the request concerning her eyes can be understood in a playful manner and he refers to 4:9; but the danger and mystery of woman is an old motif.

THE UNIQUENESS OF THE BELOVED, 6:8-10

Structure

I.	The lover compares the beloved to the royal harem and finds her unique	8-9a
II.	The harem also acknowledges her superiority	9b
III.	Cry of acclamation (by the harem) concerning the appearance of the beloved	10

Although v. 10 (cf. 6:4) may originally have been separate (Horst, 176-77, regards it as an admiration song), it is commonly interpreted as the words of the women of the harem in praise of the beloved; so Würthwein, Loretz, Rudolph. Gordis takes it with vv. 11-12 as the beginning of a new unit. The repetitions, "who is this . . ." (3:6; 6:10; 8:5) do not seem to have any significant relationship with each other.

Genre, Setting, Intention

Gerleman and Horst (p. 183) consider this section as a BOAST (*Prahllied*); Würthwein calls it a "song of praise" (*Preislied*). There is no need to postulate a setting in a royal harem. The theme is the uniqueness of the beloved.

THE NUT GARDEN, 6:11-12

Structure

I. The beloved describes her visit to a nut garden   11
II. She alludes to an unexpected happening in connection
    with the visit   12

Gerleman takes 6:11–7:1 as the unit. The meaning of v. 12 is obscure, and the text seems certainly corrupt (cf. commentaries). In addition, there is no agreement about the identity of the speaker of these lines, nor of the meaning of the garden (a real garden, or is it a symbol of the girl's charms, as Würthwein believes?). The purpose of the visit to the garden (v. 11b) is echoed in 7:13 (*RSV* 12).

Genre, Setting, Intention

This is a DESCRIPTION OF AN EXPERIENCE (*Erlebnisschilderung*, Horst, 184), a surprise rendezvous between the lover and the beloved in a garden, that seems to break off at the end. No particular setting can be claimed (although Würthwein thinks it has to do with the consummation of the marriage on the first night of the seven-day marriage celebration). The beloved, if she is the speaker, wishes to put on record an important experience that became determinative of their love.

A DESCRIPTION OF THE DANCING SHULAMMITE, 7:1-6 (*RSV* 6:13–7:5)

Structure

I. Introduction   1
  A. The onlookers invite the Shulammite to dance   1a
  B. The Shulammite remonstrates with the onlookers   1b
II. The onlookers (daughters of Jerusalem? or the lover?)
  describe the physical charms of the dancer   2-6
  A. A cry of admiration for her dance steps   2a
  B. Thighs   2b
  C. Navel and belly (euphemisms)   3
  D. Breasts   4
  E. Neck, eyes, and nose   5
  F. Head, and the hair that captivates a king   6

Several questions arise: the identity of the onlookers, of the Shulammite, of the speaker(s) of the *wasf* in vv. 2-5. The description of the girl goes in the ascending order, from feet to head.

Genre, Setting, Intention

This is a *wasf*, or description of the physical beauty of the woman (vv. 2-6), to which an introduction (v. 1a, which is highly alliterative) has been prefaced. The setting can be inferred from the introduction: a dance by a maiden that the song in vv. 2-6 accompanies. Commentators have attempted to be more specific: a wedding dance (Rudolph, Würthwein, Krinetzki), a "sword" dance (originally proposed by J. Wetzstein on the analogy of the practice of modern bedouin of Syria), the "strut" dance (*Paradiertanz*, so Staerk, 294, and Horst, 181-82). The meaning of the *maḥănāyim* dance (*RSV*, "a dance before two armies") remains uncertain. Whatever the nature of the dance, it provides the occasion for a description of the parts of the body of the woman. The mention of a king in 7:6 ties the song in with the "king" fiction expressed elsewhere (e.g., 1:4, 12).

A DIALOGUE, 7:7-11 (*RSV* 7:6-10)

Text

The text of v. 10 is uncertain. "For my lover" (*lĕdôdî*, omitted in the *RSV*) can be spoken only by the woman. Hence many commentators emend the text in such a way that all of v. 10 is spoken by the man. The structure below follows the MT and attributes the rest of v. 10 to the girl, who turns his compliment into a statement of her belonging to him. At the end of v. 10, one should read with the *RSV* and many others "lips and teeth" for the "lips of the sleepers" of the MT.

Structure

I. The lover utters a song of admiration about his beloved	7-8
A. Cry of admiration over her beauty	7
B. Comparison of her stature and breasts	8
II. The lover expresses his yearning for physical possession of his beloved	9-10α
III. The beloved responds affirmatively	10αβ-11
A. She continues his comparison of her mouth with wine, interrupting to say that it flows for her lover	10αβ-10b
B. She concludes with a formula of mutual possession (a variation of 2:16 and 6:3)	11

Genre, Setting, Intention

Horst (p. 177) regards vv. 7-10 as an ADMIRATION SONG, in which vv. 9-10 express the effect of the beauty of the beloved upon the lover: his yearning to possess her. On this view, her affirmative reply is given in v. 11. This dialogue could derive from many occasions in the experience of lovers, and it expresses the deep yearnings the man and the woman have for each other. The sexual desire (*tĕšûqâ*) attributed to the woman in Gen 3:16 is now attributed to the man in v. 11.

THE BELOVED YEARNS TO SHARE THE BLOSSOMS WITH HER LOVER, 7:12-14 (*RSV* 7:11-13)

Structure

I. The beloved invites her lover to the fields and vineyards (cf. 6:11) to see the blossoming	12-13a
II. She promises to give him her love there	13b
III. She describes the "fruits" she has preserved for him	14

Many commentators (Würthwein, Rudolph, Loretz, Krinetzki, Gerleman) separate v. 14 (a fragment from a larger piece?) from vv. 12-13, as though the "spring" situation in v. 13 eliminates the already ripe fruits mentioned in v. 14. But the fruits of v. 14 can be understood symbolically of herself, especially after her statement in v. 13b (cf. 2:17 after 2:16).

Genre, Setting, Intention

This is a SONG OF YEARNING (Horst, 186), expressed in an invitation that the beloved addresses to her lover. The request that they be together in their experience of the awakening of nature (a theme expressed already in 2:11-13 and 6:11) is a thinly veiled allusion to their exchange of love, and the beloved assures him of her devotion (v. 13b); v. 14 is, as it were, the promise of what awaits him in the vineyards (v. 13). No specific setting (against Krinetzki who finds here a certain homesickness and desire to escape from the week-long marriage festivities) can be established. This is a simple invitation in which she declares her desire to share herself and her love with her lover.

IF MY LOVER WERE MY BROTHER, 8:1-4

Structure

I. The beloved expresses a yearning, and the advantages of it	1-2
A. The yearning: that her lover were her brother	1a
B. The advantages of having such a wish fulfilled	1b-2
II. A reprise or refrain (=2:6-7; 3:5)	3-4

There is a play on a key word, '*šqk* ("I would kiss you"/"I would give you to drink") in v. 2; 8:3 is to be taken as a statement, not as a wish (*RSV*).

Genre, Setting, Intention

This is a SONG OF YEARNING (Horst, 186). The desire of the woman for intimacy with her lover is clearly expressed. Gerleman notes that the refrain (vv. 3-4) occurs at the end of a description of a rendezvous in 2:4-7, and in 3:5 (cf. the reference to the house of the mother in 3:4). The refrain serves to indicate that her desire is capable of fulfillment or actually fulfilled.

THE AWAKENING OF LOVE, 8:5

Structure

I. Cry of admiration, expressed in a rhetorical question (cf. 3:6; 6:10)	5a
II. The lover reminisces concerning a rendezvous with the beloved	5b

The identity of the speakers is not certain; v. 5a is given to a "chorus" or to the daughters of Jerusalem (*NAB*); v. 5b seems to be uttered by the lover, although Gordis puts these lines on the lips of the girl. The catchwords binding this with the previous section are "mother" (vv. 5 and 2) and "awaken" (vv. 5 and 4). Rudolph joins v. 5 with vv. 6-7 as an admiratory or descriptive song about the *married* couple, which is followed by dialogue. Würthwein considers vv. 5a and 5b as fragments, perhaps of separate poems.

Genre, Setting, Intention

On the analogy of 3:6 and 6:10, the first part of the verse may be classified as the genre of ADMIRATION SONG. As the lover and beloved approach the home of her birth, she is admired (v. 5a) and he reminisces about their first love encounter. The identity of the beloved is made plain in v. 5b. No setting can be determined for this enigmatic verse.

THE POWER OF LOVE, 8:6-7

Structure

I. The beloved makes a request for continual presence ("seal") to her lover	6aα
II. The reasons: statements about the power of love	6aβ-7
A. Love is compared to the power of death/Sheol	6aβ
B. Love is compared to flames, the flames of Yah	6b
C. Love is unconquerable	7a
D. Love is unpurchasable	7b

Many translations fail to bring out the point of the comparison of love with death/Sheol; for example, "cruel" (*NEB, RSV*) is not an adequate rendering of *qāšâ* in v. 6a; it should be "unyielding" or "relentless," in order to convey the idea of love's pursuit of the beloved (as death/Sheol pursues every living person). The word for "love" (*'ahăbâ*) occurs three times.

Genre, Setting, Intention

Horst (p. 185) describes this as a SONG OF YEARNING, followed by a description of human love. Loretz calls it a "song of praise" concerning love. Certainly the main theme is love: the presence of the lovers to each other, and the power and value of love. The lines deal with the universal, not with the particular, and no particular setting can be postulated. These lines are by their nature climactic and hence belong to a critical point in a love situation, where the beloved can sing of the power of love. Even if the statement about love's power has the ring of an aphorism (cf. Robert-Feuillet-Tournay on v. 7) it is incorporated here in the work as a kind of climax to the love relationship that has been celebrated throughout the poem. The text affirms the powerful, indomitable character of a love that is beyond all price. For similar passages in Egyptian love poetry, cf. Simpson, 311 (seal ring).

OUR SISTER, 8:8-10

Structure

I. The brothers present a program toward the eventual espousal of their sister	8-9
A. Statement of the problem: "our sister" is not yet nubile—what is to be done?	8
B. Two alternative ways of dealing with her	9

II. The sister's triumphant reply to her brothers   10

    Since the girl's brothers occur elsewhere only in 1:6, this passage may function as an inclusion or at least as a pendant to 1:6, since it shows the same irony and independent spirit of the girl. "Door" and "wall" are to be taken as contrasts (against Gordis); "breasts" is obviously a key word in this poem. "One who brings (finds) peace" of the *RSV* is one possible rendition of a difficult phrase. Exum (p. 76) ascribes vv. 8-9 to the daughters.

Genre, Setting, Intention

Horst (pp. 182-83) classifies this section as a self-description (also, 1:5-6) in which a short description follows upon the statement of the brothers' plan (in direct quotation). Gordis (pp. 32-33) accepts Tur-Sinai's view that a love charm or incantation is the background of vv. 8-9, but he has to admit that no incantation is even implied. On the whole, this song is better classified as a BOAST: to the "program" envisioned by the brothers, the beloved proclaims triumphantly her own independence and integrity, intimating that she belongs to her lover. An appropriate original setting would be one in which the beloved justifies her conduct against the programmatic supervision of her brothers. Thus, it could be part of a marriage celebration (is this song an indication of the girl's independence of her own family at the approach of marriage?). The intention of the text is to affirm the integrity of the beloved vis-à-vis the timorous supervision of her brothers. She has gone her own way and has found "peace" (*šālôm*, v. 10b; see commentaries for various interpretations of this word). The calculations of the brothers are doubtless motivated by considerations of the bride price, but her motivation is based upon true love.

THE VINEYARD OF GREAT PRICE, 8:11-12

Structure

  I. The lover acknowledges the highly priced vineyard that
     belongs to Solomon   11
  II. In contrast, he claims his own vineyard (=the beloved) is
     even greater in value   12

    Most commentators ascribe these lines to the man, despite the phrase "my own vineyard," with which the woman describes herself in 1:6. The key to these obscure verses is the word "vineyard," which is used for the maiden in 1:6 and 2:15 (cf. 4:12-16). "Silver" is the catchword that connects vv. 11-12 with vv. 8-10.

Genre, Setting, Intention

Horst (p. 183) and Würthwein classify this as a BOAST, and several commentators understand it as a sort of parallel to 6:8-10. The speaker mentions the rich vineyard of Solomon, perhaps an allusion to the royal harem in Jerusalem (=Baal-hamon?), only to contrast it with his own vineyard (his beloved) that is far more valuable. Such a boast, and compliment to the woman, might originate outside of, as well as within, a marriage celebration.

FINALE, 8:13-14

Structure
I. The lover requests (cf. 2:14) the beloved to let her voice
   be heard   13a
II. She replies (with a motif taken from 2:17)   13b

Genre, Setting, Intention
Perhaps these lines can be classified as a SONG OF YEARNING, since this note is
sounded in both the request and the reply; he desires some expression of her
presence, even just her voice, which others ("companions") also find attractive.
M. van den Oudenrijn suggests that such lines derive from a game of "hide and
seek" in which only the bridegroom, and not the "companions," is allowed to
find her by the sound of her voice. These lines lay stress on the mutual desire for
the presence, or sign of presence, of the one loved. In the context of the entire
work, it is a deliberate reprise of earlier motifs (2:14, 17), which serves as an
ending to Canticles.

ECCLESIASTES (QOHELET)

Bibliography

S. de Ausejo, "El genero literario del Eclesiastes," *EstBib* 7 (1948) 369-406; A. Barucq, *Ecclesiaste* (VS 3; Paris, 1968); A. Bea, *Liber Ecclesiastae* (Rome, 1950); R. Braun, *Kohelet und die frühhellenistische Popularphilosophie* (BZAW 130; Berlin, 1973); G. Castellino, "Qohelet and His Wisdom," *CBQ* 30 (1968) 15-28; F. Ellermeier, *Qohelet I/I* (Herzberg, 1967); L. di Fonzo, *Ecclesiaste* (La Sacra Bibbia; Rome, 1967); K. Galling, *Der Prediger* (HAT 18; 2nd ed., Tübingen, 1969) 73-125; H. L. Ginsberg, "The Structure and Contents of the Book of Koheleth," in *Wisdom in Israel and in the Ancient Near East* (ed. M. Noth and D. W. Thomas; VTSup 3; Leiden, 1960); E. Glasser, *Le procès du bonheur par Qohelet* (LD 61; Paris, 1970); R. Gordis, *Kohelet—The Man and his World* (3rd ed.; New York, 1968); H. Hertzberg, *Der Prediger* (KAT XVII/4; Gütersloh, 1963) 21-238; R. F. Johnson, "A Form-Critical Analysis of the Sayings in the Book of Ecclesiastes" (Diss., Emory University, 1973); R. Kroeber, *Der Prediger* (Schriften und Quellen der alten Welt 13; Berlin, 1963); J. A. Loader, "Qohelet 3:2-8—A 'Sonnet' in the Old Testament," *ZAW* 81 (1969) 240-42; idem, *Polar Structures in the Book of Qohelet* (BZAW 152; Berlin, 1979); O. Loretz, *Qohelet und der alte Orient* (Freiburg, 1964); R. E. Murphy, "A Form-Critical Consideration of Ecclesiastes 7," in SBLASP I (ed. G. MacRae; Missoula, 1974) 77-85; F. Nötscher, *Kohelet* (Echter-Bibel; Würzburg, 1954); G. S. Ogden, "The 'Better'-Proverb (Tôb-Spruch), Rhetorical Criticism, and Qoheleth," *JBL* 96 (1977) 489-505; idem, "Qoheleth's Use of the 'Nothing is Better'-Form," *JBL* 98 (1979) 339-50; E. Podechard, *L'Ecclésiaste* (EBib; Paris, 1912); R. Scott, *Ecclesiastes* (AB 18; New York, 1965); G. Sheppard, "The Epilogue to Qohelet as Theological Commentary," *CBQ* 39 (1977) 182-89; A. Strobel, *Das Buch Prediger (Kohelet)* (Dusseldorf, 1967); A. Wright, "The Riddle of the Sphinx: The Structure of the Book of Qoheleth," *CBQ*, 30 (1968) 313-34; idem, "The Riddle of the Sphinx Revisited: Numerical Patterns in the Book of Qoheleth," *CBQ* 42 (1980) 38-51; W. Zimmerli, *Prediger* (ATD XVI/1; Göttingen, 1962) 123-253; idem, "Das Buch Kohelet—Traktat oder Sentenzensammlung?" *VT* 24 (1974) 221-30.

THE BOOK AS A WHOLE

Structure

There is simply no agreement concerning the structure of Ecclesiastes, as can be seen by the surveys of opinion in Ellermeier (pp. 131-41) and in A. Wright's article (esp. pp. 315-17). It seems to lack any order from the point of view of logical progression of thought, but of course that depends upon whose "logic" is at issue. Hence many commentators have settled for an atomistic approach, treating the work as a collection of isolated units. Others have attempted to find some unity and progression, often by recognizing later hands (words attributable to various "correctors," such as a pious man or a sage) at work in the book. The title of an article by W. Zimmerli captures the dilemma of the structure of Ecclesiastes: "treatise or collection?" ("Das Buch Kohelet—Traktat oder Sentenzensammlung?"). His final point of view is that one cannot make a black-and-white decision for one or the other. From one point of view, collection seems an apt term because of the abruptness that marks the connection between various units, and because of the similarities between Ecclesiastes (esp. 7:1ff. and 10:1ff.) and Proverbs. Yet many larger sections can be recognized in the work, and are not to be atomized (e.g., 6:10–7:14; 11:9–12:7). There is more here than a mere collection, yet the material is too disparate to claim with Loretz that this is a treatise on "vanity." Zimmerli ("Das Buch Kohelet," 230) remarks:

> The book of Qohelet is not a treatise with clearly recognizable structure and with one definable theme. At the same time it is more than a loose collection of sayings, although in some places indications of a collection are not to be overlooked. . . . It follows that the exegete of Ecclesiastes must work on more levels than the exegete of Proverbs. He must first of all discover the primary form-critical units. Then (as is also the duty of the exegete of Prov 24:30-34, as well as 22:17ff.), he must inquire after the possible combinations of two or more of these primary units. There is still a further task, and here the exegesis of Ecclesiastes resembles more that of Job than of Proverbs. He must ask how the content determines the sequence of the complex form-critical units. The element of uncertainty is the greatest precisely at this point, and the exegete must also have the courage to register a "non liquet."

More recent attempts to capture the structure of Ecclesiastes have been made by J. Loader (*Polar Structures*) and A. Wright ("The Riddle of the Sphinx Revisited"). The thought of Ecclesiastes is indisputably polar ("patterns of tension created by the counterposition of two elements to one another," as Loader defines it, p. 1). Thus we have talk and silence, toil and joy, etc. Loader claims that these contrasts in thought, which are scattered throughout the book, are constitutive of structure. A. Wright has refined his 1968 study by establishing a numerical pattern in the book, such as:

(1) The numerical value of the *inclusion* (1:2; 12:8, *hbl hblym hkl hbl*) is 216, and there are in fact 216 verses in 1:1–12:8, at which point the editor's epilogue (12:9-14) begins, to yield a total of 222 verses.

(2) The threefold repetition of *hbl* in the inclusion (1:2; 12:8) yields the numerical value of 111 (3×37), which is the number of verses in the first half of the book (1:1–6:9), as it came from Qohelet. Both Qohelet and the editor intend the middle of the book to be at 6:9/10, and the editor has built up the second half of the book to match the 111 verses of the first half.

These and other numerical patterns indicated by Wright can hardly be dismissed as coincidental, and thus they form a strong argument for a structure that goes beyond content and thought divisions.

In the light of the uncertainty underscored by Zimmerli, and to escape subjectivity as much as possible, the analysis here will adopt the outline proposed by A. Wright, with only slight differences. In the style of the New Critics, he has looked for repetitions, catchwords, refrains which can function as divider-phrases, symmetry, etc., and has allowed the structure to evolve out of these data. With the majority of scholars, Wright recognizes a prologue (title and poem on toil, 1:1-11), and an epilogue (12:8-14). The introductory poem on toil could have been written by Qohelet, but 12:9-14 (as is generally admitted) betrays editorial hand(s). On the basis of the repetition of key phrases, Wright divides the body of the work into two parts: 1:12–6:9, and 6:10–11:6. The eightfold repetition of "vanity and a striving after wind" marks off eight units. In 6:10–11:6, two directions are pursued. In the first (6:10–8:17), four sections end with "not find out"/"who can find out," after the introduction in 6:10-12. In the second (9:1–11:6), six sections end with "do not know"/"no knowledge." The final poem (11:7–12:8) is clearly about youth and old age. This structure orients itself by fixed phrases in the text rather than by presumed content. At the same time, it allows for a succession of literary genres within a unit (e.g., two instructions and a reflection in 4:17–6:9 [*RSV* 5:1–6:9]).

The structure of the book follows:

I. Introduction	1:1-11
A. Superscription	1:1
B. Motto	1:2
C. Reflection about human *'āmāl* ("toil")	1:3-11
II. Body	1:12–12:7
A. First unit	1:12–6:9
1. Introductory reflections	1:12-18
2. Reflection upon pleasure	2:1-11
3. Reflection upon the merits of wisdom and folly	2:12-17
4. Reflection upon human toil (*'āmāl*)	2:18-26
5. Reflections upon toil and time	3:1–4:6
6. Reflection concerning "two"	4:7-16
7. Varia: instructions and a reflection	4:17–6:9
	(*RSV* 5:1–6:9)

As indicated above, this structure is based upon the occurrence of key phrases as structural dividers or determinants. The phrase "(vanity and) a striving after wind" ends sections 1-7 in the first unit (II.A). Actually Wright recognizes a "double introduction" in 1:12-15, 16-18 because of repetition of the phrase. In the second unit (6:10–11:6), the phrases are "not find out"/"who can find out" which occur at the end of the sections a-e in 6:10–8:17, and "do not know"/"no knowledge" which occur at the end of the sections a-e in 9:1–11:6. The above structure deviates slightly from that of A. Wright in that it recognizes the unit in 10:16–11:2 (Wright) as properly being 10:16–11:6. There is no claim that this is a logical structure; it is based on form, not content. The instruction on old age (11:7–12:7) stands outside this form, as does the reflection about man's toil (1:3-11) in the introduction.

Genre

The designation of the proper literary genre of the book of Ecclesiastes still escapes us. Some commentators have spoken of a "royal testament." The fiction of the wise king Qohelet is unmistakable in 1:12–2:11, but the purpose and teaching of the book does not fit the genre of royal testament in the Egyptian writings, such as the Instructions of Merikare and Amenemhet, with which it is supposed to compare. The adoption of Solomonic authorship (1:1, 12) is simply due to the tradition about Solomon the wise.

Ellermeier (p. 49) says that "one can designate the genre of the book Ecclesiastes simply as *mashal*." But this term (commonly, "proverb") is far too elusive in meaning to be helpful, and Ellermeier deals principally with sayings and reflections as genres that are constitutive of the book. One need not adopt, as genres, his further refinement of reflection as "unified" and "broken" (pp. 89-91). R. Braun deals with three basic genres: meditative reflection (*betrachtende Reflexion*), meditation (*Betrachtung*), and instruction (*Belehrung*). While he does not urge any determination of the genre of the book as a whole, his frequent comparisons with the Greek diatribe would suggest that he favors that term, which was proposed already by S. de Ausejo in 1948.

At the least, then, there has been some success in recognizing the various subgenres that enter into the composition of this book. Three principal types emerge: the WISDOM SAYING (e.g., as in the collections of 7:1ff.; 9:17ff.); the commands and prohibitions which form the heart of the INSTRUCTION; and finally the REFLECTION. At the present time, it does not seem possible to distinguish adequately different genres within the reflection, as done by Ellermeier and Braun.

The saying and the instruction have been treated elsewhere (→ Introduction to Wisdom Literature and Proverbs). The REFLECTION is characteristic of Ecclesiastes and needs further discussion. The term designates a text that is characterized by observation and thought, and hence has a fairly loose structure. It will utilize phrases such as, "I said in my heart" (1:16-17; 2:1,15; 3:17), "I gave my heart to know" (1:13,17; 8:16), "I saw (again)" (1:14; 2:14,24, passim), "I know" (1:17; 3:12,14; etc.), and rhetorical questions (e.g., 2:2, 12,15,19,22,25). The REFLECTION will actually incorporate several subgenres, such as a saying or proverb (2:14; 4:5-6, etc.). R. Gordis (pp. 95-108) has called attention to Qohelet's use of quotations. Thus, a proverb may be quoted to support an argument (5:2 [*RSV* 3]), or to provide a text for further commentary (7:2a commented on in v. 2b; 4:9 commented on in vv. 10-12). Sometimes the quotation sets up the opinion which Qohelet wants to dispute (8:12-13 is negated by the framework provided in vv. 11-14). Or two proverbs may be simply contrasted, with the preference of Qohelet, if any, to be derived from the context. Another genre that appears is the EXAMPLE STORY (*Beispielerzählung*), as in 9:13-16 (cf. 4:13-16), in which Qohelet narrates a story in order to make his case (cf. also Prov 7:6-23; 24:30-34). The WOE ORACLE appears in 2:16; 4:10; 10:16, and the BLESSING in 10:17.

A form-critical treatment of Ecclesiastes would not be satisfactory if it omitted the indications of the unusual style of this book. More than one-third of the work (total: 222 verses) is in poetry. There are countless repetitions of phrases: "pursuit after wind," "under the sun," "eat and drink," etc. In addition, there are certain favorite words that are used over and over: vanity, do/deed, wise/wisdom, good, time, know/knowledge, toil, evil, fool/folly, rejoice, profit, wind/breath, die/death, sin/sinner, justice/just, power, remember/memory, portion, vexation, affair (*ḥpṣ*), skill (*kšr*), etc. O. Loretz, who has listed these occurrences (pp. 166-79), goes on to point out that such terms constitute about one-fifth of all the words in the book (from 1:4 to 12:7).

The most conspicuous of the examples of paronomasia is "vanity of vanities" (1:2; 12:8). But there are many other instances, "the toil at which I had toiled" (2:11,18,22; 5:17 [*RSV* 18]; 9:9), "the deeds that are done" (cf. 1:9,13,14; 2:17, passim). The wordplay in 7:1 (*ṭôb šēm miššemen ṭôb*) is outstanding, and cannot be reproduced in translation. Comparisons abound, especially the "better" saying (4:6,9; 5:4 [*RSV* 5]; 6:3,9; 7:1-8; 9:16,18).

A very important stylistic feature is to be found in the "yes, but" (*Zwar-Aber Aussage*) passages, recognized by Zimmerli (*Prediger*, 130), Kroeber (p. 37), and especially H. Hertzberg (p. 30), but denied by Ellermeier (pp. 125-238). These commentators recognize a certain suppleness in the development of Qohelet's thought, in which one statement modifies another without simply contradicting it. Thus, one has the affirmation of divine justice in 3:17 after the statement of the existence of injustice in 3:16. Similarly, in 8:11-12a Qohelet remarks that the sinner survives, and in 8:12b-13 states that it will be well for the God-fearer, but otherwise for the wicked. The recognition of this stylistic feature allows one to escape the uncertainty of attributing certain passages to glossators. However, many commentators (Podechard, Galling), on exegetical grounds, and in the name of consistency, have attributed certain parts of the work to later hands, especially to a more conservative writer (or even writers) who would have toned down the radicalism of Qohelet. It seems best with more recent exegetes (Gordis, Hertzberg, and, in the main, Kroeber), to explain the work as one piece, except for the epilogue in 12:8-14, where Qohelet is written *about* (third person).

In conclusion, one may say that no single genre, even diatribe, is adequate as a characterization of Qohelet's book. This seems due to the fact that it is the publication of his teachings, which would have embraced many different genres of writing. Explicit form-critical analyses of Ecclesiastes can be found in Eller-meier (pp. 66-79), in Braun (pp. 155-58), and in Loader (*Polar Structures*, 18-28).

Setting

In its final form the work has been edited and presumably published by other(s) than Qohelet, as is suggested by the tenor of 12:9-14. Whether or not these verses are to be ascribed to one person (Gordis, Loretz), or to two redactors (so Galling, Zimmerli, Braun, Kroeber: vv. 9-11 and vv. 12-14), or even to three (Hertzberg: vv. 9-11, v. 12, vv. 13-14), they do provide the setting in which Qohelet's thoughts were finally circulated. Speculation about more proximate settings of one or another section in the book is hardly fruitful; for the most part they can all fit into a didactic situation.

Intention

The work is clearly at odds with the views of traditional wisdom teaching, especially the doctrine of retribution. The thrust of Qohelet goes deeper than merely contradicting favorite theses of the sages. His claim is that there is simply no profit for man in his achievements in this life; all is vanity. Moreover, mankind cannot make sense of any of God's action (*ma'ăśeh*) in this life. This negative stance should not be allowed to conceal certain important emphases: the insistence upon God's transcendence and sovereignty, and upon the task of man to meet the present as it is, as it comes from the hand of God, with joy (cf. Hertzberg, 222-38, and, concerning Qohelet's emphasis on Sheol and death, N. Lohfink, *The Christian Meaning of the Old Testament* [Milwaukee, 1968] 140-55).

CHAPTER 2

THE INDIVIDUAL UNITS

SUPERSCRIPTION, 1:1

Structure

I. Title of book ("The words of . . .")	1:1a
II. Identification of Qohelet	1:1b

Genre, Setting, Intention

The SUPERSCRIPTION is a literary device adopted for the written edition of biblical works. The title, "words of . . ." is paralleled especially in other wisdom collections, e.g., Prov 22:17; 30:1; 31:1, and it is comparable to the introductions to the Egyptian instructions (e.g, Ptah-hotep; *ANET*, 412). The title should be understood in the sense of "teaching," therefore, and not in the sense of "history," or "chronicles," as in 1 Kgs 11:41, etc.

The identification of Qohelet as "son of David, king in Jersualem" (v. 1, specifying the data of v. 12), is in accordance with the tradition of ascribing wisdom books (Proverbs, Canticles, Wisdom) to Solomon, who was honored as the sage par excellence. The practice of pseudonymity was fairly widespread in the postexilic period. The superscription itself serves an editorial purpose—a claim for authorship for Qohelet. While the juxtaposition of an unknown Qohelet and a (Davidic) king is to be understood in the light of the pseudonymity practiced in the world of Judaism, the thrust of the title is to exalt the wisdom and importance of the author.

MOTTO: "VANITY OF VANITIES," 1:2

Structure

I. An exclamation containing the motto, "vanity of vanities"	2aα
II. Attribution of motto to Qohelet	2aβ
III. Repetition of the motto	2bα
IV. A final judgment on the vanity of everything	2bβ

Genre

The saying emphasizes a motto which distills the message of the book. The word *hebel* ("vanity") occurs over thirty times in this work, and it deserves to be considered a key word, but the motto is found only here and in 12:8. "Motto" is the term adopted by F. Nötscher, but refused by W. Zimmerli; Loretz (*Qohelet*, 138) approves of "leitmotif."

Setting

The verse is repeated almost exactly in 12:8 (*inclusio*), which marks the beginning of the epilogue appended by the editor. Hence one may accept 1:2 as an editorial interpretation. However, there is no reason to deny that the phrase "vanity of vanities" is original with Qohelet in his oral teaching ("says Qohelet"). The editor seems to have used it deliberately in the introduction and ending (1:2; 12:8), since these are the only instances.

Intention

The verse sums up the message of Qohelet: all human efforts and human life itself are ephemeral (*hebel* = "breath, vapor"), and hence vain.

REFLECTION ABOUT HUMAN TOIL, 1:3-11

Structure

I. Poem about toil	3-8
A. Thesis: there is no profit in man's toil	3
B. Thesis illustrated	4-8
1. An endless round of events	4-6
a. Generation	4
b. Sun	5
c. Wind	6
2. Failure of creation to be filled	7-8
a. Sea	7
b. Man	8
II. Prose commentary on the poem	9-11
A. Thesis: nothing is new	9
B. Reasons proving nothing is new	10-11

After the motto (1:2), a new beginning is made, and a thesis is stated that there is no profit in man's toil (1:3)—a point that the author proceeds to show from the absence of any progress in natural phenomena. The endless activities of the agents in vv. 4-6 are tied together by the inclusion, *hôlēk* ("goes"). Another inclusion, *mālē'/timmālē'* ("fill"), holds together the sea and the man (vv. 7-8), which are never filled or satisfied. The prose commentary anticipates the objection that new things contradict the thesis; the fact is that nothing is new; there is simply no remembrance of what has been (an inclusion perhaps in vv. 10,11; *hāyâ/yihyeh*, ["is"]). On 1:3-11, see A. Wright, 333.

Genre

This section is a REFLECTION, expressed in a poem about the uselessness of toil (vv. 3-8) and justified by a prose comment (vv. 9-11).

Setting

Whether or not originally composed for this book, the poem and commentary contain an analysis of life that is characteristic of a wisdom teacher (note the examples drawn from the world of nature). Within the book, this unit serves to highlight one of the main themes: no profit (*yitrôn*, 2:11,13; 5:8,15 [*RSV* 9,16]; 7:12; 10:10,11, only in Ecclesiastes).

Intention
The uselessness of human toil is illustrated from events in nature and in human experience, and from the failure of man to remember.

INTRODUCTORY REFLECTIONS, 1:12-18

Structure
I. Identification of author in a self-presentation formula	12
II. First reflection	13-15
A. Statement of the vanity of pursuing wisdom	13-14
B. A proverb quoted in support	15
III. Second reflection	16-18
A. Statement of the vanity of pursuing wisdom	16-17
B. A proverb quoted in support	18

Even if this unit be taken, as Wright insists, as a double introduction (vv. 12-15; vv. 16-18), the structure is clear: the pursuit of wisdom is described as *rĕ'ût rûaḥ* (v. 14) and *ra'yôn rûaḥ* (v. 17) ("a striving after wind")—this gives perfect balance, and both statements are followed by proverbs (vv. 15,18) which serve to establish the author's claim.

Genre, Setting, Intention
This is a REFLECTION, as indicated by the opening words (*lēb* ["mind"]) in vv. 13 and 16. The reflection is characteristic of the style of Qohelet (see introduction above). At this point of the book, this unit is important because of the theme which will be reiterated: the bankruptcy of wisdom. Wisdom, despite its theoretical superiority to folly, is vain.

REFLECTION UPON PLEASURE, 2:1-11

Structure
I. Declaration of intention to experiment with pleasure	1a
II. Judgment about experiment—anticipated	1b-2
III. Description of calculated ("with wisdom") experiment with pleasure	3-10
IV. Judgment about experiment	11

Most commentators consider 2:1-11 as a new unit, although Galling and Ellermeier join it with 1:12-18 as part of the "king-fiction." The section ends with the recurrent phrase, "vanity and a striving after wind." There is an inclusion in vv. 1 and 11 (*wĕhinnēh . . . hebel* ["and behold . . . vanity"]), and perhaps in "pleasure" (*śimḥâ*) in vv. 1 and 10.

Genre, Setting, Intention

This is a REFLECTION upon an experiment with pleasure. Within the book, this is one of many tests made by Qohelet to determine what might be deemed of value, and not as vanity. The identification with Solomon (1:12) gives a certain verisimilitude to the experiment. The intention is clear: concentration on pleasure does not bring any profit to mankind.

REFLECTION UPON THE MERITS
OF WISDOM AND FOLLY, 2:12-17

Structure

I. Statement of search	12a
II. Complaint	12b
III. Claim for theoretical superiority of wisdom, supported by a proverb	13-14a
IV. A "yes, but" statement: wisdom is no better than folly, because there is one lot (*miqreh*) for all	14b-16
V. Conclusion (note ending: "vanity and a striving after wind")	17

The transition from v. 12a to v. 12b is difficult, as all commentators note; v. 12b may belong in another context, or perhaps it should be inverted with v. 12a (Nötscher, Kroeber, and many others).

Genre, Setting, Intention

This is a REFLECTION concerning wisdom and folly. The theoretical superiority of wisdom is negated by the fact that the wise man dies, just like the fool.

REFLECTION UPON HUMAN TOIL (*'āmāl*), 2:18-26

Structure

I. First argument	18-19
A. Statement of hatred of toil	18a
B. Reason: fruits left to successor, whether wise or foolish	18b-19a
C. Concluding evaluation: a divider phrase	19b
II. Second argument	20-23
A. Statement of despair over toil	20
B. Reasons	21-23
1. Fruits of toil left to someone else who has not toiled for them	21abα
2. Evaluation: a divider phrase	21bβ
3. (Rhetorical) question relative to toil	22
4. Reply: nothing but pain, even at night	23aα
5. Evaluation: a divider phrase	23aβ-b
III. Conclusion (ending with "vanity and a striving after wind")	24-26
A. Accept whatever enjoyment God gives	24

B. Reasons   25-26
   1. Nothing is done apart from him   25
   2. He disposes as he pleases   26abα
   3. Evaluation   26bβ

The first word, "I hated," matches the "I hated" of the previous conclusion (v. 17). The entire unit is structured around the notion of toil (verb and noun, eleven times). Many commentators (Zimmerli, Braun, Galling) separate vv. 24-26 from the preceding, but the subject of toil is continued in v. 24. Rhetorical questions in vv. 19,22,25 serve to develop the argument and conclusion: the second argument (vv. 20-23) is really an "explanatory repetition" (Galling).

Genre, Setting, Intention

This is a REFLECTION concerning toil: Since the fruits of toil are left to another, toil is futile, and the only conclusion is to accept whatever enjoyment God gives man for all his toil (ba'ămālô, v. 24).

REFLECTIONS UPON TOIL AND TIME, 3:1–4:6

Structure

I. Poem on time   3:1-8
   A. Introduction: thesis   1
   B. Elaboration of thesis: fourteen opposites on the theme
      of time   2-8
II. Application of the poem to toil: man knows neither the
    right time nor God's action   3:9-11
III. Conclusion as to how man should act: accept the
     pleasures God gives   3:12-13
IV. A description of God's judgment   3:14-22
    A. God's action is fixed and complete   14-15
    B. Divine judgment in the face of iniquity   16-17
       1. Observation that injustice prevails   16
       2. A "yes, but" statement affirming divine judgment   17
    C. Comparison of the lot (miqreh) of man with that of
       beast   18-21
    D. Conclusion   22
V. A consideration of oppression (ending with a "better"
   saying)   4:1-3
VI. Conclusion about toil (ending with a "better" saying)   4:4-6
    A. Statement of the conclusion   4
    B. Conclusion supported by two contrasting proverbs   5-6

The length of this section is guided by the occurrence of the phrase, "vanity and striving after wind" in 4:4 and 4:6 (partially). There is only a loose conceptual unity, in that toil and human activity (cf. 'āmāl, 'āśâ, in 3:9-13; 4:4,6) are treated from the point of view of time, God's judgment, and human injustice. Divine activity, which man cannot understand (v. 11), is taken up in vv. 14-15. Other significant repetitions are 'ôlām ("eternity," "forever") in vv. 11 and 14, and 'ēt ("time") in vv. 1-10 and 17. Most commentators, on the basis of content, break down this section as follows: 3:1-15, 16-22; 4:1-3, 4-6 (so Galling, Zimmerli, Ellermeier, and with a slight variation, Hertzberg).

Genre

A REFLECTION that combines a poem on time with several observations about divine action and the human lot in a general treatment of man's toil.

Setting

Some individual units (e.g., 3:1-8, the poem on time; 4:5-6, wisdom sayings about human industry) could very well have been independent compositions current in the wisdom tradition. They have been brought together here in the teaching of Qohelet.

Intention

Because man does not know the right time for things (which has been fixed by God) and does not understand justice, his own death, and oppression, all his toil adds up to nothing.

REFLECTION CONCERNING "TWO," 4:7-16

Structure

I. An argument that toil is fruitless when man is alone	7-8
A. A "vanity under the sun": a solitary man, always toiling	7-8a
B. Reason, expressed in rhetorical question: "For whom . . ."	8bα
C. Evaluation: a divider phrase ("this also is vanity")	8bβ
II. Arguments that two are better than one	9-12
A. A "better" saying: two better than one	9a
B. Reasons	9b-12
1. A good wage for their toil	9b
2. Mutual aid	10a
3. Solitary man lacks helper (expressed by woe oracle)	10b
4. Three examples	11-12
a. Warmth from two sleeping together (expressed by rhetorical question)	11
b. A saying: strength from resistance of two	12a
c. A saying: strength of a three-ply cord	12b
III. An example story, drawn from royal succession	13-16

This unit is held together by the repetition of the key word, "two" (*šēnî*, vv. 8,10,15; *šěnayim*, vv. 9,11,12), and the characteristic phrase, "vanity and striving after wind," terminates the unit. Many commentators (Hertzberg, Zimmerli, Ellermeier) separate vv. 13-16 from vv. 7-12 because of the content. However, the interpretation of vv. 13-16 is admittedly problematical, and the term "two" does appear in v. 15. The phrase, "no end to," in vv. 8 and 10 seems to be an inclusion, and "vanity" is an inclusion in vv. 7-8. "Toil" is again a prime consideration (v. 8 twice, v. 9).

Genre, Setting, Intention

This is a REFLECTION that adduces arguments in favor of the thesis that two are better than one (vv. 7-12). However the obscure vv. 13-16 are interpreted, they are deliberately associated with vv. 7-12, although the meaning of vv. 13-16 has to do with succession to the throne.

VARIA, 4:17– 6:9 (*RSV* 5:1-20; 6:1-9)

Structure

I. Instruction about speech	4:17–5:6
A. Command urging caution	17aα
B. Comparative saying about fools' sacrifice (with reason)	17aβ-17b
C. Prohibition about hasty speech to God (with motivation and conclusion)	5:1
D. Quotation of proverb supporting the folly of verbosity	2
E. Prohibition concerning hasty vows (with a motivation and command)	3
F. A "better" saying (in support of the prohibition)	4
G. Two prohibitions about sincere speech	5a
H. Reasons for prohibition (in form of rhetorical question)	5b
I. Quotation of proverb (supporting the prohibition; possibly a dittography of 5:2?)	6a
J. Command to fear God	6b
II. Instruction concerning injustice in high places	5:7-8
A. Prohibition (with reason)	7
B. A saying about the king (in support of the prohibition?)	8
III. Reflection about possessions	5:9–6:9
A. Three wisdom sayings (couplets) concerning riches with divider phrase—v. 9b, "this is vanity"— between the first and the second	9-11
B. An example story about the uncertainty of riches, for all one's toil	12-16
C. Conclusion about enjoying life and toil as gift of God	17-19
D. A second example story about the uncertainty of possessions	6:1-6
1. The case where a man's riches are enjoyed not by himself but by another	1-2
2. The case where an untimely birth is better than a life that is not fulfilled	3-6
E. Conclusion about toil and desire (*nepeš* ["appetite" or "desire"] is an inclusion)	7-9
1. Wisdom saying about human appetite	7
2. Two rhetorical questions relative to the wise and the poor	8

3. A "better" saying about desire 9a
4. "Vanity and a striving after wind"—evaluation, to
   end the section 9b

Genre, Setting

This long section obviously does not constitute one genre. In accordance with our view of the structure of the book (see above), the length of this section is determined by the key phrase with which it ends (6:9) and there are several genres: two INSTRUCTIONS and a REFLECTION. The instruction in 4:17–5:6 is set off from the brief instruction in 5:7-8 by reason of its clear content (speech), and by the fact that the PROHIBITIONS and reasons, and the SAYINGS, are constructed in a fairly consecutive manner. The instruction about injustice in 5:7-8 serves as a transition to the topic of man's desires. The reflection in 5:9–6:9 incorporates WISDOM SAYINGS and EXAMPLE STORIES, and the topic in the beginning (5:9-11) is taken up at the end (6:7-9): man's insatiable desires.

Intention

This must be determined by the disparate topics: the warning against verbosity, and the reflection upon the uncertainty of riches as far as man's happiness is concerned.

REFLECTION CONCERNING DIVINE CAUSALITY AND HUMAN IMPOTENCE, 6:10-12

Structure

I. Statement of theme 10
II. Reason for man's impotence: his talk is vanity, without profit 11
III. Rhetorical question concerning man's ignorance of what is good for him 12a
IV. Reason (in form of rhetorical question): man does not know what will come after him 12b

There are inclusions in vv. 10,12: *nôdā', yôdēa'* ("know"), *'ādām* ("man"); also "whatever has come to be," and "what will be."

Genre, Setting, Intention

This is a REFLECTION that serves as an introduction to the principal themes of 7:1–11:6: (1) what is good for man to do (these he cannot find out) (7:1–8:17); (2) he cannot know the future (9:1–11:6). Thus, man is assessed before God, and is found to be ignorant in essential respects.

COLLECTION OF SAYINGS AND INSTRUCTION, 7:1-14

Structure

I. Collection of seven sayings about "good" 1-12
   A. First saying (day of death is better than day of birth) 1

For the above structure see especially the commentary of W. Zimmerli; in general, also see Murphy. The length of this unit is determined by the occurrence of the phrase "cannot find out" in v. 14. In 6:12 Qohelet asked what is good (ṭôb) for man. Now in 7:1-6 he tests a collection of sayings about what is good, or better, for man. It is obvious that the word "good" unites the sayings in vv. 1-12, where it occurs eight times. But there are also other significant repetitions: ka'as ("sorrow," "anger," vv. 3,9); lēb, ("heart," vv. 2,3,4 twice, 7); bêt 'ēbel ("house of mourning," vv. 2,4); ksl, ("fool," vv. 4-6); ḥkm ("wise," vv. 4,5,7,10-12); rûaḥ ("spirit," vv. 8,9, and notice the rhymed ending with yānûaḥ ["lodges"]. Finally, as Wright points out (p. 330), there seems to be an inclusion in the appearance of yôm ("day") and ṭôb ("good") in vv. 1 and 14. There are clear instances of a play on words in v. 1a (šēm and šemen, "name" and "ointment"); and again in v. 6a (hassîrîm ["thorns"], hassîr ["pot"], hakkĕsîl ["fool"]). It should also be noted that in v. 7 lēb ("heart") picks up the same word in vv. 2-4 and ḥākām ("wise") picks up the terms in vv. 4-5. The adverse verdict in v. 7 (after "vanity" in v. 6b) nullifies the would-be wisdom of vv. 1-6.

The sayings continue in vv. 8-12 in a logical way. The "end of a thing" (v. 8a) is a reprise of v. 1, and there is a moral application of it in v. 8b. The prohibitions in vv. 9-10 and the sayings about wisdom in vv. 11-12 prepare for the moralizing reflection in vv. 13-14 about the day of prosperity/adversity. The adverse situation is mirrored in vv. 9-10 (anger, foolish praise of the past), and the good situation is indicated in vv. 11-12 (advantages of wisdom). The conclusion (v. 14) is to recognize that God has made the one as well as the other.

Genre, Setting, Intention

It is difficult to give a name to this unit; perhaps INSTRUCTION is the most adequate term, since the instruction in vv. 13-14 is a comment upon, and thus governs, the concatenation of the SAYINGS and PROHIBITIONS in vv. 1-12. The intention is indicated in the above analysis of the structure.

WISDOM RELATIVE TO JUSTICE AND WICKEDNESS, 7:15-24

Structure

I. Reflection upon the just/wicked paradox	15-18
A. Observation of the paradox	15
B. Quotation of admonitions concerning "too much" justice	16
C. Quotation of admonitions concerning "too much" wickedness	17
D. Qohelet gives his judgment	18
1. It is "good" to held to both admonitions	18a
2. But the one who fears God succeeds	18b
II. Two contrasting quotations	19-20
A. Saying about wisdom's strength (apropos of wisdom in v. 16)	19
B. Saying about man's moral frailty (apropos of wickedness in v. 17)	20
III. An instruction about listening to "talk" (apropos of human frailty; cf. v. 20)	21-22
A. Prohibition	21a
B. Motivation	21b-22
IV. Qohelet's description of his search for wisdom	23-24
A. His resolution to be wise	23abα
B. The reasons for his failure	23bβ-24

The length of this unit is determined by the phrase "who can find" in v. 24. The structure is loose, and sections II and III have to be understood as building out of the preceding section, as indicated in the structure. Several commentators (Galling, Braun, Ellermeier) see the search for wisdom continued in vv. 25-29, where ḥokmâ ("wisdom") would be the catchword.

Genre, Setting, Intention

The outline indicates the various genres, but there is considerable difference of opinion here. Braun interprets vv. 15-22 as an INSTRUCTION and vv. 23-29 as a meditation, while Ellermeier characterizes 15:22 and 7:23–8:1 as REFLECTIONS. In 7:15ff. much depends upon the exegesis of the PROHIBITIONS in vv. 16-17; are these meant seriously by Qohelet (so that he is urging the "golden mean") or does he have tongue in cheek? They are not taken as "quotations" by Gordis, with whom the quotation theory is original, and who recognizes vv. 19-20 as quotations.

REFLECTION CONCERNING HUMANKIND, 7:25-29

Structure

I. Qohelet's resolution to search for wisdom	25
II. What Qohelet found	26-29
A. First finding	26
1. The adulteress "more bitter than death"	26a
2. The type that escapes her, or is caught by her	26b

As with the previous section, the length is determined by the occurrence of the phrase "I have not found" (v. 28). This section is dominated by the theme of "(not) finding" (seven times). In addition, the term *ḥešbôn* ("the sum," "devices") is found three times (vv. 25,27,29). Translations differ on the correct version of v. 28. Here v. 28b is understood as a quotation of what Qohelet did not find to be true (so Kroeber, Loretz, Strobel, and Bea; against Podechard, Zimmerli, Gordis, Barucq, Braun, *NAB*, *RSV*, *NEB*). The Hebrew text is ambiguous and could be translated also as an expression of Qohelet's opinion of woman, and not as a quotation which he rejects.

Genre, Setting, Intention

This is a REFLECTION which intends to make a comment upon humankind as v. 29 makes clear. Qohelet claims that the saying—concerning one man in a thousand but not one woman—is not true; hence he does not make a qualitative difference between man and woman. The woman of v. 26 is a topos of wisdom literature, the adulteress (Prov 6:26; Sir 9:3). No moral qualification should be read into *ṭôb lipĕnê hā'ĕlōhîm* ("whom God pleases") or *ḥôṭē'* ("one who misses the mark," "sinner") in v. 26b.

VARIA: INSTRUCTION AND REFLECTIONS, 8:1-17

Text

In 8:2, read *'et* for *'ănî*, and include "be not dismayed" from 8:3.

Structure

I. Instruction concerning conduct before the king	1-4
A. Introductory saying extolling the wise man	1
B. Commands and prohibitions	2-3a
C. Motivations	3b-4
II. Reflection upon time and judgment	5-8
A. Quotation of wisdom sayings	5-6a
1. About keeping a command	5a
2. About time and judgment	5b-6a
B. Counterstatements to these sayings	6b-8
1. Introduction (an evil for man)	6b
2. First statement: man's ignorance of future	7
3. Second statement: man's impotence and subjection to death	8

The length of this section is determined by the occurrence of the phrase "cannot find" in v. 17 (twice). Commentators are not agreed on the place and meaning of 8:1. Does it end the thought of 7:25 (Hertzberg, Ellermeier, Galling), or begin a new section (8:1-5, Braun, 134; 8:1-8, Barucq, Zimmerli; 8:1-15, Kroeber)? As far as meaning is concerned, does 8:1a introduce a wisdom saying that is quoted in 8:1b (so Kroeber, Hertzberg)? If 8:1 is taken as an introduction to what follows, the topos of conduct before the king, where does this unit end (v. 4,5,8,15)? Here 8:1-4 is taken as a unit concerning conduct relative to the king. There is a catchword that explains the succession of vv. 5-8 upon vv. 1-4: *dābār rā'* ("a bad situation") in vv. 4 and 5. The phrase "all this I observed" (v. 9) is the beginning of a new reflection upon injustice (vv. 9-15) that differs from the topic of time and judgment in vv. 5-8. But again, a catchword (*šilṭôn*, *šlṭ* ["power"]) accounts for the succession of vv. 9-15 after vv. 5-8 (without making them *one* unit). The final unit is vv. 16-17, dealing with the "doing" of God. Again, a catchword ("do," "doing" ['*śh, ma'ăśēh*]) unites vv. 16-17 with vv. 9-15. An inclusion is formed within v. 14 by the repetition of "vanity," but the repetition of "wise man" in vv. 1 and 17 provides an inclusion for the whole section. Many commentators (Podechard, Galling, Strobel, Ellermeier, Braun) consider a new section beginning at 8:16 (for Hertzberg, 8:10) and extending to 9:10 (for Zimmerli, 9:12).

Genre, Setting, Intention

The INSTRUCTION and three REFLECTIONS are clearly indicated in the above structure. The instruction takes up a common theme in wisdom, the relationship between man and the king (Eccl 10:4; Prov 14:35; 20:2). The three reflections are at one in agreeing about the absence of justice and (divine) judgment in the affairs of this world and man's impotence in all this.

REFLECTIONS, 9:1-6

Text
Read *hebel* ("vanity") for *hakkōl* ("everything") in v. 2, and include it in v. 1.

Structure

I. Reflection upon a wisdom claim	1-3
A. Statement of Qoheleth's understanding of a wisdom saying	1a
1. Introduction	1aα
2. The wisdom saying: the just and wise are in the hand of God	1aβ
B. Qohelet's objection to the saying	1b-3a
1. Man cannot tell God's love from hatred	1bα
2. Verdict of "vanity"	1bβ
3. A further objection: the same lot (*miqreh*) happens to all alike in all that is "done"	2-3a
C. Conclusion: bad effects upon man	3b
II. Reflection upon the living and the dead	4-6
A. Affirmation of advantage for the living	4a
B. Arguments in support of this:	4b-6
1. Quotation of proverb	4b
2. Living know at least they will die	5a
3. Dead know nothing, have no recompense (*śkr*) or memory (*zkr*)	5b
4. Further disadvantages of those who are dead	6

The general outline of the book given above has already indicated that the units in 9:1–11:6 are determined by the occurrence of "do not know"/"no knowledge" (9:5-6, 10, 12; 10:14-15; 11:6). As indicated in the structure of 8:1-17, there is a wide division of opinion on the way in which ch. 9 is associated with ch. 8. Here we regard the section as ending in 9:5-6, where "not know" occurs (Wright, 331). The repetition of "love" and "hate" in vv. 1 and 6 seems to be an inclusion. The catchword joining vv. 1-3 with vv. 4-6 is "the dead" (vv. 3,4).

Genre, Setting, Intention

The structure clearly indicates that the genres here are REFLECTIONS. The second reflection (vv. 4-6) grows out of the first (vv. 1-3), where the common fate (v. 3, *miqreh*) for all is underlined. The intention of vv. 1-6 illustrates the ambivalence of Qohelet. While he decries the easy opinion that the just and wicked are in the hand of God as solving the situation in this life, he also chooses life (vv. 4-6, and these lines prepare for vv. 7-10), even in the face of a contrary opinion expressed earlier in 4:2.

INSTRUCTION CONCERNING ENJOYMENT OF LIFE, 9:7-10

Structure

I. Commands to enjoy life	7-9a
II. Reasons	9b-10

The length of this short section is determined by the occurrence of the phrase "no knowledge" in v. 10.

Genre, Setting, Intention

The recommendation to enjoy life is one that has been voiced several times already in the book. This is perhaps the most emphatic example, and bears comparison with the advice given to Gilgamesh by Siduri (*ANET*, 90). The horizon in both is the same: the inevitability of death.

REFLECTION CONCERNING TIME AND CHANCE, 9:11-12

Structure

I. Observation of five unexpected results	11a
II. The reason for the results: time and chance affect all	11b
III. Elaboration of the reason	12
A. Man does not know his "time"	12aα
B. Like trapped fish and birds, men are suddenly caught	
by an "evil time"	12aβ-12b

The length of this section is determined by the occurrence of the key phrase "not know" in v. 12.

Genre, Setting, Intention

This is a REFLECTION which provides another treatment of man's ignorance about the work of God (8:16-17). Man is unaware of the (evil) time that "falls" (*tippôl*, v. 12) upon him. "Time and chance" (*'ēt wāpega'*, literally, "time and accident") is a time of calamity.

VARIA: THE LIMITATIONS OF WISDOM, 9:13–10:15

Structure

I. An example story about the wise man and a besieged city
(see Prov 21:22)   13-16
   A. Introduction   13
   B. Story of the besieged city (which could have been?)
saved by the poor wise man, who is forgotten   14-15
   C. Moral of the story   16
     1. Quotation of a (comparative, *min*) wisdom saying   16a
     2. Modification of the saying by reality exemplified
in the story   16b

II. A collection of sayings about wisdom   9:17–10:4
   A. Sayings in favor of wisdom   17-18a
     1. Comparative (*min*) saying, in antithetic parallelism   17
     2. "Better" (*ṭôb min*) saying   18a
   B. Sayings modifying the advantages of wisdom   9:18b–10:1
     1. Saying about the sinner (in opposition to v. 18a)   18b
     2. Proverb about dead flies and a little wisdom   10:1
   C. Sayings about the wise and foolish   2-3
   D. Prohibition relative to conduct before kings, with
motivation   4
   E. Reflection upon a breakdown in right order   5-7
     1. Observation of an evil, which is compared to a
ruler's mistake   5
     2. The instances   6-7
      a. The fool exalted over the rich   6
      b. Slaves ride while princes walk   7
   F. Sayings about what may accidentally happen   8-9
     1. Falling into a ditch one has dug   8a
     2. Being bit by a serpent when breaking through a
wall   8b
     3. Being hurt by the stones one removes   9a
     4. Being injured by the wood one chops   9b
   G. Sayings about the wise use of one's ability   10-11
     1. Use of a dull instrument   10
     2. Snake-charming (note paronomasia: *lḥš* ["bite"],
nḥš ["snake"], *lāšôn* ["charmer"])   11
   H. Sayings about the fool   12-15
     1. Contrast between words of wise man and fool   12
     2. Characterization of the words of a fool   13-14a
     3. Statement of man's ignorance of what is to come   14b
     4. The futility of the fool's toil   15

The length of this unit is determined by the key phrase "not know" in 10:14,15. Note the inclusion ("ruler") in 9:17–10:4 and the play on words in 10:11; the repetition of "city" in 9:14 and 10:15 is another inclusion.

Genre

The structure reveals the varied genres that appear in this section, which is primarily a collection of SAYINGS. The likely setting for this wisdom is the school. A logical thread that might be termed "limitations of wisdom" runs through several units. The EXAMPLE STORY about the wise man (vv. 13-16) is another instance of 9:11, and it points forward to the sayings that deal with wisdom and also the ruler (9:17–10:4, with *môšēl* ["ruler"] an inclusion in first and last verses). The following REFLECTION (10:5-7; see Prov 30:21-23 and the teaching of Ipuwer, *ANET*, 441) has also to do with court figures and illustrates once more the uncertainty in life. The theme of uncertainty appears again in the SAYINGS which follow (10:8-11,14).

MISCELLANY, 10:16– 11:6

Structure

I. A collection of sayings relative to the political order	10:16-20
A. About kings	16-17
1. "Woe" oracle	16
2. "Blessed" saying	17
B. About diligence	18
C. About good living	19
D. Admonition about curbing one's tongue with respect to the king, with motivation	20
II. Sayings about the uncertainty of human industry	11:1-6
A. Casting bread upon the waters	1
B. Making several portions	2
C. Rain comes when clouds are full	3aα
D. Trees fall where they will	3aβ-3b
E. About weather signs	4
F. The "doing [*ma'ăśēh*] of God" is as mysterious as gestation	5
G. Admonition to diligence, because one knows not what will happen	6

Again, the length of this unit is determined by the phrase "not know" (11:5,6). Although A. G. Wright makes two units (10:16–11:2; 11:3-6) because of "not know" (and the inclusion, "land," in 10:16 and 11:2) in 11:2, it seems best to regard this as more or less parenthetical, and the unit extends to 11:6, an appropriate ending before the clearly new beginning in 11:7. It should be noticed that *rûaḥ* ("spirit") is the catchword that serves to join vv. 4 and 5.

Genre, Setting, Intention

The genres are indicated in the structure above. With Hertzberg, Strobel, and others, it seems correct to recognize that the context or setting of 10:16-20 is the court (*melek* ["king"] is an inclusion in vv. 16,20). The drift of the sayings in 11:1-6 is similar to those in 9:8-9: uncertainty. Here v. 5 takes up a theme previously treated by Qohelet (7:13; 8:17): the greatest uncertainty of all is the work of God.

INSTRUCTION CONCERNING YOUTH AND OLD AGE, 11:7–12:7

Structure

I. Youth	11:7-10
A. Statement of a thesis about the goodness of life	7
B. Recommendations to enjoy life, with reservation	8
C. Commands to enjoy life in one's youth, with awareness of God's judgment	9
D. Two recommendations to put away grief, with motivation	10
II. Old Age	12:1-7
A. Command to remember the creator (grave? spring?)	1a
B. Specifications of time	1b-7
1. Before (*'ad 'ăšer lō'*) unpleasant old age comes	1b
2. Before the signs of approaching death appear	2-5
3. Before death itself	6-7

The structure and movement of thought is built around the sequence of *śmḥ* ("rejoice") and *zkr* ("remember"). Youth should rejoice (11:8a), but remember (11:8b). The command to rejoice (11:9) is again followed by a "remember" (12:1), in view of old age.

Genre, Setting, Intention

Because of the commands, this section should be read as an INSTRUCTION, although the description of old age taken by itself might be viewed as a REFLECTION. Many commentators understand the description of old age as an allegory, in which each detail (v. 3, "keepers of the house," etc.) has a transferred meaning. Others insist that it is a parable, a description of a winter storm, or the end of a day and the beginning of night. The setting of this instruction, precisely at the end of the book, serves to highlight the importance Qohelet attaches to the enjoyment of life, despite vanity. It is an insistent recommendation to live fully, in view of old age and death that lie ahead (cf. 9:10).

EPILOGUE, 12:8-14

Structure

I. Repetition of motto (which forms inclusion with 1:2)	8
II. Editorial remarks about Qohelet	9-11
A. Qohelet's activities as a wise man	9-10
B. A quotation of a wisdom saying concerning the wise men	11
III. Instructions to the reader	12-14
A. Command to be cautious, with motivation (a wisdom saying)	12
B. Commands to fear and obey God	13-14

1. Introduction   13a
2. Commands   13bα
3. Motivations   13bβ-14

Genre, Setting, Intention

The work closes with this epilogue, which treats of Qohelet in the third person (as opposed to first person in 1:12–12:8). The positioning of these observations is clearly the work of an editor who is putting forth the work to a larger public. Commentators differ concerning the number of "editors" responsible for these remarks. But the burden of the epilogue is clear: the identification of the author and the tenor of his book and life. Moreover, real concern about the possible effects of the book on the reader is reflected in v. 12 and in the injunctions of vv. 13-14.

ESTHER

BIBLIOGRAPHY

B. W. Anderson, *The Book of Esther* (*IB* III; New York, 1954) 821-74; H. Bardtke, *Das Buch Esther* (KAT XVII/5; Gütersloh, 1963); idem, "Neuere Arbeiten zum Estherbuch," *JEOL* 19 (1965-66) 519-49; Sandra B. Berg, *The Book of Esther: Motifs, Themes and Structure* (SBLDS 44; Missoula, 1979); G. Botterweck, "Die Gattung des Buches Esther im Spektrum neuerer Publikationen," *BibLeb* 5 (1964) 274-92; D. Daube, "The Last Chapter of Esther," *JQR* 37 (1946-47) 139-47; W. Dommershausen, *Die Estherrolle* (SBM 6; Stuttgart, 1968); H. Gunkel, *Esther* (Tübingen, 1916); G. Gerleman, *Esther* (BKAT XXI/1–2; Neukirchen-Vluyn, 1973); A. Meinhold, "Die Gattung der Josephsgeschichte und des Estherbuches: Diasporanovelle II," *ZAW* 88 (1976) 72-93; C. A. Moore, *Esther* (AB 7B; New York, 1971); L. B. Paton, *Esther* (ICC; Edinburgh, 1951); H. Ringgren, *Das Buch Esther* (ATD 16; Göttingen, 1958) 371-404; H. Striedl, "Untersuchungen zur Syntax und Stilistik des hebräischen Buches Esther," ZAW 14 (1937) 73-108; F. Stummer, *Das Buch Esther* (Echter-Bibel II; Würzburg, 1956) 555-87; S. Talmon, " 'Wisdom' in the Book of Esther," *VT* 13 (1963) 419-55; E. Würthwein, *Die Fünf Megilloth* (HAT 18, 2nd ed.; Tübingen, 1969) 165-96.

CHAPTER I

THE BOOK AS A WHOLE

Structure

Some commentators divide the book into three or four sections. H. Striedl (pp. 98-101) has presented four main divisions: (1) Setting-the-stage (*Exposition*): 1:1–3:1; (2) the main action (*Haupthandlung*): 3:2–9:15; (3) etiology of the feast of Purim, 9:15-32; (4) conclusion: 10:1-3, an imitation of the Deuteronomistic model in Kings (e.g., 1 Kgs 14:29). E. Würthwein follows this closely: (1) chs. 1–3; (2) 3:1–9:19, composed of twelve scenes; (3) conclusion: 9:20–10:3. Other commentators (Bardtke, Dommershausen, Moore) follow a broader unit division that takes each scene separately. It makes little difference whether one adopts the broad or narrow approach; the important thing is to recognize various scenes that succeed each other. In certain cases there will be room for a legitimate difference of opinion. The following structural analysis, based upon sequence of plot, has been adopted here.

I.	The royal banquets	1:1-9
II.	Vashti's disobedience and the result	1:10-22
III.	Esther becomes queen	2:1-20
IV.	Mordecai's discovery of a palace conspiracy	2:21-23
V.	Mordecai brings down upon himself and his people the wrath of Haman	3:1-7
VI.	Xerxes approves and proclaims the pogrom proposed by Haman	3:8-15
VII.	Mordecai commissions Esther to intercede with the king	4:1-17
VIII.	Esther's (first) dinner invitation	5:1-8
IX.	Proud Haman's plot to hang Mordecai	5:9-14
X.	Mordecai is honored, Haman is humiliated	6:1-13
XI.	Esther's (second) dinner invitation	6:14–7:10
XII.	The elevation of Mordecai	8:1-2
XIII.	Esther and Mordecai achieve the deliverance of their people	8:3-17
XIV.	The (first) victory of the Jews (13th Adar) over their enemies	9:1-10
XV.	Through Esther's request, a (second) victory of the Jews (14th Adar) is achieved in Susa	9:11-19
XVI.	Mordecai establishes the feast of Purim	9:20-28
XVII.	Esther's regulation for the Purim celebration	9:29-32
XVIII.	Epilogue	10:1-3

Genre

The wide variety of opinion concerning the genre of Esther has been canvassed by G. Botterweck: historical fiction, a festal legend, a history, a novella, haggadic midrash, a liturgical-political text, a historicized wisdom tale. Botterweck presents the arguments put forth by those who favor these varied interpretations. Thus, the judgment of historical fiction is based upon the free style of composition, as well as the remarkable knowledge of the Persian world and its customs. H. Bardtke thinks that the book was written as the legend for the Purim feast, and that it combined originally separate traditions (this aspect is also recognized by H. Ringgren and others) concerning Vashti, Mordecai and Haman, and Esther. Very few would regard the genre of Esther as history proper. Much has been made of the author's knowledge of Persian culture, and of the topography of Susa and the empire, but these factors are not enough to determine the genre. There is reason to speak of a "kernel" of historical fact lying behind the story, but it is almost impossible to determine the kernel. Although the term "midrash" has been applied to Esther, based apparently on the implausible and improbable traits in the story, there is a lack of consistency about the meaning of the term "midrash." S. Talmon (p. 426) has defined the work as a "historicized wisdom tale," and adduced arguments drawn from OT wisdom sources. His analysis incorporates new insights, but whether this evidence really determines the genre is debatable. Most recently, G. Gerleman has proposed that the book of Esther is a counterpart to the Exodus narrative (Exodus 1–12): the foreign court, the threat of death, the deliverance, the triumph, and the establishment of a feast (Purim, Passover). Mordecai and Esther correspond to Moses and Aaron. It is doubtful if wide assent will be given to the detailed correspondences which Gerleman purports to have found. He grants that Esther is the legend for the feast of Purim, and it is fiction, whose literary background is in the book of Exodus: the old tradition has been turned into a novella ("Novellisierung," p. 23). The term "novella" is favored by Würthwein, who quotes Goethe's definition of it as "an unheard-of event" (*unerhörte Begebenheit*). The work does not develop the picture of a world or of a period, but concentrates on a single event that rushes on toward an unforeseeable climax.

A general criticism of the various genre determinations is that the reasons advanced to characterize the genre are either not adequately presented or else they are not convincing (Talmon, Gerleman; at the most, these two scholars have presented evidence for the possible literary background of Esther). For example, it is not enough to say that the book is historical fiction. That it contains fiction, enough evidence is forthcoming. But what is the degree of its historicity? No solid judgment can be given because there is no evidence of a specific pogrom to which the book, on the basis of its own data, must be referred. Without such evidence, it is hard to justify the phrase "*historical* fiction." It is reasonable to suppose that there is a historical kernel, but the kernel is simply irrecoverable at the present time. All the arguments concerning the author's knowledge of Persian ways, etc. prove nothing about the genre of the work that he has written. The only certain affirmation is that the story of Esther and Mordecai is related as background for the celebration of the feast of Purim. Hence, as the book stands, it can be considered a reading for the Purim celebration. But the characterization as historical fiction is problematic.

There is, however, solid evidence on literary grounds to support the fictional aspect of the work. Many reasons have been offered in the past, and they can be briefly reviewed here. The ages of Mordecai and also of Esther cannot be reconciled realistically with the date of Xerxes' reign in 486-465 B.C. (since Mordecai was taken into exile in 597 according to Esth 2:6). Other improbabilities are the sumptuous feast of 180 days (1:1-3); the royal letter ordering all men in the empire to be masters in their own homes (1:22); the royal permission for the slaughter and plunder of a people within the empire, on a year's notice (3:8-15); and the reversal of this decree in a manner that would bring about anarchy in the empire (8:1–9:19). The point is not that such things could not happen; rather the frequency of these and other improbabilities and the manner in which they are woven into the narrative suggest fiction.

Even more impressive than a list of unlikely events is the book's literary style, which of its very nature suggests fiction and literary creation. One may recall the possible literary background in Exodus 1–15 (Gerleman) or in the wisdom literature (Talmon). The studies of Striedl and Dommershausen are particularly valuable in illuminating the style of the author and thus in providing a basis for the designation of genre as fiction. The use of conversation is an indication of fictional reality, since one can hardly surmise there were court reporters, and about one-fourth of the events described are expressed in dialogue (Dommershausen, 148). In this respect the questions of the king are both very frequent and important (1:15, 6:6; 5:3,6 with 7:2 and 9:12; 5:3, 7:2,5; 6:3-5). In the case of Esther, her requests of the king keep lengthening in expression (introductory formulas) as the suspense itself heightens (5:4,8; 7:3; 8:5).

The motif of concealment is a hallmark of the author's style. Thus, ignorance of the fact that Esther is a Jew and related to Mordecai enables Haman to conceive of his pogrom and attempt to hang Mordecai. This ignorance makes possible his misinterpretation of the queen's invitation to dine. The king is kept in ignorance that the Jews are the people who are to be slaughtered; hence he can plan the highest honor for Mordecai. Ch. 6 is a particularly good example of the motif: Haman comes to the king for the purpose of hanging Mordecai, but does not know the king intends to honor Mordecai; similarly the king is unaware of Haman's intentions. It is against that background that the conversation in 6:6-10 is so effective. Again, in ch. 7 Haman sits at a meal with the queen, totally unaware of the identity that Esther will reveal and the ensuing wrath of the king.

Another feature is the antitheses which extend throughout the work. The entire book is governed by two great counterpoints: the Jews and their enemies. The pogrom of the Jews on the 13th of Adar becomes the slaughter of their enemies. Mordecai is opposed to Haman (the Saulite against the Agagite, 1 Samuel 15) and replaces him as head of state while Haman replaces Mordecai on the gallows. In fact, several minor contrasts are associated with the basic opposition between these two men: Mordecai's defense of the king goes unnoticed, while Haman is exalted (2:21–3:2); Haman feasts, while Mordecai fasts (3:15–4:1), etc. The speeches of Haman's family and friends are in artful contrast in 5:14 and 6:13.

Particularly dramatic is the principle of delay, which is at work in 5:3-8. Just after the suspenseful moment of the king's acceptance of Esther, she puts off answering the king's generous request, and even postpones an explicit dinner engagement to which the king and Haman are invited! The vivid scene at the dinner in ch. 7 retains its suspense in no small way by the delaying of the name of Haman until a climactic moment (7:6). Similarly, there is a delay factor at work in the description of Esther's agreement to intercede with the king (4:4-16).

But the delaying tactic is admirably balanced by acceleration in action. The tempo in chs. 5–6 is particularly fast. The king and Haman answer at once Esther's invitation to dinner (5:5-6). Mordecai passes from the threat of gallows (5:9-14) to royal honors (6:10-11) within twenty-four hours. Haman's humiliation is followed in rapid succession by a visit to his home, the summons to Esther's dinner, and his own hanging on the gallows (6:14–7:10); and on the same day Mordecai replaces him. The first three chapters linger over events that fill a nine-year period (1:3; 2:16; 3:7), but then the story is concentrated within a year, the twelfth of Xerxes' reign, according to 3:7. Within this year, the most decisive events take place in two days! The undoing of Haman is described in a very rapid tempo (chs. 6–7).

Dommershausen (p. 153) has pointed out various motifs: (1) the woman who by her beauty wins the heart of her husband-king and achieves the extraordinary; (2) a Jew becomes a courtier of a foreign king and influences him to save the Jews; (3) a king who had previously decreed the destruction of a people becomes the friend of the people. One may recall also the possible literary references to Exodus and the wisdom literature that are offered by Gerleman and Talmon.

This description of the manner in which the writer has put together the development of the Esther narrative provides solid evidence that the genre of the book is fiction. Dommershausen has distinguished various subgenres within the book. The most frequent is the STORY (*Erzählung*), for this carries the movement of the book. Throughout the analysis below other subgenres recognized by Dommershausen have been indicated, such as the "speech" in 2:1-4, or the "battle report" in 9:1-4. But the minute assigning of a genre is not always helpful. The comment of C. A. Moore (p. LV) is apropos: "as Goethe's Faust long ago observed, to name a thing is not necessarily to explain it."

Setting

The question of the setting of Esther is easier to answer than the genre. It is the Purim celebration. The book was written to explain why the feast of Purim, which does not have the authority of the Torah behind it, came to be, and must be, celebrated. Hence it can be considered a reading for the feast of Purim.

Much has been written about Purim and its origins. It seems best to regard the term itself as derived from an Akkadian word for "lot" (*pûr* is interpreted as *gôrāl* in 3:7). The feast itself is probably of non-Jewish origin, although there is no certainty on this score. It would have been adopted by the Jews, and provided with the Esther story as an explanation of the feast and the dates and manner of its celebration.

Intention

On one level, the intention of the book coincides with the explanations given above for its setting. One may note further that within the book itself is an effort to explain why urban Jews have a two-day celebration, in contrast to the country

Jews (9:15-19). Moreover, the specification of fasting is the preoccupation of 9:29-32.

However, on the level of the story which forms the main part of the book, one may ask about the intention. There is a delicate tension between chance and Providence in the story. Esther happens to become queen, the king's sleeplessness leads to the "discovery" of Mordecai's loyalty. On the other hand there is a basic conviction that the Jewish people are being cared for. If Esther does not intercede with the king, help will surely come "from another place" (4:14). Whether or not one agrees with Gerleman that Exodus 1–15 forms the precise literary background of the book, the similarity between the situations and the theology is obvious. The election and protection of Israel remain. Although the word "God" is not to be found, and the sacred name is also absent from the text, the reality is present (and the Greek additions to Esther make this clear).

CHAPTER 2

The Individual Units

THE ROYAL BANQUETS, 1:1-9

Structure

I. Xerxes gives a banquet for the leaders of his kingdom	1-4
A. Three temporal indications, leading up to the banquet	1-3
B. Description of rich display at banquet of 180 days	4
II. Xerxes gives a second banquet, of seven days, for the people of Susa	5-8
III. Queen Vashti gives a banquet for the women	9

Some of the prime characteristics of the structure of this work appear in these first verses: the indication of time (vv. 1-3), the double action (the leaders, the people, Susa; compare the two days celebration of Purim, 9:15-21), repetition of key words and phrases (*melek* ["king"] thirteen times; *'āśâ mišteh* ["give a banquet"]).

Genre, Setting, Intention

This section is a "tendentious description" (Dommershausen), drawn from the style of court history (as in Judith, 1 Esdr 3:1-3, etc.). The purpose is to celebrate the opulence and power of the Persian court, while a mise-en-scène is set up for the developments to follow. Thus, already there is a distinction between Susa and the provinces, and Vashti's separate banquet is noted in preparation for 1:10-22.

VASHTI'S DISOBEDIENCE AND THE RESULT, 1:10-22

Structure

I. The king's request and Vashti's refusal	10-12
A. On seventh day of banquet, Xerxes orders the seven eunuchs to have Vashti show herself	10-11
B. Vashti's refusal, and the king's anger (note chiastic structure in v. 12b)	12
II. The king's recourse to the seven	13-15
A. Xerxes addresses the seven, whose relationship to him is described in detail	13-14
B. Xerxes' question: what is to be done?	15
III. Memucan gives the answer	16-20
A. Vashti has wronged king, princes, and peoples	16

158

B. Effect of her wrongdoing upon women of kingdom   17-18
C. Verdict: Vashti to come before king no more, but to
    be replaced, so that women will honor their men   19-20
IV. Xerxes sends out verdict to kingdom, so that "every man
    be lord in his own house"   21-22

Several structural features appear: the indication of date (v. 10) the explicit mention of names (of seven eunuchs, of seven princes), the predilection for the number seven. The structuring of the titles of the seven princes is striking; they are described as wise, knowers of times, versed in law (then follow the names of those "next to him"), princes, viewers of the royal face, sitting in first place. Thus, seven terms for seven princes. In Memucan's speech a marked structure appears: *yēṣē' dĕbar hammalkâ* ("the queen's deed will go forth," v. 17a) is balanced by *yēṣē' dĕbar malkût* ("a royal order will go forth," v. 19a). In both of those verses there is also a repetition of Vashti's "coming" before the king.

Genre, Setting, Intention
Dommershausen characterizes this as a "wisdom narrative" on the basis of the following elements: Xerxes is a type of the "foolish king" (Eccl 10:16; Prov 19:12); merely one factor (Vashti's disobedience) can undo all (Eccl 9:18–10:1); the talion law (Vashti did not appear, now she is to disappear); the phrase "that every man be lord in his own house" (v. 22) recalls a wisdom ideal about the husband-wife relationship (Prov 31:10ff.; Sir 9:2; etc.). While there may be wisdom motifs underlying the book of Esther (see Introduction above), these characteristics in vv. 10-22 do not make it a specific wisdom narrative. More simply, it is a NARRATIVE, and it moves the story along in order to bring Esther on the scene. There may also be a latent contrast between Vashti, who is disobedient to Xerxes, and Esther, who is obedient to Mordecai. There seems to be a humorous intent, even ridicule, in the portrayal of the danger to the kingdom stemming from the rebellion of all the wives.

ESTHER BECOMES QUEEN, 2:1-20

Structure
I. The proposal for the choice of a new queen   1-4
  A. General indication of time and circumstances   1
  B. The proposal of royal servants for the replacement of
    Vashti receives the approval of Xerxes   2-4
II. Mordecai's adopted daughter is brought to the harem   5-11
  A. Identification of characters: Mordecai and Esther   5-7
  B. Esther is placed under Hegai's supervision and wins
    his favor   8-9
  C. Esther's silence about her Jewish descent   10
  D. Mordecai's daily activity, solicitous for Esther   11
III. Esther is chosen by Xerxes as queen   12-20
  A. The procedural rules for the selection of queen   12-14
  B. Manner of Esther's success   15-20

Several characteristic stylistic features appear in this section. The introduction begins with a general designation of time, "after these things," which serves to join separate scenes together (cf. 3:1). The triple use of the particle '*ēt* (the grammatical object marker) in 2:1 is quite effective in making the connection with the events in ch. 1. The speech of the servants in vv. 2-4a follows the "reverent" style in which the king is mentioned in the third person, and the plan is expressed in very compact manner. The motif for the "search of a maiden" is reminiscent of 1 Kgs 1:2-4. The movement in the narrative is momentarily stopped with the introduction of Mordecai and Esther; the identity of Mordecai as a Benjaminite prepares for the later identification of Haman as an Agagite (cf. 1 Sam 15:7-9). A similar lull in the movement of the narrative comes in vv. 10-11, where the motif of silence concerning Esther's Jewishness is introduced, despite Mordecai's daily concern for her. Both traits are important for the later development of the story, and the silence motif is taken up again in v. 20. V. 19 is a *crux interpretum*, and commentaries propose various solutions for this gathering "a second time." As the text stands, the verse can be understood as a stylistic "repetition of a situation in order to introduce something new" (Striedl, 99, and he compares it with 8:3; 9:29).

Genre, Setting, Intention

Several subgenres appear as the story line develops in this NARRATIVE: the SPEECH of the servants is in the genre characteristic of speeches made by servants to the king; there is a BIOGRAPHICAL RECORD in vv. 5-7 about Mordecai and Esther; a REPORT is at the basis of vv. 8-20 concerning Esther's entrance to the palace, her favor with Hegai, and then with the king. The author is gradually bringing events and characters together to prepare for the eventual dramatic conflict of the work.

MORDECAI'S DISCOVERY OF A PALACE CONSPIRACY, 2:21-23

Structure

I. Report of the attempted assassination	21
II. Through Esther, Mordecai alerts the king	22
III. Punishment of the guilty, and record made in the chronicles	23

This section narrates an important event that will be taken up later on (ch. 6). It is introduced by the vague "in those days" and the mention of Mordecai at the gate (v. 21) ties the section with v. 19. The style is very spare; the author has no interest in the manner of Mordecai's discovery, the king's reaction, etc.

Genre, Setting, Intention

This section is a short REPORT that is placed here in view of the events in ch. 6. The indication of Jewish concern for the head of state is not without irony in view of the charge to be made against the Jews in ch. 3.

MORDECAI BRINGS DOWN UPON HIMSELF AND HIS PEOPLE THE WRATH OF HAMAN, 3:1-7

Structure

I. Xerxes' exaltation of Haman leads to obeisance from all the royal servants	1-2a
II. Mordecai refuses obeisance	2b
III. Reaction of servants: dialogue with Mordecai and report to Haman	2b-4
IV. Haman's reaction: anger, but exterminate the Jews rather than handle only Mordecai	5-6
V. A note about Pur	7

As often in Esther, the temporal indication ("after these things," as in 2:1) indicates the opening of a new section. This well-constructed scene sets up the hostility of Haman (the "Agagite," as Mordecai was described as the Benjaminite in 2:5; see I Samuel 15) against Mordecai and the Jews. Although v. 7 seems to interrupt the sequence between vv. 6 and 8 (Gerleman), and is joined by some (Würthwein) to vv. 8-15, it is appropriate to see it as a note concerning the day determined by Haman before he has recourse to the king (Bardtke).

Genre, Setting, Intention

This section is called a "short narrative" by Dommershausen: it is the opening scene of the great conflict between Haman and the Jews, and described with no little subtlety. Haman is not directly said to be the enemy, but the "Agagite." The issue of being a Jew emerges emphatically after the apparent curiosity of the servants (v. 4; the author never addresses himself to the meaning of Mordecai's refusal; the language in v. 4a is reminiscent of Gen 39:10). Onomatopoeia is striking in v. 5b: *wayimmālē' hāmān ḥēmâ* ("and Haman was filled with fury"). And the threefold repetition of the name of Mordecai is stylistically effective: twice the Jews are called the "people of Mordecai," and the plan is to kill "all" in "all" the kingdom. The notice about the casting of lots for the day of the pogrom ties in with 8:12; 9:24ff.

XERXES APPROVES AND PROCLAIMS THE POGROM PROPOSED BY HAMAN, 3:8-15

Structure

I. Haman's request	8-9
A. Haman's description of the Jews: dispersed and different, disobedient	8
B. Proposal for their destruction, and his offer of ten thousand talents	9
II. The king's affirmative reply	10-11
A. Handing of signet ring to "the enemy of the Jews"	10
B. Xerxes returns the money to Haman and the people	11
III. Execution of the royal decision by edict throughout the provinces	12-15a
A. Detailed preparation of edict by secretaries	12

B. Notices sent to provinces designating Adar 13 for the
   day of slaughter of Jews   13
C. Manner of proclamation, in readiness for the day   14
D. Dispatch of couriers, and issuance of decree in Susa   15a
IV. Reactions of Xerxes, Haman, and the people of Susa   15b

Although the structure is somewhat repetitious in vv. 12-15, the whole is marked by subtlety and style. The people to be slaughtered is never explicitly identified (but the diaspora conditions are neatly indicated in alliteration: *mĕpuzzār ûmĕpōrād* ["scattered and dispersed"]). From now on Haman is named "the enemy of the Jews" (3:10; 8:1; 9:10). The king replies to Haman's address in inverse order: money, then people (v. 11), after his extraordinary granting of the signet ring that is described in words taken from Gen 41:42 (a kind of "parody" of the salvation history, according to Bardtke). The date which begins v. 12, "in the first month, on the thirteenth day," is reminiscent of Lev 23:5, "in the first month, on the fourteenth day," that introduces the celebration of the Passover in connection with the exodus from Egypt. Chiastic parallelism and alliteration characterize the seven words in v. 12b. The author is not concerned to explain why such a decree would be published eleven months before the date of execution. The description of the conduct of Xerxes and Haman in v. 12b (sitting down to a meal!) and the confusion in Susa may be merely "narrative motifs" (Bardtke), but they are also a bitter commentary.

Genre, Setting, Intention

Dommershausen classifies this section as a "NARRATIVE" that incorporates a "description" of the content and proclamation of the royal decree. The text underlines the insensitivity and criminality that lies behind the pogrom.

MORDECAI COMMISSIONS ESTHER TO INTERCEDE WITH THE KING, 4:1-17

Structure

I. Description of the lamentation of Mordecai and the Jews   1-3
II. Description of Esther's dealings with Mordecai   4-17
  A. She sends Mordecai garments to replace his sackcloth
    (cf. v. 2) and he refuses   4
  B. She sends Hathach to Mordecai seeking an
    explanation, and Mordecai informs him and charges
    him to have her intercede with the king   5-9
  C. Again through Hathach Esther indicates this is
    impossible because one cannot approach the king
    without running the risk of death   11-12
  D. Mordecai's message to Esther: warning, threat,
    encouragement   14
  E. Esther's compliance and request for Jews in Susa to
    fast   15-16
  F. Mordecai carries out Esther's request   17

Although the author has put great emphasis upon the lamentation scene (vv. 1-3), there is no need to separate it from vv. 4-17, as Dommershausen does. The structure is obviously built around the three exchanges between Mordecai and Esther, each of which increases the tension, till finally the words of Mordecai and Esther are directly quoted (vv. 11, 13b-14, 16; note the anacoluthon in v. 11).

Genre, Setting, Intention

Dommershausen classifies this section as a "NARRATIVE" (vv. 4-17). The artistry consists in the building up to the final exchange between Mordecai and his adopted daughter: the movement is deliberately slowed by Esther's initial refusal, and then the climax is presented with a mysterious allusion to help "from another place" (against Bardtke, it should be said that the reference is to God). The "who knows . . . ?" of v. 14 does not express doubt; rather it is an expression of belief that the Providence which made her queen will see her through to the end with the salvation of herself and her people. Esther's final words are an anadiplosis, in the style of Gen 43:14—"if I perish, I perish!"—and are a moving finale to the section. As so often in this story, the author pays no attention to certain details, such as the manner of Mordecai's communication with Esther, or the reason, if any, why Esther was ignorant of the decree against her people.

ESTHER'S (FIRST) DINNER INVITATION, 5:1-8

Structure

I. Esther prepares herself to approach the king	1
II. Esther is received favorably by the king who wants to grant whatever request she makes	2-3
III. Esther invites the king and Haman to a banquet and they come	4-5
IV. The king repeats (cf. v. 3) his readiness to grant her wishes	6
V. Esther's reply is to invite them again to banquet on the morrow when she will indicate her request	7-8

This scene is so structured as to build tension in the events and in the reader. The sixfold repetition of the root term *mlk* ("king") in v. 1 underlines the solemnity and the seriousness of the forthcoming encounter: will the king accept or reject her? He accepts her enthusiastically in a formula which will be repeated three more times with variations (5:3,6; 7:2; 9:12). And in this climactic moment, she merely issues an invitation to a banquet! Her naive request is followed immediately (!) by the presence of the king and Haman for the banquet. When for the second time she invites them to a banquet on the following day, the reader begins to see that there is a "delay factor" working in the presentation of the story that is deliberately utilized in order to build up tension. And the delay will also provide time needed for the *entr'acte* which will be related in 5:9-14. The terms "petition" and "request" (vv. 3,6,8) are used effectively for symmetry and assonance. The threefold occurrence of "and Haman" (vv. 5,6,8) is striking; Esther has not forgotten the pogrom!

Genre, Setting, Intention

On the basis of contents, Dommershausen classifies this section as a "wisdom narrative," but his references to Ben Sira to support this are farfetched (Sir 26:13-14; 36:27). This is simply another scene in the eventual deliverance of the Jews that Esther will achieve. Naturally, her cleverness is underscored, but the NARRATIVE is interested more in building up tension and suspense, leading to the climactic deliverance, than in any didactic purpose.

PROUD HAMAN'S PLAN TO HANG MORDECAI, 5:9-14

Structure

I. Haman's good humor turned to wrath at the sight of Mordecai's refusal of obeisance	9
II. Haman's consultation with his wife and friends concerning his predicament	10-13
III. Their advice to him to build a gallows and execute Mordecai is agreeable, and he has the gallows built	14

Several traits add to the suspense of the story: this time (cf. 3:2, 5) Mordecai's total indifference to Haman, even after the decree of extermination of the Jews, is minutely described (v. 9). The details about Haman's exaltation climax in the dinner invitation of Queen Esther (v. 12), but the exquisite torture of Mordecai's refusal wipes all this out (v. 13). The reader may wonder if perhaps Esther, with her delaying tactics, may have misjudged the situation! But in fact, Haman's misinterpretation of Esther's invitation is, as Gunkel remarks (p. 30), one of "the most effective traits in the book." Dommershausen remarks perceptively that the mixture of certainty and optimism on the one hand with so much uncertainty and pessimism (in v. 14) is an example of the author's remarkable artistry. The term *śmḥ* ("joy," vv. 9,14) forms an inclusion.

Genre, Setting, Intention

Dommershausen characterizes this as an ANECDOTE with wisdom teaching. Anecdote it is, and an important one leading to the undoing of Haman. But it is somewhat heavy-handed to speak of wisdom teaching. It is true that the episode illustrates that pride goes before a fall (Prov 16:18), and that the one who digs a pit will fall into it (Prov 26:27), but this is not the major concern of the narrative.

MORDECAI IS HONORED, HAMAN IS HUMILIATED, 6:1-13

Structure

I. The king makes the discovery of Mordecai's unrewarded loyalty (see 2:21-23)	1-3
II. Entry of Haman, intent upon Mordecai's death	4-5
III. Misinterpreting the king's question, Haman prescribes the honor to be shown to "one whom the king delights to honor"	6-9
IV. Haman carries out the commission of the king to honor Mordecai	10-11

V. Mordecai returns to the king's gate; Haman, to his house   12
VI. The judgment of Haman's wife about the situation   13

This structure needs to be fleshed out by indications of the dialogue that the author uses cleverly to heighten the tension and increase the rapid tempo of events (cf. Striedl, 87). The dialogue between the king and his servants (vv. 3-5) concerns the absence of any reward for Mordecai's loyalty, the presence of a visitor in the court (Haman), and the royal invitation for him to enter. At this point the irony is greatest: Haman is intent upon Mordecai's death, and now becomes the unsuspecting instrument for Mordecai's exaltation. The gross misunderstanding is made possible by several silences: the name of the one to be honored, the king's ignorance of the Haman/Mordecai conflict (although Mordecai is called "the Jew" for the first time by the king in v. 10), Haman's ignorance of the fact that the one to be honored is one who has saved the life of the king. Although the king acts unsuspectingly, he has become the instrument of divine Providence. There are many small but significant touches in literary expression: alliteration (*lamed*) in describing the purpose of Haman's visit (v. 4); the sixfold repetition of the neatly indefinite phrase, "one whom the king delights to honor" (vv. 6-11); the understatement in v. 12; the contrast between the scene at home the day before (5:10-14) and now (v. 13). The verdict of Zeresh and the wise men concerning Mordecai as a member of the Jewish people (v. 13) is an anticipation of the final outcome; the verdict has been made possible by the bitter irony of Haman himself prescribing the honor to be shown to his enemy.

Genre, Setting, Intention
Dommershausen classifies this section as a STORY with a "wisdom saying" (v. 13) as its climax. One may question the emphasis on wisdom; the statement of Zeresh and the "wise men" in v. 13 is hardly a wisdom saying. It serves as an anticipation of the eventual deliverance of the Jewish people, and this is clearly its intention. The story itself, with its remarkable tensions and surprises, is an omen of Haman's eventual undoing, the exaltation of the just man over the proud man.

ESTHER'S (SECOND) DINNER INVITATION, 6:14–7:10

Structure
I. Introduction: Xerxes and Haman arrive for the banquet   6:14–7:1
II. Esther grants the king's request, and informs him of the
   situation of herself and her people   2-4
III. Reactions of the king and Haman when Esther reveals
   Haman as responsible for this   5-7
IV. The king interprets Haman's action as assaulting the
   queen   8a
V. Judgment falls for Haman: hanging on the gallows
   prepared for Mordecai   8b-10

This structure analysis cannot bring out all the nuances in the story. In the very introduction (6:14) is a link with the preceding section, "while they were yet talking with him. . . ." The events proceed at a very fast tempo, almost unnaturally so, and hence there is a sense of eeriness about what is to happen at the second dinner. Although Esther begins with a stereotyped formula of royal etiquette, she continues in the second, not the third, person. The assonance of šě'ēlâ and baqqāšâ ("petition" and "request," noted above in ch. 5) is again effective in 7:2-3. Again there is the motif of concealment, as Striedl (p. 104) points out: the king is ignorant of the fact that Haman's decree is against the Jews, and that Esther is a Jewess. Similarly, Haman is ignorant of Esther's Jewish identity, and now sits at her table unaware. There are several fine touches: Esther is called "Queen Esther" five times to emphasize her position in this critical moment; the irony of Haman's begging a Jewess on his knees (esp. when Mordecai's refusal of obeisance was the reason Haman initiated the pogrom) for his life—only to have this be taken by the king as "assault"; the readiness of Harbona the eunuch to suggest a proper use of the gallows! There is an effective chiastic expression in v. 8b concerning the work of the king and the covering of Haman's face. There is obvious irony in Haman's dying on the gallows which he prepared for Mordecai. For the sake of a fast-moving story, the author skips over certain details (did Esther know of Mordecai's recent triumph?), as he has done many times before (e.g., 4:1-17).

Genre, Setting, Intention

With Dommershausen, this may be classified as a STORY, and the remarks above concerning its structure underscore the care with which it has been conceived and written. This scene is surely a climactic one in the resolution of the Jewish situation: Esther has saved them, and their enemy is dead. In comparison to this fact it seems inconsequential to speak, as Dommershausen does, of just retribution, or that "a king's wrath is a messenger of death" (Prov 16:14), or that a person falls into the pit he digs for another.

THE ELEVATION OF MORDECAI, 8:1-2

Structure

I. The king disposes of Haman's house to Esther, and
   Haman's royal signet ring to Mordecai   1-2a
II. Esther places Mordecai over Haman's house   2b

Genre, Intention, Setting

With Bardtke (against Würthwein and Gerleman), this section deserves to be set off as a separate unit; it is in the genre of REPORT. As Dommershausen remarks, this forms a certain "resting point" in the narrative, and it rounds out ("on that day," v. 1) the hectic events at the court. The contrast between Mordecai and Haman is completed now as Mordecai receives the signet ring formerly worn by Haman, and also all his possessions. Of course, the reader might ask: and what about Haman's plan? This is likewise to be reversed, as the following verses show. Bardtke remarks correctly, however, that from this point on the narrative is without the tension and drama that has marked it thus far; it now becomes a report of how Esther and Mordecai worked out the deliverance of the people.

ESTHER AND MORDECAI ACHIEVE THE DELIVERANCE OF THEIR PEOPLE, 8:3-17

Structure

I.	Esther requests of Xerxes the cancellation of Haman's letters	3-6
II.	Xerxes grants the requests, authorizing a new edict	7-8
III.	Mordecai attends to the new decree in favor of the Jews	9-14
IV.	The Jews rejoice over their deliverance	15-17

A natural sequence justifies this structure, although various genres are involved. The literary style is unusual. As Dommershausen remarks, there is frequent repetition of previous sentences or scenes, with only infrequent (in contrast with the earlier chapters) temporal references. Esther's performance before the king (v. 3) is much more effusive than in 5:1-2, but there is the same detail about the putting forth of the royal sceptre. Her speech (cf. Striedl, 88-89) is marked by four conditional clauses before she comes to the heart of the affair: revoke the letters written by Haman (whose full description is deliberate here). Dommershausen and Gerleman compare 3:6 with Gen 44:34. Conveniently, Esther seems to know nothing about the irrevocability of Persian law (1:19)! From 8:9ff. the chapter becomes a pendant (Gerleman) to ch. 3, especially in the terminology concerning the new decree and its implementation. However, the Jews are not ordered, but are "allowed" (v. 11) to defend themselves against attackers on the 13th of Adar. The following comparisons can be made: 3:12a and 8:9; 3:12b-13a and 8:10; 3:13b and 8:11-12; 3:14 and 8:13; 3:15a and 8:14. As Würthwein remarks, "If the carrying out of the pogrom was factually doubtful, how much more the reversal in favor of the threatened Jews!" The joy of the Jews (vv. 15-17) corresponds to the lamentation described in 4:1-13.

Genre, Setting, Intention

The STORY in 8:3-8 is clearly designed to feature Esther as the intercessor for her people. The rest of the chapter is a report and description of the steps taken by Mordecai to ensure the reversal of Haman's letters. The concern of the story now is the deliverance of the Jewish people, and the presentation in 8:9ff. is modeled upon 3:12ff., without being a slavish imitation (Bardtke). Commentators rightly consider the decree of reversal as a "fairy-tale" trait (Bardtke), since no official could tolerate, much less abet, such civil war. If 8:9 is compared with 3:12 it appears that sixty days provide the temporal framework for 4:1–8:8, although some events (the downfall of Haman) occurred in rapid succession. The description of Mordecai in 8:15 seems to be in deliberate contrast with the humble figure that used to sit at the king's gate. The tenor of the chapter is set by the appearance of the term "the Jews" fourteen times.

THE (FIRST) VICTORY OF THE JEWS (13th ADAR) OVER THEIR ENEMIES, 9:1-10

Structure

I.	The reversal	1-4
	A. Announcement of the reversal on 13th Adar	1-2a

The key words governing this statement of the Jewish victory are the "reversal" (*hpk*, v. 1) and the "fear" (*phd*, vv. 2-3). There is a deliberate emphasis on the extermination of the family of Haman, mentioned explicitly by name in vv. 7-9.

Genre, Setting, Intention

Dommershausen classifies this as a BATTLE REPORT. There is a concern to stress that there was no plunder (v. 10, and again in vv. 15-16); this seems part of the evenness demanded by a reversal of the decree against the Jews.

THROUGH ESTHER'S REQUEST, A SECOND VICTORY OF THE JEWS (14th ADAR) IS ACHIEVED IN SUSA, 9:11-19

Structure

Genre, Setting, Intention

In vv. 11-15 one is dealing with another STORY reminiscent of previous encounters of Esther with the king. Here the intention is quite clear: to explain the establishment of a second day of celebration because of a second day of battle. Dommershausen's explanation of this as another instance of stylistic reprise (similar to the gathering of the maidens in 2:19, or the redundant request of Esther in 8:3) is not helpful. Instead, there is a basic etiology at work: since the Jews in the provinces celebrated 14th Adar as a day of rest after the victory over their enemies, whereas the Jews in Susa (who fought on two successive days) celebrated their respite in the 15th, provision for this had to be made in the Esther narrative. This is explained in vv. 16-19. (Purim came to be celebrated on the 14th in the provinces, on the 15th in Susa. Why?) Certain key words are repeated over and over in vv. 16-19: rest, feasting and gladness, the Jews.

MORDECAI ESTABLISHES THE FEAST OF PURIM, 9:20-28

Structure

I.	An (indirect) report of Mordecai's letters to the provinces regulating 14th and 15th Adar as the days of the joyful celebration of Purim	20-23
II.	An explanation of the name Purim	24-26a
III.	Acceptance of the feast of Purim by the Jews	26b-28

There seems to be a wordplay on Haman in v. 24, in which he has lots cast to "crush" (lĕhummām) the Jews.

Genre, Setting, Intention

This section purports to be an (indirect) REPORT of Mordecai's regulations concerning the celebration of Purim, and of the Jews' acceptance of this regulation. The themes of "rest" and "reversal" reappear (v. 22) and the joyous character of the feast is underscored (v. 23). The explanation of Purim (vv. 24-26a) is a summary, in catechism style (Bardtke, Gerleman), of the events in chs. 3–8 that form the "prehistory" to the feast of Purim: Haman's plot, Esther's intervention, the king's action, and the death of Haman and his sons. Purim is in the plural to account for the two days of the feast, and the term harks back to 3:7 and 9:24 for the etymology: the casting of lots. Bardtke notes an increasing emphasis in each of the three units in this section until finally (vv. 26b-28, which borrow phrases from vv. 21-23) the feast is commanded to be observed by all Jews and their posterity (including proselytes, "those who joined them," v. 27) for all time. The intention is quite clear: Purim is not a festival sanctioned by the Torah; nonetheless, it is to be observed by the Jews, as Mordecai's authoritative letters and Jewish acceptance indicate.

ESTHER'S REGULATION FOR THE PURIM CELEBRATION, 9:29-32

Text

Omit in v. 29: "and Mordecai the Jew" as an interpretative gloss; and omit in v. 31: "and Queen Esther" for the same reason; see the commentaries.

Structure

I.	Esther sends copies of a second Purim letter to the Jews of the provinces	29-30
II.	Purpose of the letter: observance of Purim, and especially the fasts and lamenting	31
III.	Characterization of the letter as a "command" that was put in writing	32

Genre, Setting, Intention

This purports to be an (indirect) report (cf. vv. 20-28) of Esther's regulations concerning the celebration of Purim. What is new is the legislation concerning fasts and lamenting, in keeping with 4:1-3 and especially 4:16 (in which Esther orders a fast to be held). The purpose of the section is to achieve the observance of the fast (*qyym* ["enjoin"] occurs five times) as a memory of the distress which had afflicted the Jews, thus balancing the note of joy in Purim. Striedl (p. 101) sees here a characteristic feature of the book's style: the repetition of a previous situation or event (cf. 2:19; 8:3). The glosses, which have been omitted from the structure above, tend to attribute everything in a blanket manner to both Mordecai and Esther.

EPILOGUE, 10:1-3

Structure

I. A note about the tribute exacted by Xerxes		1
II. The greatness of Mordecai		2-3
A. Expressed in the formula of the Deuteronomistic historian		2
B. The esteem enjoyed by Mordecai among his brethren		3

Genre, Setting, Intention

The book concludes as it begins with the mention of the great Xerxes (1:1-8). It is understandable that the ending of the book harks back to Mordecai, and celebrates him in the style of Solomon and other kings (e.g., 1 Kgs 11:41). Epithets in his honor are expressed in v. 3, with attractive assonance: *dōrēš tôb . . . dōbēr šālôm* ("seeking good . . . speaking peace"). This epilogue (as Daube, 145, terms it) seeks to underline the importance of Mordecai in the whole story, and orient the reader toward the future.

GLOSSARY

ACCOUNT (Erzählung, Bericht). Practically a synonym for the (→) report. Perhaps the account tends to be used where the narrative is more explanatory in nature. Cf. Judg 1:16, 17.

ACROSTIC POEM. A poem whose structure is guided by alphabetic considerations. Each unit (one-line, Psalms 111; 112; two-line, Psalm 34; eight-line, Psalm 119) begins with a consecutive letter of the Hebrew alphabet. Cf. Prov 31:10-31; Psalms 9; 10; 25; 34; 37; 111; 112; 145; and perhaps Nah 1:2-10.

Properly this term does not designate a genre, but the technique suggests a literary, scholastic background such as would have been at home in the school.

Related genre: (→) Alphabetizing Poem.

ADMIRATION SONG (Bewunderungslied). A statement that describes the physical and spiritual beauties of another, along with the subjective reaction of the speaker to these qualities. Cf. Cant 1:15-17; 4:9–5:1.

F. Horst, "Die Formen des althebräischen Liebesliedes," in *Gottes Recht: Gesammelte Studien* (TBü 12; Munich, 1961) 176-87; R. E. Murphy, "Form-Critical Studies in the Song of Songs," *Int* 27 (1973) 413-22.

ADMONITION (Mahnung, Mahnwort, Mahnrede). A genre of address that is designed to dissuade an individual or group from a certain type of conduct. It is difficult to distinguish this genre from the (→) prohibition; in fact, the prohibitive form ('*al* or *lō*' with the jussive) is used most frequently.

In the setting of wisdom or of preaching, admonition captures the mood of the statement: "the Wisdom prohibition is not really a command at all, but an admonition" (Bright, 202). Examples of the genre are Isa 1:16-17; Jer 25:1-7.

J. Bright, "The Apodictic Prohibition: Some Observations," *JBL* 92 (1973) 185-204.

ALLEGORY (Allegorie). Not strictly a genre, but rather a speech form closely related to figurative or metaphorical language. The details of an allegory are chosen and shaped against the background of the interpretation or application so that each detail of the allegory recurs in the interpretation.

The shortest form of the allegory is the metaphor, with just one motif calling for interpretation; a longer form is the allegorical story where each detail has its bearing on the interpretation. An allegorical form of speech calls for allegorical interpretation.

Allegory occurs in the OT in a dream report (cf. Gen 37:7; 41:17-24; Dan 7:2-14), in a vision report (cf. Dan 8:1-14 and the vision of Zechariah), in a Psalm (cf. Ps 80:9-20 [*RSV* 8-19]), or as a self-contained narrative like the (→) fable in Judg 9:8-15. Examples of this speech form are characteristic of Ezekiel (cf. Ezekiel 16; 17; 19; 23; 31–34).

Related speech form: (→) Figurative Speech.

L. Goppelt, "Allegorie II," *RGG* (3rd rev. ed.).

ALPHABETIZING POEM. This is not a genre term, but it describes the exterior poetic character of portions of OT poetry in which the writers "play" with letters. A good example is found in the alphabetic (→) acrostic poems (Psalms 25; 34). Both have a final verse added to the twenty-two letter acrostic device, and it begins with the letter *pe*. Thus *'aleph* is the first letter, *lamed* is the first letter of the middle verse, and *pe* is the first letter of the final verse. The whole poem is signed *'lp*, the verb stem which means "to learn" and "to teach."

In addition, there are clear signs of alphabetizing poems of twenty-two or twenty-three lines that imitate, as it were, the (→) acrostic poem. Psalms 33 and 103 are twenty-two lines each; Psalms 74 and 94 are twenty-three lines each. In the twenty-two line poem of Proverbs 2, the use of *'aleph* and *lamed* to begin strophes in vv. 1, 5, 9, 12, 16, 20 can only be deliberate. Similarly, Job 9:2-24 consists of twenty-three lines, mostly three-line stanzas, with significant use of certain letters to begin the lines (*'aleph, he, ḥet, lamed, tav*), and in 9:24c there seems to be a play, as the context allows, on the letters *'aleph, lamed,* and *pe*.

Related genres: (→) Acrostic Poem, (→) Wisdom Poem.

P. W. Skehan, *Studies in Israelite Poetry and Wisdom* (CBQMS 1; Washington, 1971) 74-75, 96-104.

ANECDOTE (Anekdote). A very short (→) narrative of an interesting or amusing episode, usually biographical, and often told to illustrate a point.

The OT anecdote is brief and usually inherently interesting (e.g., Gen 25:29-34; 2 Sam 23:11-12, 13-17, 20b), though the interest may be due primarily to the fact that the narrative explains or justifies something (cf. Josh 15:16-19, explaining the possessions of Othniel).

Grothe, Barnet et al., *Dictionary* ("Anekdote" *Sammlung Metzler*; Stuttgart, 1968).

APPEAL TO ANCIENT TRADITION. This is a genre of argument in which ancient tradition is cited in support of some point. The structure is regular, and contains the following elements: The appeal (*š'l, zkr*), often accompanied by the reason; the citation of the tradition; and application or expansion. Examples are Job 8:8-13; 20:4-29; Deut 4:32-35; 32:7-9; Jer 18:13-17; Isa 4:21-24.

N. C. Habel, "Appeal to Ancient Tradition as a Literary Form," SBLASP I (ed. G. W. MacRae; Missoula, 1973) 34-54.

AVOWAL OF INNOCENCE (Unschuldsbeteuerung). A statement in which one denies wrong-doing or even affirms good behavior. The setting can be legal, as when the avowal is aimed at an unjust accuser and before a judge; or it can be cultic, as the avowals in Psalms 7, 17, 26. Imitations of the avowal of innocence are found in Job (cf. 9:29-31; ch. 31).

BATTLE REPORT (Schlachtbericht). A (→) narrative of a war or battle organized with the following elements: Prelude (*Auftakt*), notice of initial movement (*Schlachteinleitung*), of battle (*Schlacht*), or defeat (*Niederlage*), of the extent of victory (*Aus des Sieges*), and, occasionally, of the annihilation of the enemy (*Ausrottung des Gegners*). Examples are Num 21:23-24; Judg 8:11-12; 10:17; 11:20-22.

W. Richter, "Die Überlieferung um Jeptah, Ri 10, 17–12, 6," *Bib* 47 (1966) 485-556.

"BETTER" SAYING. A wisdom saying that involves a comparison; it has two forms, "A is better than B," or "A with B is better than C with D." It is used as a rhetorical device in Qohelet to introduce and conclude certain thoughts. Cf. G. S. Ogden, "The 'Better'-Proverb (Tôb-Spruch), Rhetorical Criticism, and Qoheleth," *JBL* 96 (1977) 489-505.

BIOGRAPHICAL RECORD. This is a shortened (→) biography that serves to inform the reader of pertinent data for the development of events, as in Esth 2:5-7.

BIOGRAPHY (Biographie). In the strict sense, biography is a form of history. Its subject is the history of the life of a particular person. However, biography usually deals with more than just the bare facts. It includes an evaluation of the achievements of a person, a description of the development of ideas and their bearing on the future, etc.

There is no biography as such in the OT. However, as part of the prophetic tradition individual biographic narratives, or collections of such narratives are found that deal with events in the life of a prophet. But generally the intention is not biographical; the focus is not so much upon the person as upon what can be learned from what he experienced, how he acted, or what he said.

BLESSING (Segen). A pronouncement cast in either the imperative (cf. Gen 24:60) or the indicative (cf. Num 24:5-9), designed to release the inherent power of the spoken, preformative word.

A blessing can be introduced or concluded by a formula employing the passive participle *bārûk*, followed by the object of the blessing (cf. Num 24:9). Those formulas setting Yahweh as the object of the blessing represent a development from the formula, but nonetheless are a part of the history of this genre.

Related genre: (→) Curse.

W. Harrelson, "Blessings and Curses," *IDB*; F. Horst, "Segen and Segenhandlungen in der Bibel," *Gottes Recht: Gesammelte Studien* (TBü 12; Munich, 1961) 188-202; repr. from *EvT* 7 (1947-48) 23-37; J. Scharbert, " 'Fluchen' und 'Segnen' im Alten Testament," *Bib* 39 (1958) 1-26; S. Towner, " 'Blessed by YHWH' and 'Blessed Art Thou, YHWH': The Modulation of a Biblical Formula," *CBQ* 39 (1968) 386-99.

BOAST (Prahllied). A genre which appraises some person or thing for its value, and puts it in superior contrast to some other value. Cf. Cant 6:8-9, and perhaps also 8:11-12.

COMEDY. It is not at all certain that this is a form that is to be found in the Bible. As applied to Job it can be defined as a literary creation which consists of a vision of incongruity (the ironic, the ludicrous), and a basic story line that ultimately reintegrates the hero into his society. Cf. J. W. Whedbee, "The Comedy of Job," in *Semeia 7: Studies in the Book of Job* (ed. R. Polzin and D. Robertson; Missoula, 1977) 1-39.

COMMAND (Gebot). A direct commission, based upon authority such as custom or law. It is usually expressed by an imperative or by forms with an imperative function, and it may be accompanied by a (→) motive clause (cf. Prov 4:1-2).

A command is the opposite of a (→) prohibition and a subgenre of an (→) order.

COMPLAINT (Klage). A statement which describes personal or communal distress, often addressed to God with a plea for deliverance (Job 3; Hab 1:2-4; etc.). The description of the distress is characterized by vivid language (cf. the so-called confessions of Jeremiah, 12:1ff., etc.), and by the use of the question, "why?"

COMMUNAL COMPLAINT. → Complaint.

CURSE (Fluch). A pronouncement in the indicative (cf. Gen 27:39-40) designed to release the inherent power of the spoken, preformative word. Cursing can be introduced or concluded by a formula employing the passive participle, *'ārûr*, followed by the object of the curse (cf. Gen 27:29).

S. Blank, "The Curse, Blasphemy, the Spell and the Oath," *HUCA* 23(1950-51) 73-95; W. Harrelson, "Blessings and Cursings," *IDB*; J. Scharbert, " 'Fluchen' und 'Segnen' im alten Testament," *Bib* 39 (1958) 1-26.

CURSE FORMULA (Fluchformel). The original Israelite curse formula reads "Cursed are you" (cf. Josh 9:23; 1 Sam 26:19—*'ārûr*). Its setting is the nomadic culture where it is pronounced by the head of the community (clan or tribe), and becomes effective by the magical power of the spoken word. When this formula became part of the Yahweh religion, it was related to the power of Yahweh, and instead of a pronouncement it was understood as a wish. The personal address "you" could be replaced by the impersonal "he," or "the person" (cf. Josh 6:26; 1 Sam 26:19; Jer 11:3; 17:5).

This development presupposes a distance between the pronouncement of the curse and its taking effect, and allowed for a conditional curse depending upon a particular action which had already been committed or was likely to be committed. In this case, the person being cursed could be referred to by a participle, or by "the person" followed by a relative clause (cf. Deut 27:15ff.). As a later development, a reason for the curse and statements containing specifications could be added (cf. Gen 3:14-19; 49:7; Jer 20:14-18).

Related genre: (→) Blessing.

S. Blank, "The Curse, Blasphemy, the Spell and the Oath," *HUCA* 23 (1950-51) 73-95; J. Hempel, "Die israelitischen Anschauungen von Segen und Fluch im Lichte altorientalischer Parallelen," *Apoxysmata* (BZAW 81; Berlin, 1961) 30-113; D. R. Hillers, *Treaty-Curses and the Old Testament Prophets* (BibOr 16; Rome, 1964); W. Schottroff, *Der altisraelitische Fluchspruch* (WMANT 30; Neukirchen, 1969).

DESCRIPTION OF AN EXPERIENCE (Erlebnisschilderung). A genre described by Horst as a (→) story that is expressed in poetic form and in the first person. Thus, in Cant 2:8-13 the beloved describes a tryst with her lover; in Cant 3:1ff. and 5:1ff. a dream experience is described.

F. Horst, "Die Formen des althebräischen Liebesliedes," in *Gottes Recht: Gesammelte Studien* (TBü 12; Munich, 1961) 184-85.

DESCRIPTIVE SONG (Beschreibungslied). A statement in praise of the physical beauty of another person, usually the beloved. This is done of the women by the man in Cant 4:1-7, of the man by the woman in Cant 5:10-16, and of the woman by others (perhaps the man) in Cant 7:2-7 (*RSV* 7:1-6).

The genre has a long history in the ancient Near East (e.g., the description of Sarah in the Genesis Apocryphon), and in Arabic literature, where the term *waṣf* originated.

W. Herrmann, "Gedanken zur Geschichte des altorientalischen Beschreibungsliedes," *ZAW* 75 (1963) 176-96; F. Horst, "Die Formen des althebräischen Liebesliedes," in *Gottes Recht: Gesammelte Studien* (TBü 12; Munich, 1961) 17-87; R. E. Murphy, "Form-Critical Studies in the Song of Songs," *Int* 27 (1973) 413-22.

DIALOGUE (Dialog). There is no specific literary genre of dialogue in the OT (compare Plato's Dialogues). But there is dialogue—in the sense of exchange of speech—in the (→) disputations of Job and in the historical and prophetic narratives. Thus the term describes verbal exchange, oral or written, in a given situation (affairs of love or war, business or play, etc.).

DIRGE (Leichenlied, Leichenklage, Leichenklagelied). A funeral song, often accompanied by a flutist, bewailing the loss of the deceased, describing his merits, and calling for further mourning. The typical meter is *qînâ* (3 + 2). The most characteristic formulas employed are *'êk* (or *'êkâ*) ("how," "alas") and imperatives which call for mourning ("weep," "mourn," etc.).

The dirge was ordinarily performed by hired women or gifted individuals after the death of someone, and was usually sung in the presence of the corpse as part of the funeral preparations. Examples are 2 Sam 1:19-27; 3:33-34. In Isa 14:4-23 the dirge is used mockingly. For a prophetic adaptation of the genre, cf. Amos 5:1-3.

H. Jahnow, *Das hebräische Leichenlied* (BZAW 36; Giessen, 1923); E. Littmann, *Abessinische Klagelieder* (1949); E. Luddeckens, *Untersuchungen über religiösen Gehalt, Sprache und Form der ägyptischen Totenklagen* (1943).

DISPUTATION (Disputationswort, Streitgespräch). An argument between two or more parties, in which differing points of view are held. The disputation is an overarching genre that can designate the discussions of wise men (cf. Job), or parties in court, or prophet and people (cf. Jer 2:23-28).

In the disputation itself, a vast array of subgenres can be employed, drawn from judicial practice, worship, the world of wisdom, etc.

DRAMA. A literary composition, involving plot and conflict, and normally designed for public enactment. It is usually expressed in a (→) dialogue between two or more characters or groups of characters.

There is no drama, strictly considered, in the OT, although one may speak of dramatic elements, such as conflict, in certain books (e.g., Absalom's revolt against David). The Song of Songs has sometimes been interpreted as drama, but mistakenly; mere (→) dialogue does not constitute drama.

Many scholars (e.g., Mowinckel) have concluded from ancient Near Eastern parallels that there was cultic drama in Israel. Thus, a given piece of literature, such as a Psalm, would have been accompanied by some ritual. Mowinckel has postulated the feast of Yahweh's enthronement, in which several Psalms would have been ritually expressed (e.g., Psalm 48). It is possible that such a dramatic presentation may have been the original setting for certain Psalms.

EXAMPLE STORY (Beispielerzählung). A genre that provides a concrete example as an illustration of a point that an author, especially a sage, is making. Cf. Prov 7:6-23; 24:30-34; Eccl 4:13-16.

FABLE (Fabel). A short (→) story, usually involving animals or plants as characters, that expresses either implicitly or explicitly a moral principle. Cf. Judg 9:8-15.

FIGURATIVE SPEECH (Bildrede). A fact or state of affairs indirectly described in the form of a picture with symbolic figures. It is left to the reader or to the audience to discover the intended application. Figurative style can occur as metaphorical language in various genres, especially in poetry. Or an entire story can be told in which the acting persons represent the audience. In this case, the genre of the entire unit may be called figurative speech.

A typical example is the picture of the marriage to describe the relation between Yahweh and Israel. In Hos 1:2ff.; Jer 2:1-3; 3:6-11; Ezek 16:23 it constitutes a particular genre, figurative speech.

The instructing or advising character of a figurative speech suggests that it arose in the wisdom tradition.

FOLKTALE. → Story.

GENEALOGICAL LIST. A simple recounting of names giving an (→) account of one's descent from an ancestor or ancestors by indicating the intermediate persons.

GREETING. A genre in which individuals or groups express attitudes to each other on the occasion of meeting. The attitudes range from friendliness (Ruth 2:6; 1 Kgs 1:31) to hostility (2 Kgs 18:17; 2 Kgs 9:31).

HISTORICAL NOVEL (historischer Roman). A fictional narrative constructed to give the appearance of history. The effect is achieved by creating what seems to be a realistic setting, particularly by referring to actual historical personages who may even be actors in the narrative. Cf. the books of Esther and Judith.

E. Sellin and G. Fohrer, *Introduction to the Old Testament* (Nashville, 1968) 102.

HYMN. A song in praise of the Lord because of his interventions in the history of Israel or of the individual Israelite, or because of his creative power, or because of his kindness. These occur both in the liturgy (Psalms), and in other circumstances (Isa 12:1-6; Sir 42:15–43:33).

176

INSTRUCTION. A teaching or doctrine that gives guidance to an individual or group, setting forth certain values, or prescribing rules of conduct, answering questions, etc. It is usually given by someone of official status, such as a lawgiver, priest or teacher, and sometimes a prophet (Isa 8:16-20). Hence one can have various types of instruction: legal, liturgical, wisdom, etc.

The wisdom instruction usually prescribes a rule of conduct or some value, whether positively or negatively (→ prohibition). It may be very short and provided with a (→) motive clause (Prov 22:17-24:22). On the other hand, the instructions in Proverbs 1-9 are lengthy and exhibit influence from Egyptian instructions (cf. Introduction to Proverbs).

Related genre: (→) Wisdom Poem.

LEGEND (Legende). A (→) narrative primarily concerned with the wonderful and aimed at edification.

The legend has no specific structure of its own. It is concerned not with narrative interest, but with the impressiveness of its contents, which are supposed to stimulate its audience to believe or to do something good. Thus legends often serve to inculcate awe for holy places (cf. Judg 6:10-24), for ritual practices (cf. 2 Macc 1:19-22), and respect for men (cf. the Elijah Cycle; 2 Kgs 2:23-24) who may be models of devotion and virtue (cf. Exod 32:27-29; Deut 33:9; Num 25:6-12; Ps 106:30-31). This parallels the usage in the ancient world where legends were told to glorify shrines, the ritual practices observed in them, and the heroes whose connection with the place honored it (cf. Herodotus' *Histories* ii for Egypt; Pausanius' *Description of Greece*).

There were also civic legends which dealt with the extraordinary qualities of national heroes and places important to the nation (cf. the earlier books of Livy's *History*). Since the ancients did not really distinguish between state and religion it is impossible to separate civic legends entirely from the numinous. Nevertheless, the different emphases and attitudes of narratives like these separate them from narratives which are associated more directly with religion. Israelite legend tended even less to disassociate the civic from the religious (cf. Genesis 39-41, which glorifies the Hebrew).

A legend is distinguished from a (→) *Märchen*, a genre which shares an interest in the wonderful by virtue of two characteristics: (1) its specific practical aim (*Märchen* may have a moral, but it is concerned more with general attitudes), and (2) its claim to belief. Unlike the *Märchen*, the legend is placed in the real world and is often associated with historical characters. This latter characteristic distinguishes legend from (→) myth, which may claim belief but is essentially nonhistorical, outside time. Legend is distinguished from (→) story by (1) its specific practical aim and (2) its consequent relative indifference to narrative art. It is the marvellous and not the story line that constitutes the legend's essential claim to attention.

H. Delahaye, *The Legends of the Saints* (London, 1962); R. Hals, "Legend: A Case Study in OT Form-Critical Terminology," *CBQ* 34 (1972) 166-76; H. Rosenfeld, *Legende* (*Sammlung Metzler* 9; Stuttgart, 1972) 5-6, 15-17; S. Thompson, *The Folktale* (New York, 1946) 234-71.

LOVE SONG (Liebeslied). The overarching genre indicates the outpouring of the lover's feelings (desire, admiration, sadness because of absence, etc.) concerning the beloved. The standard OT collection is the Song of Songs, to which can be compared the love songs of ancient Egypt (examples in *ANET* and in Simpson).

Specific subgenres can be found: the (→) descriptive song is the lover's description of the physical beauty of the beloved (cf. Cant 4:1-7; 5:10-16; 7:1-6 [*RSV* 6:13-7:15]). The (→) self-description is a delineation of one's own characteristics, offered as a boast (cf. Cant 8:10), as an answer to an objection (Cant 1:5-6), or even as a challenge to the lover (cf. Cant 2:1-3).

F. Horst, "Die Formen des althebräischen Liebesliedes," in *Gottes Recht: Gesam-*

melte Studien (TBü 12; Munich; 1961) 176-87; R. E. Murphy, "Form-Critical Studies in the Song of Songs," *Int* 27 (1973) 413-22; W. K. Simpson, *The Literature of Ancient Egypt* (New Haven, 1972).

MÄRCHEN. A traditional narrative set in a mysterious world of fantasy, provoking sympathy for the principal figure. It commonly features creatures such as goblins, demons, sprites, and talking animals. A recurring motif is a concern to show how a basic injustice was finally righted (cf. Num 22:21-35). There are no *Märchen* as such in the OT, although *Märchen* motifs appear from time to time (cf. Genesis 38).
　　Related genres: (→) Fable, (→) Narrative, (→) Story.
　　A. Jolles, *Einfache Formen* (Tübingen, 1968).

MAXIM. Synonym for (→) saying or (→) proverb.

MOTIF (Motiv). The smallest element of content with the power to persist in an oral or literary tradition.
　　An example of the motif is that of the foundling hero. Normally a motif will be stated in an adjectival phrase like this, since the noun is not sufficiently defined to be distinct in the tradition without the adjective. Further definition beyond the adjective moves toward the (→) topos.

MOTIVE CLAUSE (Begründungssatz). A genre element often joined to a (→) prohibition, thus enhancing its pedagogical thrust. It is usually introduced by *kî* ("if"), *pen* ("lest"), etc.
　　B. Gemser, "The Importance of the Motive Clause in Old Testament Law," VTSup 1 (1953) 50-66.

MYTH (Mythos, Mythe). One can describe at least five major uses of the term myth.
　　(1) Any (→) narrative about gods or culture heroes. This is the terminology of the first form-critical work (cf. H. Gunkel, *Genesis* [HKAT I/1; 6th ed.; Göttingen, 1964]).
　　(2) A narrative recited to accompany a ritual. Undoubtedly myth is so used in many cultures. However, the idea, once widely held, that all myth was created to account for or accompany ritual actions (Raglan, Hyman) is untenable. Myths have many different origins and functions (Kirk).
　　(3) A symbolic expression of certain basic intuitions in which intellectual and emotional perceptions are interfused. This is the reason for the recurrence of the same symbols in diverse cultures and in separate individual psychic experiences, as in dreams (Cassirer, Jung).
　　(4) A narrative which functions in the traditions of various cultures or in individual lives to constitute world order by referring important elements of experience effectively to a higher supernatural reality of primordial events (*in illo tempore*, Eliade).
　　(5) The narrative resolution of contradictory perceptions or experiences. For example, in the Oedipus myth the hero who slays the sphinx, a symbol of the earth, and destroys his family through incest, is punished. This is not a logical resolution of the contradictory perceptions which are symbolized—on the one hand, the feeling of mankind that it is sprung from mother earth, and on the other, the obvious fact that human beings are born of sexual union, the family. However, the narrative does manage a kind of release of the tension between these two feelings by showing the negative result common to the flouting of the one and the other perception (Levi-Strauss).
　　Particularly in sense (4) and (5), myth is really alive only as long as it is believed, felt, and lived.
　　Provisionally, one may sum up some common elements in these different uses of the word myth. Myth tends to deal with the ultimate in terms of basic symbols structured in a narrative, not logical system (cf. Lewis).

However, the indetermination of the concept of myth as a narrative form means that it is a problematic designation of an OT genre. On the other hand, it must be emphasized that the OT does make extensive use of mythic elements: for example, the heavenly council (cf. Psalm 82), heroes of semi-divine parentage (cf. Gen 6:1-4), the hero who struggles with superhuman beings (cf. Gen 32:22-32), or the primeval golden age (cf. Gen 2:4b–3:24; Ezek 28:11-19).

E. Cassirer, *Language and Myth* (tr. Susanne Langer; New York, 1946); M. Eliade, *Cosmos and History: The Myth of the Eternal Return* (1954; repr. New York, 1959); S. E. Hyman, "The Ritual View of Myth and the Mythic," in *Myth* (ed. T. A. Sebeok) 136-53; C. G. Jung, *Psyche and Symbol* (ed. V. de Laszlo; New York, 1958); C. G. Jung and A. Kerenyi, *Essays on a Science of Mythology* (1949; repr. New York, 1963); G. S. Kirk, *Myth: Its Meaning and Function in Ancient and Other Cultures* (Cambridge, 1970); C. Levi-Strauss, "The Structural Study of Myth," in *Myth: A Symposium* (ed. T. A. Sebeok; 1955; repr. Bloomington, 1965) 81-106; C. S. Lewis, *An Experiment in Criticism* (Cambridge, 1961) 40-49; Lord Raglan, "Myth and Ritual," in *Myth: A Symposium* (ed. T. A. Sebeok; 1955; repr. Bloomington, 1965); P. Ricoeur, *The Symbolism of Evil* (tr. E. Buchanan; New York, 1967); T. A. Sebeok, ed., *Myth: A Symposium* (1955; repr. Bloomington, 1965).

NARRATIVE (Erzählung). An (→) account of or information about action communicated directly. This is an overarching concept which does not constitute a concrete genre itself.

It is information because it is not primarily or directly concerned with moving an audience to action or creating an attitude (as in an → admonition or a → song). It is about action because its subject is event or movement—even if the action is emotional or intellectual it will involve the development or interplay of emotions or ideas in action, not their simple description or logical progression (as in exposition). It is communicated directly because it is spoken to the audience, not acted out before a group which "overhears" it (as in a → drama).

OT narrative has many concrete forms. From the point of view of narrative technique, there is the (→) story, which moves from created tension to its resolution, the (→) report, which simply describes events with no overt effort to create tensions and resolution, and the (→) legend, which seeks to edify. From the point of view of content, when these techniques are used to narrate facts organized in terms of the chronology or causes they constitute history, but when the content is fictional, they are (→) historical novel or (→) novella. (→) Anecdote and (→) Märchen are other forms of narrative with special techniques and content.

R. Scholes and R. Kellogg, *The Nature of Narrative* (New York, 1966).

NARRATIVE FRAME. A form of inclusion in which some element from the beginning of a (→) narrative is taken up again at the end of a unit to mark it as a completed whole.

Thus Josh 21:43-45 notes that the plan for the conquest in 1:5-6 has been fulfilled. Also, Job 42:12-17 reports the reparation of the evils recounted in 1:1–2:10.

NOVELLA (Novelle). A long prose (→) narrative produced by a literary artisan for his own particular purposes.

The structure depends on the ability of the author to develop suspense and resolve it in particular directions. Toward that end, subplots and interweaving (→) motifs provide depth to the major plot line. Even in the major plot, multiple structures can facilitate a wider range of goals than would normally be the case in traditional narrative. Moreover, characterization can develop subtle tones. Thus the entire piece gives the reader a total impression of events as a complex and subtle process. Figures in the process are subordinated to the crucial character of the process itself.

The setting for the novella lies in the literary activity of the author, who may draw on traditional narratives with settings in various institutions. However, the qualifying characteristic of the novella is the unique shape given to the subject matter by the author. In

179

that sense, the novella is not simply a stage in the history of typical traditional material, but an original creation (cf. Genesis 37–47).

A. Jolles, *Einfache Formen* (Tübingen, 1968); H. W. Wolff, *Studien zum Jonabuch* (BibS[N]47; Neukirchen, 1965).

NUMERICAL SAYING (Zahlenspruch). A (→) saying characterized by a numerical pattern which consists of a title-line and a list. The title-line mentions the feature(s) which the items listed have in common. The number is usually two, three, or seven, and sometimes two numbers (cf. Prov 30:18) are mentioned in the title-line (a graded saying: x and x plus 1). In an inverted numerical saying (cf. Exod 21:10-11), the title-line follows the list. Cf. Jer 15:3; Amos 2:1, 4, 6; Prov 6:16-19; 30:18-20, 21-23, 24-28, 29-31.

The pattern is found in many types of literature: historical, ritual, wisdom, etc. Thus the pattern is used in genealogical groupings and also in reflective sayings about humanity, society, and nature.

The origin of the numerical saying in the (→) riddle is a moot question.

M. H. Pope, "Number, Numbering, Numbers," *IDB*; W. M. W. Roth, *Numerical Sayings in the Old Testament* (VTSup 13; Leiden, 1965).

OATH. A pronouncement, either in cohortative or indicative, binding the swearer to a particular course of action or a particular stance.

ORDER (Befehl). A forthright expression of will (e.g., *miṣwâ*), which may be positive (→ command) or negative (→ prohibition). Like all expressions of will, an order can have several settings, as in legal narratives, wisdom teaching, etc.

PARANESIS (Paranesis). An address to an individual (or group) that seeks to persuade with reference to a goal. It may be composed of several genre elements and characteristic stylistic features, in a flexible arrangement (cf. Deut 6–11; Prov 1:8ff.). Hence one finds (→) commands, (→) prohibitions, (→) instructions, etc. mixed into a paranetic address. Paranesis may exhort, admonish, command, or prohibit in its intent to persuade; (→) motive clauses are frequently included.

PROHIBITION (Verbot). A direct forbiddance of an action or thing, based upon an authority such as custom or law. It is usually expressed by *lō'* or *'al* with the jussive (vetitive or prohibitive form). It carries its force in itself, but is frequently accompanied by a (→) motive clause (cf. Prov 22:22ff.). A prohibition can appear alone (cf. Exod 22:17) or in a series (cf. Exod 20:2-17).

The opposite of prohibition is (→) command; both are subgenres of (→) order (cf. 2 Sam 13:28).

The prohibition occurs frequently in the wisdom teaching (→ instruction, admonition), as well as in the legal narratives; hence it can have several different settings.

J. Bright, "The Apodictic Prohibition: Some Observations," *JBL* 92 (1973) 185-204; E. Gerstenberger, *Wesen und Herkunft des "apodiktischen Rechts"* (WMANT 20; Neukirchen, 1965); W. Richter, *Recht und Ethos* (SANT 15; Munich, 1966).

PROVERB. Strictly speaking, a (→) saying that is purely observational, derived from experience as opposed to a (→) wisdom saying. Examples are Prov 11:24; 28:16; Eccl 1:15; 10:8-9. Wordplays, onomatopoeia, and other literary devices are often characteristic of the proverb (as well as of other genres, such as the [→] wisdom saying and the [→] riddle). The OT proverb derives its didactic character from its context (e.g., the wisdom sayings in Proverbs 12ff.).

It may be presumed that proverbs were handed down orally in Israel, and thus gained currency among the people (in this sense they may be called folk proverbs). But a deliberate cultivation of this genre is to be presupposed in the court and in the teachings of the postexilic sages (Qohelet, Ben Sira). In this stage especially the stress would have been on artistic expression in written form (in this sense it may be called an artistic saying or *Kunstspruch*).

H.-J. Hermisson, *Studien zur israelitischen Spruchweisheit* (Neukirchen, 1968); A. Jolles, *Einfache Formen* (Halle, 1956).

PURIFICATORY OATH (Reinigungseid). A declaration which backs up the veracity of a claim by invoking an evil upon oneself if the claim is not true. It is used to show that one is innocent, as in Job 31. It is comparable to the "negative confession" in the Egyptian mortuary texts (cf. *ANET*, 34-36).

H. J. Boecker, *Redeformen des Rechtslebens im Alten Testament* (WMANT 14; Neukirchen-Vluyn, 1964) 37-40; F. Horst, "Das Eid im Alten Testament" in *Gottes Recht: Gesammelte Studien* (TBü 12; Munich, 1961) 292-314.

REFLECTION (Reflexion). A genre that is characteristic of the book of Ecclesiastes (cf. 2:1-11, 12-17, 18-26). The reflection states a thesis or goal which the writer considers and evaluates in a very personal way. It captures "the course of thought" (Ellermeier), and has a loose structure, depending upon the author's personal style. Characteristics are quotation of (→) wisdom sayings, employment of (→) rhetorical questions, and giving examples.

R. Braun, *Kohelet und die frühhellenistische Popularphilosophie* (BZAW 130; Berlin, 1973) 153-59; F. Ellermeier, *Qohelet* (Herzberg, 1967) 50-92; R. E. Murphy, "A Form-Critical Consideration of Ecclesiastes 7," SBLASP I (ed. G. W. MacRae; Missoula, 1974) 77-85.

REPORT (Bericht). A (→) narrative, usually brief, that tells what happened without trying openly to arouse interest by creating tension looking to resolution (contrast → story). Cf. Judg 1:16, 17.

(→) Account and report are usually synonymous. They have the same definition, but account may imply a less impersonal tone than report.

RHETORICAL QUESTION (rhetorische Frage). A question asked for its rhetorical or telling effect, which does not require a reply. It is found frequently in argument and persuasion, and occurs as a subgenre in all parts of the OT. The supposition is that the answer is clear, usually the only one possible, and a deeper impression is made upon the hearer by the question form than by a statement.

RIDDLE (Rätsel). A statement (question or proposition) that is worded in such an ambiguous or intriguing way that it provides conjectural interpretation or solution. In the OT, *ḥîdâ* ("riddle") is often interpreted broadly (cf. Prov 1:6; Ps 49:5 [*RSV* 4]), but there is a classic example in Judg 14 (Samson).

The setting of the riddle is varied: a feast or celebration, a school, etc. The riddle is both a game and a test of wisdom in which there is a matching of wits, and it is often humorous. The relationship between the riddle and the (→) numerical saying is a moot point.

H. P. Müller, "Der Begriff 'Rätsel' im Alten Testament," *VT* 20 (1970) 465-69; H. Torczyner, "The Riddle in the Bible," *HUCA* 1 (1924) 125-40.

SAYING (Spruch). This term is used in a neutral sense to indicate a one-line or two-line (sometimes more) unit, such as can most readily be seen in the collections that make up the book of Proverbs.

Saying is not a form-critical term in itself, but it can describe such form-critical genres as (→) wisdom saying and (→) proverb.

A saying can be described as experiential or observational when it merely registers a fact; any didactic character it has derives from the context (as in Prov 10ff.). When the saying inculcates a value, it is properly didactic (→ wisdom saying).

SELF-DESCRIPTION (Selbstbeschreibung). A personal statement of one's physical properties, ordinarily in praise of them. This genre occurs in Cant 1:5-6; 2:1; 8:10.

F. Horst, "Die Formen des althebräischen Liebesliedes," in *Gottes Recht: Gesammelte Studien* (TBü 12; Munich, 1961) 176-87; R. E. Murphy, "Form-Critical Studies in the Song of Songs," *Int* 27 (1973) 413-22.

SHORT STORY. A composition of distinctive literary style (artistic prose and poetic rhythmic style), probably transmitted orally until fixed in writing. In content short stories combine interest in typical people with interest in mundane affairs. They serve a combination of purposes, such as entertainment and instruction. This definition has been culled from Ruth by E. Campbell.

    Related genre: (→) Novella.

    Cf. E. Campbell, *Ruth* (AB 7; New York, 1975) 5-6.

SONG (Lied). A poetic composition intended for public performance by an individual singer and/or group (choir). The performance of songs could be accompanied by musical instruments.

    The OT preserves a number of noncultic types:

    (1) Working songs (Num 21:17-18; Judg 9:27)

    (2) Love songs and wedding songs (Canticles; Psalm 45)

    (3) Songs of yearning (Cant 2:4-5; 8:6-7)

    (4) Drinking songs (Isa 5:11-13; Amos 6:4-6)

    (5) Battle songs (Exod 15:20-21; Num 10:35ff.; 1 Sam 18:6-7)

    (6) Funeral songs (→ dirge)

    (7) Mocking songs (Isa 23:15-16; 47; Num 21:27-30)

    For a discussion of cultic songs used in religious ceremonies, see the subsequent volumes on Psalms in this series.

    F. Horst, "Die Formen des althebräischen Liebeslieder," in *Gottes Recht: Gesammelte Studien* (TBü 12; Munich, 1961) 176-87; T. H. Robinson, *The Poetry of the Old Testament* (London, 1947); G. A. Smith, *The Early Poetry of Israel in its Physical and Social Origins* (London, 1912).

SPEECH (Rede). Not a precise definition of genre, since any kind of longer oral presentation can be called a speech. The form of a speech depends on many factors, including position of the speaker, topic, setting, and intention. A setting which recurs again and again, especially when it is part of an institution, can produce a particular genre of speech like a (→) disputation, sermon, or a speech as part of a legal procedure. Other speeches, however, are not so formalized, but grow out of particular customs. At a special point in life, or when a particular situation occurs, one gives a speech, like the farewell speech, or the speech before a battle (2 Sam 2:25-26; 2 Chr 13:4-12).

    In Proverbs Wisdom is personified as a woman who gives public speeches (Prov 1:20-33; 8:1-36; 9:3-9); similarly Dame Folly delivers a speech in Prov 9:13-17.

STORY (Sage, Erzählung, Geschichte). A (→) narrative whose structure is controlled by a plot, moving from introduction of characters through complication in relationships to denouement and conclusion.

    The setting for story cannot be controlled with as much precision as it can be for other genres. Stories that belong to popular literature can be told in multiple settings (cultic celebrations, family entertainment, etc.). Yet one particular setting demands attention: entertainment such as the singer of tales (cf. Peterson). The intention of such literature lies in entertainment. But entertainment impacts upon people in various directions: didactic, ethical, propagandistic, etc.

    The story may be independent of all other contexts. If so, it may reveal typical elements of narration identified as parts of a (→) saga by Olrik. Or, the story may function as a typical theme or episode in a larger whole. If so, it may show a variety of typical subjects, such as marriage story, etc.

Related genres: (→) Saga, (→) Legend.

R. Hals, "Legend: A Case Study in OT Form-Critical Terminology," *CBQ* 34 (1972) 166-76; A. Jolles, *Einfache Formen* (Tübingen, 1958); A. Olrik, "Epische Gesetze der Volksdichtung," *Zeitschrift für deutsches Altertum und deutsche Literatur* 51(1909) 1-12; C. Westermann, "Arten der Erzählung in der Genesis," in *Forschung am Altem Testament* I (TBü 24; Munich, 1964) 9-91.

SUMMARY-APPRAISAL FORMULA (Zusammenfassende Abschlussformel). A statement attached to the end of a literary unit that offers both a summary and an appraisal of the preceding material. The formula consists of a demonstrative pronoun (*zeh*, *zō't*) and usually has a bi-colon structure. It has a reflective, didactic bent, often containing technical wisdom terms. Its original setting seems to have been the wise man's reflections and instructions (cf. Prov 1:19; Job 8:13; 18:21; 20:29; Ps 49:14 [*RSV* 13]), but it also was utilized by some of the prophets (cf. Isa 14:26; 28:29; Jer 13:25).

B. S. Childs, *Isaiah and the Assyrian Crisis* (SBT 2/3; London, 1967) 128ff.; J. W. Whedbee, *Isaiah and Wisdom* (Nashville, 1971) 75ff.

SUPERSCRIPTION (Überschrift). A statement prefixed to a literary work. The term refers to the place of this statement in the structure of a work, namely, anteceding its body (as opposed to the subscription which follows the conclusion of the body).

As such, the superscription may consist of a variety of elements, e.g., author, addressee, (→) title, date, location. While the composition of most of these elements can vary among texts, superscriptions in the OT ordinarily indicate the character of the work, either in the concise, definitional form of a title ("This is the book of the generations of Adam," Gen 5:1; 2:4a; "A Psalm of David," Ps 101:1), or in a more elaborate form (Jer 1:1-3).

Gene M. Tucker, "Prophetic Superscriptions and the Growth of a Canon," in *Canon and Authority* (ed. Burke O. Long and George W. Coats; Philadelphia, 1977) 56-70.

TEASE (Scherzgespräch). A genre in which one party speaks against the will or desires of another party in a jesting manner. Cf. Cant 5:3, and perhaps 1:7-8.

F. Horst, "Die Formen des althebräischen Liebesliedes," in *Gottes Recht*: *Gesammelte Studien* (TBü 12; Munich, 1961) 176-87.

TITLE (Titel). A word or a concise phrase that constitutes the name of a particular literary work. A title ordinarily characterizes the work in terms of itself ("A Psalm," Ps 98:1) and/or its (supposed) author ("A Psalm of David," Ps 110:1; "The Proverbs of Solomon," Prov 10:1).

Titles in the OT ordinarily occur as (→) superscriptions or as elements of superscriptions.

TOPOS (Topos). An ordered constellation of (→) motifs characteristic of a tradition. The topos includes a number of motifs connected among themselves so that it forms a relatively complete unit. The general connection among motifs within a topos is usually fixed by the nature of things. For example, in the tale of the foundling hero—a widespread topos—the infant hero must be taken into someone's protection. However, the particular form of the motif used to realize this need is fixed by the tradition. Sargon is rescued by a gardener, Moses by a princess, Romulus and Remus by a wolf.

The topos, although relatively complete in itself often also prepares for or connects with other topoi which belong together in a narrative tradition, if not in strict logic (e.g., in Yugoslav epic the marriage feast normally issues not in a "they lived happily ever after" scene, but in a bloody battle).

Because it is traditional, the topos is the subject of more than one telling or singing about the same hero. Thus, the youth of the hero (a typical heroic narrative topos) is described in several versions in 1 Samuel 16–17.

A. B. Lord, *The Singer of Tales* (Harvard Studies in Comparative Literature 24; Cambridge, 1960) 68-98 (using the word "theme" for topos); R. Scholes and R. Kellogg, *The Nature of Narrative* (New York, 1966) 26-28.

TRAVESTY or LITERARY FICTION (Travestie). A term used to designate a recurring literary phenomenon in which one assumes another role in human relationship, one that is lived in fantasy, all the while remaining what one is. In western literature, the "knight," the "shepherd," and the "rogue" (Picaro) exemplify such literary fiction. The same phenomenon seems to be at work in Canticles, where the lover is both king (1:4, 12) and shepherd (1:7).

A. Hermann, *Altägyptische Liebesdichtung* (Wiesbaden, 1959) 111-24; A. Jolles, "Die literarischen Travestien," *Blätter für deutsche Philosophie* 6 (1932) 281-94.

WARNING (Drohwort). An address that pressures an individual or group toward a given point of view or action. It is often accompanied by an indication of a danger or threat.

The warning can assume various coloring from its context. In the (→) instruction of the sage it is usually more tempered than in the speech of the prophet (contrast Prov 5:1-14 with Amos 4:9-11).

Related genres: (→) Prohibition, (→) Paranesis, (→) Admonition.

WAṢF. A technical term for a (→) descriptive song.

WISDOM POEM (Lehrgedicht). In contrast to the discrete (→) wisdom saying (Proverbs 10ff.), this phrase describes a structured, consecutive piece of poetry dealing with wisdom themes (e.g., the poems in Proverbs 1–9). It does not designate a genre, but it is descriptive of poems with wisdom themes that often have stylistic features that seem to have been cultivated by the sages (→ Introduction to Proverbs, Introduction to Job), e.g., the (→) acrostic poem (Prov 31:10-31), and the (→) alphabetizing poem (Prov 2:1-22; Job 9:2-24).

WISDOM SAYING (Weisheitsspruch). A didactic (→) saying, based on experience and/or tradition, that inculcates some value or lesson. It is found most commonly in Proverbs 10ff., and is expressed in various kinds of parallelism. In contrast to the (→) proverb, the wisdom saying may not have common currency; it is directly didactic; it teaches, and does not leave an issue as an open question. Sometimes the lesson found in the saying is expressed in another way, as in an (→) admonition (contrast Prov 16:20 with 16:3).

H.-J. Hermisson, *Studien zur israelitischen Spruchweisheit* (Neukirchen, 1968).

WOE ORACLE (Wehruf). A genre which is used in the prophetic literature to criticize particular actions or attitudes of people, and to announce punishment upon them. Woe oracles are found as individual units (Isa 1:4; 3:11; 10:5) or in a series (Isa 5:8-24).

The typical woe oracle has two parts: (1) the exclamation *hôy* ("woe") followed by a participle denoting the criticized action, or a noun characterizing people in a negative way, and (2) a continuation with a variety of forms, including threats (Isa 5:9, 13-14, 24; 28:2-8), accusations (Isa 1:4), or rhetorical questions (Isa 10:3-4; Amos 6:2). This genre was adopted by the prophets from wisdom circles (Gerstenberger, Wolff, Whedbee); according to Westermann it is a milder form of (→) curse.

E. Gerstenberger, "The Woe Oracles of the Prophets," *JBL* 81 (1962) 249-63; W. Janzen, *Mourning Cry and Woe Oracle* (BZAW 125; Berlin, 1972); G. Liedke, *Gestalt und Bezeichnung alttestamentlicher Rechtssätze* (WMANT 39; Neukirchen, 1971) 147-48;

Wanke, "אוי und הוי," *ZAW* 78 (1966) 215-18; C. Westermann, *Basic Forms of Pro-*
etic Speech (tr. H. C. White; Philadelphia, 1967) 190ff.; J. W. Whedbee, *Isaiah and*
sdom (Nashville, 1971) 80ff.; H. W. Wolff, *Amos geistige Heimat* (WMANT 18; Neu-
chen, 1964) 12ff.

Made in United States
Orlando, FL
25 October 2023